WRITING FICTION

Gotham Writers' Workshop®
WRITING FICTION
THE PRACTICAL GUIDE FROM NEW YORK'S ACCLAIMED CREATIVE WRITING SCHOOL

WRITTEN BY GOTHAM WRITERS' WORKSHOP FACULTY
EDITED BY ALEXANDER STEELE

B L O O M S B U R Y
NEW YORK · LONDON · OXFORD · NEW DELHI · SYDNEY

Bloomsbury USA
An imprint of Bloomsbury Publishing Plc

1385 Broadway   50 Bedford Square
New York   London
NY 10018   WC1B 3DP
USA   UK

www.bloomsbury.com

First U.S. editon 2003

ISBN: TPB: 978-1-58234-330-3
ePub: 978-1-59691-791-0

Library of Congress Cataloging-in-Publication Data

Writing fiction : the practical guide from New York's acclaimed creative writing
school / written by Gotham Writers' Workshop faculty ; edited by Alexander
Steele.—1st U.S. ed.
p.cm.
Includes index.
ISBN 1-58234-330-6 (pbk.)
ISBN-13 978-1-58234-330-3
1. Fiction—Authorship. I. Steele, Alexander. II. Gotham Writers' Workshop.
PN3355.W75 2003
808.3—dc22
2003057739

20 19

Interior and cover design by 2x4, New York City
Typeset by Palimpsest Book Production Limited, Polmont, Stirlingshire, Scotland
Printed and bound in the U.S.A. Berryville Graphics, Inc., Berryville, Virginia

To find out more about our authors and books visit www.bloomsbury.com.
Here you will find extracts, author interviews, details of forthcoming events,
and the option to sign up for our newsletters.

Bloomsbury books may be purchased for business or promotional use.
For information on bulk purchases please contact Macmillan Corporate and
Premium Sales Department at specialmarkets@macmillan.com.

FROM GOTHAM WRITERS'
WORKSHOP'S FOUNDERS

Gotham Writers' Workshop began with a single class taught in a living room on the Upper West Side of New York City. The class was free. After three hours, everyone had a choice. They could leave, or, if they felt they had learned something worthwhile, they could pay for the rest of the course. Everyone decided to stay, and the first semester at Gotham Writers' Workshop had begun.

Those original students spread the word. So we offered more classes. Word of mouth traveled wider. We hired teachers, rented an office. Soon we were teaching classes in various locations throughout New York City. Eventually we expanded into online classes, and we drew students from all over the world. Today we employ over a hundred instructors who teach more than six thousand students a year.

Despite our growth, we still think of ourselves as a grassroots organization. Class size remains small enough to fit into a New York living room. Our teachers continue to bring their passion for writing to every class. Our founding principles are unchanged.

Simply put, we believe anyone can write. We believe writing is a craft that can be taught. True, talent cannot be taught, only nurtured, but the craft of writing *can* be taught. We're devoted to teaching the craft in a way that is so clear, direct, and applicable that our students begin growing as writers during their very first class.

There's no easy formula for creating great fiction, but a fundamental knowledge of writing craft is, more than anything, what will allow your talent to blossom on the page. Such knowledge is what we offered in that first class, and it's what our teachers—who are all writing *and* teaching professionals—continue to offer every one of our students.

Now we've put the Gotham style of teaching into a book. The ability to write—to write with excellence—is in your hands.

Jeff Fligelman and David Grae
February 2003

HOW TO USE THIS BOOK

You shouldn't just read your way through this book, but write your way through it as well. After all, you're reading this book because you want to write.

Sprinkled throughout every chapter, you'll find numerous writing exercises, indicated by the words *Your Turn*. Quite literally, this means it's your turn to apply the knowledge you've just learned to your own writing. You shouldn't worry about turning these exercises into brilliant works of fiction. Rather, you should simply focus on experimenting and having fun with the task at hand. If one of the exercises spawns a wonderful idea that you would like to expand into a longer piece of writing, a piece you hope to finish and perhaps publish, by all means help yourself. In fact, toward the end of the book you'll be advised to do just that.

You also might find it useful to keep your work on these exercises in a notebook, either the paper kind or the computer kind. If you do all or most of the exercises in this book—and you should—you'll have a wide resource of ideas and fragments from which to draw or be inspired the next time you're looking for a fiction project.

Not that we want to make things too easy for you, but at the back of this book you will find a "cheat sheet" that gives you a checklist of many of the key points on writing craft that appear in this book. You may want to keep the cheat sheet handy when writing your next work of fiction.

You will also find numerous passages from works of fiction cited throughout this book. If one or more of these works looks interesting to you, you should get your hands on a copy and read it. If the work is a novel or novella the title will appear in *italics,* and if the work is a short story the title will appear in "quotes." A number of the short stories that appear in this book can be found in *The Vintage Book of Contemporary American Short Stories,* edited by Tobias Wolff.

In particular, you should read the short story "Cathedral" by Raymond Carver, preferably in tandem with reading this book. "Cathedral" is referred to repeatedly throughout this book, and having read the story will enhance your understanding of these references. You will find "Cathedral" reprinted in its entirety in the Appendix.

Last, you'll find additional information on the art and business of writing at the Gotham Writers' Workshop Web site: www.writingclasses.com.

CONTENTS

CHAPTER 1
FICTION: THE WHAT, HOW, AND WHY OF IT

BY ALEXANDER STEELE

Hello, you look familiar.

As the dean of faculty at Gotham Writers' Workshop, I'm surrounded by people with a desire to create fiction. On a daily basis I work with our fiction teachers, folks so talented and intelligent they could have made a killing in most any field, but instead have opted to pursue the precarious life of a fiction writer. Frequently I observe our fiction classes, some in regular classrooms filled with students from New York City and the surrounding areas, some in cyberspace classrooms, filled with students from all over the United States, and from as far away as Africa, China, and Australia. I see the whole wide world in these classes—doctors, lawyers, accountants, janitors, policemen, undertakers, housewives, retirees, students, psychics, zookeepers, and everything else.

It's a fact: a staggering number of people out there harbor an intense desire to create fiction.

Why?

Though this chapter will cover more than a philosophical inquiry into why we write fiction—as the title promises—let me see if I can find an answer to this vexing question, preferably by the chapter's end.

A BRIEF DEFINITION OF FICTION

Let's start with a simpler question: what is fiction? In the broadest sense, fiction is simply a made-up story.

The business of making up stories has been going on for a long time. Somewhere in the shadowy past, our cave-dwelling ancestors began conjuring stories and telling them to each other. The tradition grew, and some of these stories eventually attained the "best-seller" status of myths, tales destined to be passed on through generations and to migrate across continents and to shape the way people thought. At some point, some of these stories started to get written down with the intention that they would be *read.* An enterprising Mesopotamian writer chiseled *The Epic of Gilgamesh* into stone tablets some four thousand years ago, and if you think revision was difficult on a typewriter . . .

Anyway, this brings us to the more narrow definition of fiction: a made-up story told in prose with words alone.

Words alone.

That's the unique challenge and wonder of written fiction. There's no actor or storyteller using gesture and inflection. No painter or filmmaker showing settings or close-ups. Everything is done with those little symbols we call letters, which are melded into words, which multiply to form sentences and paragraphs. And by some alchemical process those words interact with the reader's imagination in such a way that readers are taken inside the reality of a story—like Alice stepping through the looking-glass—and once there they can experience and feel and care about this alternate reality as deeply as they do for the meanderings and heartbreaks of their own lives.

For us humans this process is strangely important. We seem to have a primal need for fiction, or really any kind of story, that is as deeply rooted as our need for food, shelter, and companionship. I see two reasons for this.

The first reason: entertainment. We crave entertainment, and stories are one of the key ways we satisfy this desire. The second reason: meaning. Our curiosity, and perhaps insecurity, compels us to explore continually the who, what, where, when, and why of our existence. Some call this lofty goal a search for *Truth.*

A good piece of fiction will satisfy one or both of these needs extremely well and do so in a miraculously low-tech manner. All fiction ultimately requires is words interacting with the reader's imagination, a combination that provides, for many people, the most powerful form of storytelling possible, not to mention the most portable.

A MATTER OF FORM

We'll come back to entertainment and meaning shortly, but now let's take a brief look at the basic forms of fiction.

First, the novel. Typically a novel runs at least eighty thousand words (about 320 pages of double-spaced typing). Some novels run a bit shorter than this and many run way longer. Novels are usually broken into chapters, which give the reader a much-needed mental break.

A novel is the literary equivalent of a symphony, the big, ambitious form of fiction. Novels aren't just longer than other forms of fiction. They generally have more of everything: more characters, more scenes, more developments, more *heft*. They may have a central story, but the story is usually surrounded by a whole swirling world of activity. Someone once told me she could tell if a work was a novel or short story simply by hearing the first sentence. Interpret that as you may.

Some novels are sprawling. Leo Tolstoy's *War and Peace* is an ocean, bearing countless characters over numerous years and thousands of miles, immersing the reader in a span of history, encompassing all aspects of humanity. But J. D. Salinger's *The Catcher in the Rye* covers only a few days and never leaves the side of that mixed-up teenager, Holden Caulfield. And then there's James Joyce's *Ulysses,* which staggers on for almost eight hundred pages, weaving in and out of various minds and styles, but staying within the confines of a single Dublin day.

Writing a novel is a long haul that can swallow years of a life, a test of endurance for even the hardiest of souls. Nevertheless, for many an aspiring writer, the novel is the great white whale of fiction, and these people will not rest until they have spilled the blood of several hundred pages. Godspeed to them all.

Next, there's the short story. Short stories tend to run no longer than fifteen thousand words (about sixty pages of double-spaced typing), and most run shorter than this. The average short story is about the length of the chapters in the book you're holding, though recently flash fiction—stories that run only a page or two—has come into fashion. Short stories are the literary equivalent of songs. They are not necessarily less emotionally complex than novels, just as "Amazing Grace" is no less powerful than Beethoven's Ninth Symphony, but the scope of a short story is narrower. Often short stories focus on a single event, or at least a single aspect of a character's life.

"The Swimmer" by John Cheever stays focused on a man's dogged attempt one summer afternoon to travel home via the neighboring swimming pools. "A Bullet in the Brain" by Tobias Wolff stays focused on a few significant minutes while a book critic stands in line at the bank. "Carried Away" by Alice Munro stretches from World War I to World War II but stays focused on a librarian's strange relationship with a man who loses his head, literally. These stories dig deep yet never wander outside their tightly focused spotlights.

Sometimes, related short stories are written to be collected in a book, as in Sherwood Anderson's *Winesburg, Ohio,* where the stories feature different characters, all of whom live in the same small town, or as in Denis Johnson's *Jesus' Son,* where the same misfit character drifts through every story. The stories here can be enjoyed individually, but read together they have a cumulative effect.

Short stories are perhaps the best first step for the beginning fiction writer simply because they demand less time commitment than a novel does. But short fiction is an exacting form. Whereas a novel may be forgiven a bit of flabbiness, short stories must be kept on a strict diet. Every word *counts.* The best short stories employ a precision and economy reminiscent of poetry.

Then there's the novella, which hovers in between the novel and the short story. In length, novellas run from about fifteen thousand words to about eighty thousand words. Some novellas combine the broader scope of a novel with the lean telling of a short story, as with Joseph Conrad's *Heart of Darkness,* which covers a long river journey by steamer through Africa. Other novellas combine the narrower scope of a short story with the leisurely unfolding of a novel, as with Franz Kafka's *The Metamorphosis,* which covers a few weird days in the life of a man who wakes up to discover he's been turned into an insect.

To generalize any further about these forms would do them an injustice. They are elastic forms and can be many things to many different writers. The only indisputable difference is length, and no one really agrees on that either. Perhaps the only truly indisputable difference is that the titles of novels and novellas are italicized while short story titles are put in quotation marks.

Which form should you focus your efforts on? Well, a story should take the form it wants to take, the form in which it is most comfortably told. For example, you may start writing a short story and then discover that the characters and situations demand a much larger canvas. They won't stay within the small frame of short fiction. Then you'll either need to narrow your focus or cancel that summer trip and start working on a novel. Some writers choose one of these forms and stick with it, while others bounce back and forth between the forms.

LITERARY AND GENRE FICTION

Fiction can be further subdivided into two camps—*literary fiction* and *genre fiction*. Literary fiction refers to stories with some aspiration of being considered "art." Most of the stories here appeal to a somewhat elite readership, especially in the case of short fiction. Genre fiction refers to stories that usually fall within the popular genres of mystery, thriller, horror, fantasy, science fiction, western, and romance. Here you'll find stories geared for a broader audience. (Sometimes you'll hear the term *mainstream fiction,* which usually refers to literary fiction that has broad commercial appeal.)

The easy distinction is to say that genre fiction is fun, popular, and less important than literary fiction, which strives for layers of depth and artistic heights. There is some truth in this notion. Most genre writers will proudly admit that their chief motive is to keep their readers entertained. Most literary writers will readily affirm that they're trying to express something about the human condition. Both types of fiction are equally valid, with plenty of readers in both camps to prove it.

There is nothing terribly wrong with this division in the fiction house. *Vive la différence.* We now have several hundred channel choices on our TV sets. Why shouldn't we have as wide a range of options with our fiction?

Some prefer, say, the stylish prose of Amy Tan, a prize-winning literary author, while others prefer, say, the screaming terror of Stephen King, the big daddy of genre writers, while others still enjoy moving their tent between camps.

Actually, there is much common ground here. The literary writers need not view the genre writers as slackers and the genre writers need not view the lits as snobs. In fact, they can learn a great deal from each other. A literary work should keep readers entranced and turning pages well past bedtime, and an entertainment work will be all the more entertaining if it has some real insight and resonance.

This book will mostly focus on writing literary fiction, as is true of the GWW Fiction classes. We have separate classes for the various genres of fiction. However, while the genre classes deal with the specific needs of their genre, the majority of what is taught in these classes is exactly the same as what is taught in the Fiction classes. The same elements of craft apply. And, really, when it comes to fiction—good is good.

AT ITS BEST

If you look at the great works of fiction throughout the ages, you will notice just how brilliantly these stories have satisfied the dual need for entertainment and meaning. A few examples from the past two centuries:

Pride and Prejudice by Jane Austen (1813)
With fairy-tale charm, the romance between Elizabeth and Darcy develops, enlivened by the push-pull of two magnetic personalities. Cold realities intrude too, in the form of gossip, suspicion, money, and meddling, and several couples in this English countryside fall prey to recklessly bad romances. Step by intricate step, the mating dance is revealed with such wit and precision, the book may almost serve as a relationship primer. Ultimately hope of true love shines through, and we take joy that Elizabeth and Darcy are still living happily ever after.

"The Tell-Tale Heart" by Edgar Allan Poe (1843)
Right away, we're sucked inside a nightmare. Trapped in a house with an old man who has a sickening vulture eye. Leaping against our will into murder.

Chatting with policemen while the heart beats relentlessly louder, louder, LOUDER. We sweat through a terror made all the more terrible because the psychotic villain is inside our very own mind. It's one of the most frightening tales ever told, and no one loves it more than children.

The Adventures of Huckleberry Finn by Mark Twain (1885)
The most engaging (and revolutionary) thing about this book is the way it's told in the believable voice of an uneducated backwoods kid. It really wasn't okay to use bad grammar and slang until this book came down the pike. What a break-the-rules joy it is rafting up the Mississippi River with Huck and his companion, the escaped slave Jim, watching these two get themselves in and out of all sorts of trouble, some vaudevillian, some quite serious. We also gain miles of insight into the less noble sides of human nature by seeing it all through Huck's innocent eyes.

"The Lady with the Dog" by Anton Chekhov (1899)
A life-weary man from Moscow begins an affair with a young woman in a seaside resort. Both are married, neither expects the affair to last. Yet, for the first time, the man is caught in the undertow of genuine love. It's a tale of adultery told in shades of gray. No one wears a scarlet *A* or commits suicide with a rushing train. Instead we see the quiet yearning and uncertainty of the human heart, and while waiting to see where things will lead, the suspense overwhelms.

The Great Gatsby by F. Scott Fitzgerald (1925)
First there's the vicarious pleasure of spending the summer among the elite of Long Island, attending the lavish parties, listening to jazz in the moonlight. Then, like Nick, the narrator, we become intrigued by this enigma of a man, Gatsby. Who is he? Where did he come from? What does he most desire—the elusive Daisy, the kind of class money can't buy, or simply the dream of life? Like a perfectly cut jewel, every facet shimmers and hypnotizes and reflects differently upon each observation. And it's nice to be reminded that rich people aren't always happy.

"A Good Man Is Hard to Find" by Flannery O'Connor (1955)
A tough old bird of a grandmother takes a car trip through the American South with her grumpy son, his snooty wife, and their two obnoxious

children. And, oh, yes, Grandma has secretly smuggled her cat along. It's a hilarious ride, bound to conjure memories of your own hellish family trips. But when the family meets up with a dangerous escaped convict, things take a sharp turn down the darkest of roads. There lies both evil and salvation.

One Hundred Years of Solitude by Gabriel García Márquez (1967)
The saga focuses on a single family in a single town in a single century, but the whole of history seems to roll by in a biblical flow of passion, sadness, absurdity, and miracles. The Latin American town begins an Eden but is soon overrun with business, politics, war, and a quagmire of family scandals that would make a soap opera blush. It's nearly impossible to keep track of the time or the characters or to separate the magical from the mundane, but if you "listen" patiently at the storyteller's heels, you'll see all the butterflies and blood of our world.

"The Things They Carried" by Tim O'Brien (1990)
A platoon of soldiers trudges through Vietnam. Much of the story is simply a litany of "things" the soldiers carry with them, a list that evolves from equipment to personal items to emotion, told with a mesmerizing mix of documentary fact and poetic meter. Amid the baggage, a young lieutenant ponders his past and future back home in New Jersey with a girl he barely knows. After reading this story, in some sense, you have been to war.

These stories entwine entertainment and meaning so artfully that you could read them for either of these purposes without failing to let the other get under your skin. Don't pressure yourself to write a classic, a sure way to stifle creative freedom, but challenge yourself, as these writers have done, to keep your readers breathlessly turning pages and then give them something that lingers and reverberates even after they finish that last word. Isn't that what usually satisfies us most as readers?

> YOUR TURN:
> Choose a work of fiction that you cherish. In a single sentence, try to state the major reason why you love reading this work. Then list several ways with which you think the author achieved this effect. The reasons don't have to employ any fancy terms and they don't

have to make sense to anyone but you. You're simply trying to tune in to the source of the magic.

SEE THE SEEDS

"As Gregor Samsa awoke one morning from a troubled dream he found himself transformed in his bed into a monstrous insect."
—*The Metamorphosis,* Franz Kafka

In the beginning is an idea. Ideas are seeds from which the mimosa tree or watermelon or delphinium of a story will arise. There are no rules about what constitutes a proper seed. It can be a character, a name, a situation, structure, overheard dialogue, a setting, a theme, even a vague feeling.

While passing through an obscure nook of Notre Dame cathedral, Victor Hugo noticed the Greek word for *fate* carved in the stone. He imagined a tormented soul driven to engrave this word. From this seed sprang his monumental novel *The Hunchback of Notre Dame.*

Ideas are everywhere. The writer of fiction must learn to search the world for these seeds.

Probably the most fertile place to look for ideas is right inside the backyard of your own life. Herman Melville drew on his whaling adventures for *Moby-Dick* and Philip Roth has drawn endless inspiration from his crazy Jewish family. You've got stuff to draw on too. If you don't think so, look a little harder. There are probably hundreds of things in your seemingly mundane existence that, if looked at with a little insight and whimsy, could be turned into good material. Your home life, relationships, work, hobbies, chance encounters. Sure, the eccentric and exotic make for good stories, but so does the ordinary, especially in contemporary fiction, where the ordinary flourishes like a spider plant in ample sunlight. (See, I drew that image from my very own window.)

Even the little things in your life can spark a story. Let's say you're having technical problems with your computer, so, horror of horrors, you have to call Tech Support. Telephone hell—pushing buttons, eternal waiting, trying to reason with computerized voices, trying to explain to computer people, contemplating throwing your computer out the window. But you know what? This very situation could prove useful in a story. Perhaps a character must send a life-or-death message that can be received only by e-mail but the tech problem is making this impossible. Or perhaps the frustration of dealing with Tech Support triggers all the other frustrations in a character's life, causing a major emotional crisis, perhaps poured out to the puzzled person on the other end of the line. You see, even the tiniest seed can sprout multiple story ideas.

Flannery O'Connor said, "Anyone who has lived to the age of eighteen has enough stories to last a lifetime." Zoom in for a close look at some of the events and people in your past, things that have haunted you, things you thought you had forgotten. Remember that girl from the other side of the tracks in your third-grade class whom you and your friends made fun of, until you caught a poignant glimpse of her eating alone in the lunchroom, after which you bought her a bracelet? Good seed.

Search your thoughts. Fyodor Dostoyevsky's changing philosophical views led him to write *Crime and Punishment* (and he was lucky enough to have spent time in a Siberian prison to help with the last section of the book). What are the things you most love? What are the things you most hate? If you were to make a list of answers to either of these questions, you would have a collection of ideas that are of passionate interest to yourself.

But the fictional version of *You* doesn't have to be the whole story, or even any part of the story. Indeed, if you're too egocentric with your ideas, your work may take on the yawning indulgence of that person who is always trying to give elaborate descriptions of her dreams (though dreams can certainly be a rich source for stories). A good writer must keenly observe things outside of himself or, as Henry James said, develop "the power to guess the unseen from the seen." Look around at other people and imagine who they really are and what it would be like to walk around in their shoes, whether the footwear is designer heels or clunky orthopedics.

One of the pleasures of reading fiction is the way it gives a secret peek into the lives of others—those people in the passing cars or at the cash registers or on the television screens—people we may never meet. This is a bit like stealing a glimpse of a person in the nude through a window or overhearing an argument between lovers in a restaurant. Whether these glimpses are enticing or unsettling, they usually provide a certain voyeuristic thrill. On a deeper level, it's actually very comforting to see that other people are just as lost and flawed as we are. In a way, fiction is firm affirmation that We Are Not Alone.

Learn to see, and then reveal, those secret peeks, be they about someone like yourself or someone entirely different. This is another fringe benefit of being a writer. As you search for ideas, your powers of observation (and other senses as well) will intensify. The world around you will become more alive, vibrant, multidimensional, entertaining, meaningful.

Feel free to search for seeds far from home too. You can look in a newspaper any day of the week and chances are you'll find a multitude of seeds for stories. I'll do it myself, right now. Granted my local paper happens to be *The New York Times,* but I'll bet you could do this with most any newspaper.

Let's see, on the front page there's an article about the fellow who painted those dog pictures, the most famous of which shows a poker-playing pug slipping a pawed ace to a pal. This man has won very little respect or reputation, but his art is probably better known to many people than that of Cézanne or Van Gogh. Certainly there's a story in there somewhere.

Here's an article in the sports section about a pitcher who is expected by his team to bean (hit) a batter in an upcoming game because this player beaned a player from the pitcher's team two seasons ago. But the pitcher seems reluctant. To bean or not to bean? That's a story.

Elsewhere. A faulty carnival ride left seventeen people hanging upside down for a period of time. A substitute teacher attacked his class with a broom. The obituaries report the passing of a gentleman who belonged to five country clubs. Story, story, story.

You may have heard the old maxim *Write what you know.* The advice has merit, but it's not the whole truth. If you want to write about a famous fashion model who befriends a lame penguin while on a magazine shoot in Antarctica, go for it, even if it has absolutely zero relationship to your own life. You may have to do some research on models and penguins and Antarctica, but it may be intriguing. How could it not be? And I would guess that even if you write about things totally alien to your existence, you will still be writing, in some way, about what you know. The tone or emotions or perspective will be your own. The truest maxim in this respect might be *Write what ignites your interest.*

Don't shy away from surprising seeds. GWW teacher Jess Row somehow got himself stuck on the idea of echolocation, the sound-detection technique used by bats to navigate. Though he didn't really know much about echo-location, he liked the idea and began imagining a girl who believed she had the power of echolocation, which she used to pursue the spirit of her departed mother. Following this bizarre seed, Jess created the much-acclaimed story "The Secrets of Bats."

History is an incredibly rich source of story ideas. Toni Morrison heard tell of a slave woman who murdered her child to prevent the child from being a slave herself. Out of this haunting incident grew Morrison's *Beloved.* Salman Rushdie's *Midnight's Children* was largely inspired by the contemporary history of India, the protagonist even being born at the moment of India's independence from colonialism.

So, in addition to absorbing the world that is immediately around you, feel free to absorb the world that is around you in a broader sense, even if that takes you to other time periods or the far reaches of the universe.

Ideas are everywhere, and there is literally no limit to what you can write about.

> YOUR TURN:
> Write down ten things that might possibly serve as story ideas, drawing from things that happened to you over the past week—people, emotions, thoughts, situations. Nothing is too big or small, cosmic or microscopic. Then review your list and pick the idea that looks the most promising for a story. The right idea will probably give you a buzz when you see it. Then list several ways in which this idea might be turned into a fictional story. Will your idea result in a brilliant story? Maybe, maybe not. But you'll probably discover how plentiful ideas can be.

Once you start absorbing the world as a writer, your problem will quickly shift from *I don't have any good ideas* to *I have so many great ideas I can't possibly live long enough to get all of them down.* This is a wonderful problem for a writer to have.

So how do you know when you have the right idea, the one that's truly worth pursuing? Well, you'll know. People who live in New York City know that if you're riding the subway and across the aisle from you sits a wild-eyed person wearing garbage-can couture who is clearly on his way to nowhere, you should avoid making eye contact with that person because the second you do the person will lock those wild eyes onto your soul and start jabbering about apocalypse or Porky Pig or who knows what and the conversation will continue with or without your consent for an uncomfortably long period of time. Ideas are like that person. When the right idea enters your head it will loudly and persistently announce its presence. You may acknowledge its presence right away or it may take you a few days, but you'll know when the right idea has arrived.

Bear in mind, however, that a single big idea won't give you a whole story. A fictional work is really an accumulation of many ideas. A single word may have inspired *The Hunchback of Notre Dame,* but, somehow or other, Hugo managed to cultivate some five hundred pages from this seed. He also got the idea for a noble hunchback, a gypsy girl with a dancing goat, the Festival of Fools, a mob storming the cathedral walls, and a host of other things that he skillfully wove into a multicolored, yet unified, tapestry.

Before I forget, let me remind you to write your ideas down. Most writers don't go far without a notebook handy. The "eureka" ideas may stay with you, but once you get going ideas will start popping in your head like popcorn and you can't possibly remember them all. The jottings in your notebook don't have to make any sense and you won't use every single one of them, but sooner or later some of those notes will flower into something very useful.

Now, a word of caution. The seeds you pick up from the world are just that, seeds. Once you plant your seeds in the soil of a story, let those seeds grow into fiction, not fact. Don't confine your story to the way things really were, in a literal sense. Fiction demands better storytelling than real life, even if the fiction seems perfectly "real." Often beginning fiction writers stick too rigidly to the facts and inevitably their stories feel a little flat or indulgent. (True, many memoirs are quite compelling, but one reads a memoir with a different set of expectations than one reads fiction with.)

Lorrie Moore's "People Like That Are the Only People Here" is a somewhat autobiographical story about a mother seeing her baby through a terrible illness. The real-life seed idea was certainly emotional enough. But Moore chose to fictionalize the story (even though the protagonist is a writer) so she could further deepen the story's impact. If she had not done so, the story probably wouldn't have the shape, suspense, clarity, irony, and humor (yes, humor) that make it so unforgettable.

The fiction writer must water the soil with imagination until the story yields the maximum amount of entertainment and/or meaning. The goal is to write a story that a total stranger will enjoy (though some writers find it helpful to picture someone they know as the total stranger). The stranger reading your fiction won't care about you or your life or your observations. Not a bit. All the stranger ultimately cares about is a great story well told.

Will you be sacrificing honesty along with the facts? No. By bending reality into fantasy you are not lessening the Truth inherent in your idea. Rather, you are increasing it. Life is a blur in which it is difficult to see anything clearly because a zillion things are going on all at once. Art is all about sharp focus.

Attempted Theory #1: Hey, back to our initial question. Perhaps this is the big reason why we write fiction—as a way of understanding ourselves and the world around us. The fiction writer takes a fragment of reality and examines it from several angles until it starts to make some damn sense. By focusing life through the lens of fiction, truths are revealed and magnified and understood. Order is made from chaos. It's like therapy but cheaper and more fun, and perhaps even more effective.

Yes, a good answer. But not the complete answer. If fiction were such an effective method of making sense of things, why am I generally more confused than, say, my blissfully satisfied sister who has never written a word of fiction in her life? I sense there is a more definitive reason out there, perhaps something like Descartes's sweeping proof of human existence: "I think, therefore I am." So . . . let's continue examining the creative process of a fiction writer.

SHOW UP FOR WORK

> "If I'd 'a' knowed what a trouble it was to make a book I wouldn't 'a' tackled it, and ain't a-going to no more."
> —*The Adventures of Huckleberry Finn,* Mark Twain

At some time or another, most everyone fancies they have a story to tell. As you may have just learned, ideas are rather cheap and easy to come by. But few of these people actually manage to get the story on paper, fewer still stick with it long enough to go through several drafts, and fewer still move on to complete numerous stories.

For a work of fiction to exist it must get written down. For it to be any good, a lot of work must be done. If you want to be a great writer and you have a choice between being brilliant and lazy or being a little clueless but motivated, choose the latter. You stand a far better chance. Sure, such intangibles as creativity, talent, and inspiration play a role, but work is where the real action is.

The best way to get good at writing fiction is to write and write and write. Do it enough and you can't help but get better. Watch a kid playing a quick-reflex computer game. You will never be that adept at the game because you will never put in that many hours practicing. Go to a lake and try skipping stones across the water for a few hours. I guarantee your skipping skills will improve. Frequent practice is how I made the passage from the worst writer who ever lived to someone who occasionally turns out something worth reading, and most of the fine writers I have the pleasure of knowing will tell you the same thing.

Much of your improvement will be so incremental you won't even notice it. But then one day, after x number of months or years, voilà, there is bound to be a moment where it seems a switch was flicked, instantly changing you from Bad to Good. You'll cruise through, instinctively knowing where to turn and how to hug the curves and when to downshift and accelerate. It's an exhilarating ride and well worth the long wait.

If you're serious about creating fiction, you should set aside designated writing times, preferably most days of the week. If you leave it catch-as-catch-can, it will become all too easy to catch nothing. Some writers prefer the first blush of morning, others opt for the graveyard shift. Find the time at which you feel the most free and stimulated.

Force yourself (and the other people in your life) to stick to the schedule. It's actually more important to stick to the schedule than it is to write something wonderful at these sessions. Indeed, if you work for five hours and end up with zilch, you've still done your work for the day. (Hey, creative writing isn't like most jobs.) If you simply show up for work every time, you will have developed a discipline that will become your greatest strength. Eventually progress will be made. Some writers measure their time in pages, not hours, but unless you've got plenty of spare time, you may not want to put this pressure on yourself.

Find a place where you feel comfortable creating. Don't worry if you don't have a study with bay windows on the coast of Maine. A section of your den or a stretch of your bed can work just fine. Most writers need solitude, but some prefer the stimulation of public places. I know a professional writer who uses the corner table at a little French café as his office. He works in the café every day all day long, and even takes meetings there. He doesn't even order very much.

A regular time and place for writing seems to be the key for most writers. Then again, Joyce Carol Oates claims to have no regular writing habits and she turns out more fiction than, well, just about anyone. So the real trick is to find what works best for you.

> YOUR TURN:
> Create a week-long writing schedule for yourself, encompassing at least five hours of writing time, with the installments lasting at least an hour each. Work on a piece of fiction using this schedule for a full week. (If you have a story in progress, use that. If you need a story idea, you'll find plenty of "triggers" in the exercises throughout this book.) The idea is to utilize a writing schedule, not write a masterpiece, so don't worry about the result. When the week is done, analyze how well the schedule worked. If the schedule needs adjusting, do so. If your discipline needs adjusting, do so.

There are really two kinds of writing time, what I call *hard time* and *soft time*. Hard time refers to what is normally thought of as "writing"—at the computer screen or typewriter or pad of paper. Obviously, you'll need to put in plenty of hard time since this is where the words get written. Soft time refers to the time when you are not actually writing but pondering your work. This can happen anywhere—walking the dog, buying groceries, losing money at the casino. Pondering is a major part of the job, which is one of the cool things about being a writer.

When I started writing, I used to stare at the blank page until my forehead bled (to borrow an oft-used metaphor). I thought that's what writers did. Yes, it was torturous, but I took a certain masochistic pleasure in it. As I began to write professionally and get better, my technique shifted. I began doing more soft time in the early stages of a project, letting my mind wander in a leisurely manner. Perhaps I would do relevant research or have conversations with people about my ideas. Perhaps I would just ponder. I would take notes and maybe even write fragments here and there. After a while, I had an abundance of ideas about my story. Then . . . I took the story into hard time. The work flowed with relative ease. And it was better. I seldom needed to bandage my poor forehead.

I also recommend soft time as a tool, like a crowbar, to help out when you're stuck. If you absolutely can't figure out the resolution of your story or how to describe the mysterious stranger in the alley, don't wear yourself out with worry. Go do something else while keeping the problem somewhere in your mind. Or do some really soft time where you take a complete break from your work. Instead of desperately searching high and low for that elusive solution, let the solution come to you. Like a runaway cat that grows hungry, that solution will return home when it's ready.

Perhaps the very best time for soft time is in bed at night. As you're lying there, easing into sleep, let your mind play over some aspect of your story, maybe something you're having trouble with. You'll be amazed at what brilliant ideas sneak in at this relaxed moment. You should keep a notepad and pen by your bedside and you should make yourself jot down these ideas or they may easily disappear into the mist of your dreams. Sometimes the idea is so inspiring you simply must spring to full alert and get some writing done.

Also be aware that there are two types of writer inside every person. There's Free Spirit, who wears flouncy attire and meditates at ashrams and never stops her kids from crayoning the walls. She writes whatever and whenever she wants and doesn't give a fig what anyone thinks of it. Then there's Stern Editor, who wears button-down shirts that peek out exactly one inch from the sleeves of his double-breasted suits. He won't allow a single word that isn't necessary and he can be a stickler for logic and grammar. (He's a lot like GWW Fiction teacher Peter Selgin, who you'll meet in the Revision chapter.) Both of these people are crucial to a story's success. But they seldom see eye to eye so it's best to keep them separated.

In the early stages of a work, banish Stern Editor from the room and let Free Spirit reign in chaos. Much of the work will be fragmentary, rambling, and incoherent, but you will be tapping into that deep well where your thoughts are both wise and childlike. Pump that well until you sweat. Many writers swear by the virtues of freewriting, which means you can write whatever you want just as long as you don't lift your pen from the page or your fingers from the keyboard. Free Spirit loves freewriting. At the very least, it's a great kick-start for those times when you're stuck in the mud. Sooner or later, something interesting will emerge.

> YOUR TURN:
> Take this opening phrase: *Sam wasn't sure if it was a wonderful sign or a sign of disaster but Sam knew* . . . Write down that fictional opener, then keep going. Freewrite, meaning write without stopping or even thinking too much, just scribble away however things come out. You should write for at least five minutes but feel free to go as long as you like. No one will see this but you, and you have permission for this to be nothing but gibberish. Just feel what it's like to write in a white heat.

At some point, perhaps not until after you've dashed off a complete first draft, you'll send Free Spirit out for some herbal tea and invite Stern Editor in with his set of finely sharpened pencils. Oh, he'll make you cut and correct and shape and answer a bunch of difficult questions, but pay attention, because your future readers will be every bit as demanding as he is. Then you'll probably alternate these two helpful sides of your psyche for a while, letting each have his or her say at what you deem to be the proper times. Toward the end of the process, submit yourself to Stern Editor's iron law while Free Spirit is off prancing in the meadow, hopefully conjuring up your next big idea.

Attempted Theory #2: Ah, perhaps the answer lies here. Maybe writing fiction is akin to those personal challenges we call recreation, such as playing golf or climbing mountains or doing crossword puzzles or building ships inside bottles. These things are rewarding because they're not so easy. They awaken us by making us feel the vibrations of our inner potential, regardless of the outcome. Writing is one of the best possible personal challenges because the room for growth is as limitless as outer space and you're never too young or old to give it a go.

Could this be the big reason we want to write fiction? Uh, no, wait a second . . . I know many writers who say they enjoy having written something much more than the actual writing of it and will clip their toenails twice in one day to procrastinate. How would they fit into this explanation? Sorry, let's keep going.

DON'T BE A CHIMP

"If I could have reached my rod I would have blown his guts out."
—*The Big Kill,* Mickey Spillane

So let's see where we are in the creative process. Promising ideas + hard work = good fiction. Well, not quite. Something is still missing.

To tell a story effectively, you will need some mastery of *craft*. By craft we mean the time-tested practices that have proven helpful to the construction of good fiction.

Good writing comes down to craft far more than most people realize. True, anyone can write a story without training, which separates fiction writing from such activities as performing heart surgery or piloting a helicopter. But a working knowledge of craft is almost always necessary to make a story really good, worthy of being read by all those strangers. You could build a chair without any knowledge of woodworking because you have a good idea of what a chair is like. You would cut the wood and hammer the pieces together, and sure enough you would have a chair. But it would probably be wobbly, unsightly, and destined to break. It certainly wouldn't sell. The same is true of fiction.

You should learn craft because it works. The "rules" of fiction craft weren't created by any one person in particular. They simply emerged over time as guiding principles that made fiction writing stronger, in much the same way the mortise-and-tenon joint emerged as a good way to join parts of a chair.

Let's say you learn that it's better to *show* a character trait than to *tell* about it. (*Show, don't tell* is something of a fiction mantra, like the carpenter's *Measure twice, cut once*.) So you go back to your story in progress, cross out the line "Kathy was a dishonest woman," and insert a moment where you show Kathy doing something dishonest. Perhaps Kathy realizes the teenage cashier has given her ten dollars too much in change but Kathy slips the bill in her purse without a word. Most likely the dishonesty trait will be illustrated more dramatically, more memorably. We'll gain a more dimensional sense of Kathy as a "real" person. If dishonesty comes into play later in the story, we'll be better prepared for it. You haven't grown any wiser or more intrinsically talented. You've just picked up some *craft*. And craft makes all the difference.

In addition to making fiction better, knowledge of craft can actually make the writing easier. There is a theory that if you put a bunch of chimpanzees in a room with a bunch of typewriters, eventually one of them will tap out *Hamlet*. I have some doubts about this theory but I will say this: if those chimps know something about craft, they will get there faster. When you work with craft, you're not floundering so much, waiting to stumble accidentally into something good. Once you have some craft at your fingertips, you'll look a lot less like one of those chimps, showing teeth and screeching as you maniacally play with that toy of a keyboard.

Now, I can hear what some of you are thinking. You don't want to trod the familiar paths. You're a rebel, busting to blaze some new ground, perhaps with purple ink. Good for you. But get this: you can actually break the rules better if you know a little something about them in the first place. Take Frank Lloyd Wright. He reenvisioned architecture, creating buildings and spaces that seemed to emerge out of their natural surroundings as if they were always there. (He also served as the model for the maverick architect in Ayn Rand's *The Fountainhead*.) Yet Wright knew the structural principles of architecture through and through, and this is why his Imperial Hotel in Tokyo was one of the few buildings that withstood the Great Kanto earthquake of 1923.

Rules are made to be broken. If you follow the rules of craft too scrupulously, you'll likely end up with a story that's more of an A+ assignment than a vibrant work of art. The great writers usually break a few rules, and the greater the writer the larger the transgressions. James Joyce opened the floodgates of the human mind, letting the prose gush higher and farther and weirder than ever before. Ernest Hemingway kicked all of what he called the "bullshit" out of prose (even when he wrote about bulls), making prose simpler than was ever thought acceptable.

GWW Fiction teacher Brian Dillon likes to give each of his students five pieces of different colored candy on the first day of class. Each color represents an element of craft—red/character, black/plot, green/dialogue, orange/point of view, yellow/theme. After explaining how each color corresponds to its craft element, Brian tells his students to eat the pieces of candy. There is a point to this fiction-class version of the Eucharist. The teacher wants his students to digest the elements of craft, merge them into their systems, which is very different from slavishly following the rules.

This book will mostly focus on craft. After reading this book once or twice (and doing the nifty exercises), you will have some familiarity with all the major craft elements that go into fiction writing. They are easy enough to pick up, though you can spend a lifetime learning to manipulate them to the satisfaction of yourself or the world at large. And, believe it or not, this book is not the only place you will learn about writing craft.

As late as 1920, there weren't many, if any, good books on writing craft and there were virtually no educational programs devoted to creative writing. So where did James Joyce, Thomas Mann, Willa Cather, F. Scott Fitzgerald, Ernest Hemingway, and Gertrude Stein, all of whom wrote at that time, learn their craft? They read. They read a lot. And they analyzed the hell out of what they read. They also discussed things with other writers, often in cool expatriate locations, and that's also a good thing to do.

Painters often learn their craft by studying the masters, and writers should do the same. If you want to see how to imbue a story with the dirt and essence of its setting, read William Faulkner's *The Sound and the Fury*. If you want to see how to manipulate perception through point of view, read Henry James's *The Turn of the Screw*. If you want to see how to turn everyday life into the rising action of a plot, read Raymond Carver's "Cathedral."

Read widely and adventurously. There is no telling where you might pick up something useful. You should read some of the so-called great writers, but, if you're so inclined, don't hesitate to study those lesser lights who might make a literature professor sneer. Perhaps Mickey Spillane, creator of the *Mike Hammer* detective series, didn't quite have Edith Wharton's craftsmanship, but he probably knew a few tricks.

If you read a story that leaves you a little cold, ask yourself why. What's missing? Is the plot not quite plausible? Does the story feel pointless? Are the sentences too show-offy? Sometimes you can learn volumes from a story you don't like. And it's fine, by the way, if you find yourself bored by some work that everyone else seems to think is The Greatest Story Ever Written.

Trust your own taste. As Duke Ellington said about music: "If it sounds good, it *is* good." At the end of the day, you should be writing the kind of thing that you enjoy reading. Figure out why you like what you like, then try to utilize some of the techniques that will help you get there. Following your own taste is a good way to let your true self emerge, as long as you manage to draw a line between emulation and imitation.

> YOUR TURN:
> Return to the work of fiction that you chose as a favorite. Get your hands on a copy of this story, then pick a passage that you especially like. Write out a page or so of this section, word for word, just to let yourself feel what it might have been like to create that particular arrangement of words. You may gain some insight into *how* the author did what he did. At the very least, you'll see that everyone does it the same way—one word at a time.

Once you start mastering your craft you'll be on your way to accomplishing what has been achieved by all the writers you've admired through your own reading, on your way to holding strangers in thrall with your fiction. Out of nothing—literally nothing but the invisible vapor of imagination—you will create stories that tickle, torment, intrigue, inform, entertain, and maybe even *change* your readers. All with words alone. Your words.

Attempted Theory #3: Aha! Perhaps that is the real reason why we write fiction. The satisfaction, nay, the intoxication, of creating something we sense will soon captivate legions of readers, making us like Scheherazade, who (over the course of a thousand and one nights) transformed her murderer into her bridegroom through the sheer hypnosis of a tale brilliantly told. Who knows what earthly delights may follow—prestige, adulation, fame, money, sex, travel, the respect of our parents. And now that we're getting egotistical about it, let's face it, great fiction could give us our one real shot at the impossible—immortality.

THE BIG ANSWER

Forgive me if I got carried away back there. Sometimes we scribblers do indeed become drunk with power. But now I see, with some humility, that I haven't really succeeded at my task. The flaw in my last theory is that some people write fiction with no real intention of ever showing it to anyone, and often they're deliriously happy doing so. Alas, I've come up with several possible and plausible reasons why we write fiction, good ones at that, but it seems the "smoking gun" is still missing.

So I asked a bunch of GWW students and teachers why they write fiction, in the hope of finding an obviously dominant answer. Here are some of the responses:

I like blank paper.

To meet people I find interesting.

Writing puts me into a world that has not been written yet.

I spend much of my time contemplating love and death.

When I am writing a surge of complete happiness takes over.

To make readers hear the sound of their own heartbeats, that sound that whispers up to us: you are alive.

When I manage to turn pages and pages of crap into a little bit of art, I feel like that girl in the *Diamonds Are Forever* ad.

Writing gives me permission to be a child and to play with words the way that children play with blocks or twigs or mud.

Writing makes me a god, each new page enabling me to create and destroy as many worlds as I please.

It allows me to spy on my neighbors.

It's the only socially acceptable way to be a compulsive liar.

I want to cleanse the past.

To discover, to express, to celebrate, to acknowledge, to witness, to remember who I am.

I find out what might have been, what should have happened, and what I fear will happen.

It's a means of asking questions, though the answers may be as puzzling as a rune.

This question drives me crazy.

There is nothing else I want to do more.

My soul will not be still until the words are written on paper.

Because I can.

Because I must.

I can't not.

If I don't I will explode.

I want to be good at something and I've tried everything else.

Oh, well. The question took me on such an interesting journey, I suppose I no longer care about reaching the desired destination. Suffice it to say there is no ultimate answer for why we want to write fiction. It's as mysterious as everything else about human nature, and if human nature weren't so mysterious we probably wouldn't need to write (or read) fiction in the first place.

CHAPTER 2
CHARACTER: CASTING SHADOWS
BY BRANDI REISSENWEBER

When I taught creative writing on a pediatrics ward at a hospital I met a long-term patient, a thirteen-year-old girl who had been in and out of the hospital since she was two years old. She was sharp and witty but rarely ever wanted to write with me, no matter how enticing the writing project. She eyed me from the corner of the hospital playroom as I wrote with other young people, but every time I'd approach her she would send me away, telling me that, after all, the hospital wasn't school.

One day, I found her reading a book in her room. I sat down and asked if she would read to me, which she did. That afternoon, I learned that she loved to read books, so we talked about some of our favorite stories. I asked, thinking it was a simple question: "Why do you enjoy reading?"

She looked at me, scratched her shortly cropped hair, and then opened her book again. I thought she was through with me as her eyes began to follow the lines on the pages. After a few minutes she looked up at me and said: "Because I get to meet lots of different people."

We eventually wrote a story together. It was fantastical and full of the kinds of people she wanted to be around: those who could fly, aliens who would befriend her, people who were outrageous, graceful, and courageous, just like her. But what stuck with me most was her response to my question—that she read to meet people. That answer to what I thought was a simple inquiry lies at the heart of good storytelling.

When you read fiction, you are, first and foremost, meeting people. Characters are the core of a story and interact with or influence every other element of fiction. Characters are what drive a story, carrying the reader from the first to the last page, making readers care. How exciting would Ken Kesey's *One Flew Over the Cuckoo's Nest* be without Randle McMurphy, the rabble-rouser asylum patient who shakes up the system? Without Miss Amelia, the self-reliant and cross store owner who is unlucky in love, Carson McCullers's "The Ballad of the Sad Café" would be about a dull, dusty town. And without the mysterious and glamorous Jay Gatsby, F. Scott Fitzgerald's *The Great Gatsby* would be far from great.

Good writers create a sense that their characters are people—physical, emotional, living, breathing, thinking people. The more you manage to make your characters feel real, to create the illusion of an actual person on the page, the more likely your reader is to fall into the story, past the language and the words, letting the real world recede and be replaced by the fictional world you have created. As a writer, you want your reader to feel that your characters are substantial, authentic, dimensional. Real enough to cast shadows. Creating characters that seem dimensional and lifelike requires some artistry, to be sure, but with a little knowledge such a miraculous feat is entirely possible. Let's examine the process.

THE BEAT OF DESIRE

Desire beats in the heart of every dimensional character. A character should want something. Desire is a driving force of human nature and, applied to characters, it creates a steam of momentum to drive a story forward. You may create a character with quirky habits and high intellect and vague tendencies toward adventure, but if all he does is sit on the couch and snack on lemon squares, the reader is going to find more excitement in thumb twiddling. Give that same character a desire to travel from Florida to Maine in a hot-air balloon and that begins to propel the story into motion, especially if the character doesn't know how to acquire or pilot a hot-air balloon.

A character's desire can be huge, looming, and intoxicating, like the desire to ease loneliness, to seek the revenge of a son's death, or to climb to the peak of Mount Everest. Or the desire can be smaller and simpler: to find a wedge of stellar Brie, to escape the complaining of an ailing wife, or to coax the orchids into finally blooming in the backyard garden.

The grandness or simplicity of the desire is not important as long as the character wants it badly. In Katherine Anne Porter's short story "Theft," the main character simply wants to retrieve her empty purse. However, this desire is rendered important to her and, therefore, it is important to the reader. A strong desire helps the reader identify and sympathize with the character, whereas a character without a strong desire will bore your readers, a great way to get them to abandon your story for good. After all, why should the reader care about a character retrieving a purse if she only *kind of* wants it back?

One of the benefits of spending time drawing a main character who has a strong desire is that the story line will grow organically from the character's need. In Vladimir Nabokov's *Lolita,* for example, the main character, Humbert Humbert, desires nymphets (his word for beautiful preteen girls), a category in which the youthful Lolita reigns queen. The story grows out of Humbert Humbert's attempts to possess Lolita's body and affections. If he didn't crave Lolita with such fierceness, there would be no story.

What happens when characters don't have desire? I once had a student who wrote a piece about two boys exploring their grandmother's vast mansion. The reader followed the children up creaking stairs, into the dank attic, behind a false wall, and past steamer trunks filled with old photographs.

The description was wonderful, but the story fizzled out quickly. Why? Because the characters didn't want anything. They were content with their adventures. Description, no matter how brilliantly crafted, cannot carry a story. What the piece needed was a driving force, a momentum to thrust the reader forward. If the boys found themselves trapped in the attic, the summer sun quickly heating up the small space to an unbearable degree, creating a desire for escape, that would have added some tension and interest. The gears of the story machine don't start swirling into action until characters have a desire.

Desires, however, are not always as straightforward as they are in Porter's "Theft" and Nabokov's *Lolita.* For instance, in Raymond Carver's "So Much Water So Close to Home," Claire attempts to come to terms with her husband's decision to continue with a fishing trip even after he and his buddies find a young woman's dead body floating in the river. They secure the woman's wrist to a tree trunk so her body won't float away, and it is not until they are on their way home, when they can conveniently reach a phone, that they report the body to the police.

The story revolves around Claire, who wants to understand what has happened on this weekend, and why her husband and his friends dealt with the body so insensitively. Out of Claire's intense desire to seek understanding, she questions her husband, which leads to arguments between them. She scours the newspapers for information and travels to attend the young woman's funeral. She begins to sleep in the guest bedroom and is awakened one night to her husband breaking the lock on the bedroom door, simply to prove that he can do so. Claire's desire to understand and come to terms with the decision her husband made is complex and circuitous, but no less compelling.

> YOUR TURN:
> Think of a character. If that's too vague, make this character some kind of performer—actor, singer, magician—who has hit middle age and is finding that his or her career is now mostly faded glory. Or use a parent or child who is having difficulty with his or her own parent or child. Then think of a specific desire for this character. One driving desire. Make the desire something concrete—money, a career break, the touch of a certain person—instead of an abstract desire like love or personal growth. Once you find the character and desire, jot them down. We'll be coming back to this character shortly.

HUMAN COMPLEXITY

Nothing is less compelling in a story than a character who acts like a million other characters you've encountered, exhibiting only one facet: the kindly grandma, the sinister janitor, the heroic patient. It's easy enough to fall into this trap because it's so easy to see people as types, at first. For example, the well-situated investment banker—are you picturing formal suits and a furrowed forehead? Long hours, lots of technical gadgets like handheld palm pilots and cellular phones, and a whole lot of excess cash? That's a good place to start with this character, but your specific character should transcend this type. Richard, an investment banker, might have a lot of excess cash and work long hours, but maybe he also makes anonymous donations to the local Humane Society. On evenings when he's had too much imported beer, he calls his sister's last known number, even though she hasn't lived there for at least a year.

Such distinctiveness makes Richard different from any other person who might fall into his type. When you create characters, explore the specific and unique details that will make them complex; not a type but a real person. We carry with us our histories, our experiences, our memories, each of our bundles distinctly different from anyone else's. Craft characters in the same fashion.

In Joyce Carol Oates's "Where Are You Going, Where Have You Been?" Connie, the main character, is a fifteen-year-old girl who is self-absorbed and insecure. Yet Oates didn't stop there. She gave Connie qualities that raise her beyond this type. Connie has a "high, breathless, amused voice which made everything she said sound a little forced, whether it was sincere or not." She easily abandons her friend when a popular guy comes along. She has disdain for her sister for still living at home at twenty-four years old and for not being as beautiful as Connie. She is convinced that her mother likes her better because of her beauty and that their arguments are just a front, "a pretense of exasperation, a sense that they were tugging and struggling over something of little value to either one of them." In the end, when her family is away at a barbecue and the sinister Arnold Friend pulls up and threatens to harm her family if she doesn't submit to him, Connie eventually relents, sacrificing herself by walking toward Arnold, toward what she "did not recognize except to know that she was going to it."

From the small details, like the sound of her voice, to the larger details of the ultimate decision she makes, Connie is revealed as a complex character. Not every fifteen-year-old teenager possesses this combination of traits. Not every fifteen-year-old would make the decision to walk out that door at the end of the story. Connie is not a type. She is a dimensional character, substantial enough to cast a shadow.

Writers are sometimes drawn specifically to the allure of the all-good or all-evil character, which is another version of the typecast character. Unless you're writing a fairy tale, you'll want to avoid these extremes. Aristotle once wrote that a character should be one "whose misfortune is brought about by some error or frailty." Whether your characters meet misfortune or not, flaws will make them more interesting and authentic.

Frankie Machine, the main character in Nelson Algren's *The Man with the Golden Arm,* a card dealer in the nighttime circuit of Chicago's bars, is a predominantly good character but certainly not without flaws. The most obvious flaw is his frantic struggle with drug addiction. Also, he seeks solace in an affair with Molly-O, avoiding his wife, who is cooped up at home in a wheelchair. And the crushing guilt Frankie feels over his wife's immobility eventually causes him to leave her.

Those characters who are *not* fundamentally good should also be rendered with multiple facets. Bad guys aren't bad every single second of the day. Sometimes, they're just hanging out eating their take-out Chinese food, or waiting in line with their car at the car wash, or even doing something kindly, like helping an old lady pick up apples that have fallen from her grocery bag.

Lolita stirred a lot of controversy when it was published and Nabokov spent quite a bit of time insisting that his own knowledge of nymphets was purely scholarly, unlike the fictional Humbert Humbert, who molested young girls. In *Lolita,* Nabokov committed one of the toughest acts of the fiction writer: staying true to the humanness of a reprehensible character. Humbert Humbert is as disgusting and deplorable a character as any ever written and it would be easy to cast him in a light that shows him as only horrid. Yet Nabokov allows him some appealing traits: decided charm, dazzling intelligence, a sense of shame for his weakness, and, ultimately, a genuine love for Lolita.

Literature is filled with great villains. Part of what makes them so compelling is the tiny bit of ourselves we can see in them. Usually there is something, however small, that a reader can relate to. In *Lolita,* the reader can relate to Humbert Humbert's inability to resist a desire he knows is wrong. Although Humbert's desire is extreme, that basic idea of wanting and indulging in what you shouldn't—be it greasy foods, cigarettes, or too much mind-numbing television—is a very human trait. In showing Humbert Humbert as something more than an inhuman monster, the impact of his misdeeds is much more powerful.

YOUR TURN:
Recall the worst person you've ever met.
A psychotic boss, a back-stabbing friend,
a playground bully. Or make someone up.
Next, assign one redeeming quality to this

character—kindness, courtesy, sympathy, a fondness for animals. Then write a passage with this person in action. Perhaps you show a sadistic ex-spouse helping a homeless person find shelter, or a bank robber arranging a baby-sitter on behalf of a woman he's just tied up. The result? A fully dimensional villain.

CONTRASTING TRAITS

A fascinating element of human nature is that we all possess contrasting traits, sometimes subtle, other times greatly conflicting. These contrasts provide endless opportunity to make your characters complex.

We see this very clearly in Oates's "Where Are You Going, Where Have You Been?" where Connie behaves one way with her family and another way when she's out with her friends:

> *Everything about her had two sides to it, one for home and one for anywhere that was not home: her walk that could be childlike and bobbing, or languid enough to make anyone think she was hearing music in her head, her mouth which was pale and smirking most of the time, but bright pink on these evenings out, her laugh which was cynical and drawling at home—"Ha, ha, very funny"—but high-pitched and nervous anywhere else, like the jingling of the charms on her bracelet.*

Details such as her girlish walk at home and her fluid saunter outside of home show the reader Connie's dual personality, which hints at both her childlike innocence and her devious, secretive side. This contrast in Connie's actions helps to reveal the complexity of her character, to show the struggle with her own identities—who she was as a young girl and who she will become as a woman.

You might think of contrasting qualities as places where the characterization is unexpected or not quite matching up. A college football hero bravely battling leukemia need not be cowardly in order to exhibit contrasting qualities. A more subtle option would be preferable. His pride could be wounded by a bad call in the game, or he could drive recklessly while his younger brother is in the passenger seat, or betray a friend's secret. Any of these would add a level of complexity to the character without being too predictable.

Regardless of what kind of contrasting traits you give your characters, keep in mind that contrasts do not leap forward and say, *Here I am, a contrast! Revel in my humanity!* The best contrasts are so seamlessly sewn with the characterization that they're not easy to spot; they seep into the characterization. The reader should experience the tension, not be spotting contrasts like stop signs along the road.

> YOUR TURN:
> Return to the character for whom you created a desire. Now give this person two contrasting traits. Let's say you chose an actress hoping to win an audition. Maybe she's overly considerate to people but turns into a witch if she feels slighted by someone. Jot down the contrasting traits. We'll be coming back to this character again soon.

CONSISTENCY

Unless your character swallows some kind of Jekyll/Hyde potion, you don't want to have him or her behave one way for most of the story and then change with just a snap at the end. All actions and behaviors should seem authentic and true to the character based on what you have established. Contrasting qualities are important, but your characterizations should still be consistent. Hmm . . . That seems like a contradiction: our characters should have contrasting qualities, but should be consistent.

Here's the difference. Contrasting qualities are moments of humanness. Keeping a character consistent is a general issue of good characterization. Rod may be a cocky, angry guy, defensive when someone asks the time, a person who cuts to the front of a long line at the convenience store when he has only one item. But perhaps he also stops to look, with interest, at a poster for a carnival. Something is going on there. Maybe he's putting on airs with his defensiveness and he really does like the fun, carefree things in life. Or maybe the poster reminds him of something he did with his own son before he divorced his wife and they moved to another state. Either way, it's a contrast in action: he projects an angry persona but shows interest in a carnival, a happy and rather playful event. It's believable that he could have these conflicting traits. However, if we see Rod as self-assured, gruff, and dismissive for the first nine pages of a story and then, on page ten, he starts wandering around a carnival, excited to ride the Ferris wheel *for no reason at all,* then the character has not stayed consistent.

Characters can do something "out of character" as long as you show the reader a glimmer of that tendency ahead of time. If a shy character who usually plays it safe does something courageous or risky, the reader needs to see where this is in his realm of capability before it happens.

Nothing is worse than walking away from a story thinking there is no way *that* character would have done *that* action. Even if readers are very surprised by what your character does (which is a good thing), the characterization should still be consistent.

In "Queen Devil" by Kathy Hepinstall, Nick, the narrator's brother, does something utterly surprising—he shoots and (presumably) kills his wife. Quite a shock. Nick, up to that point, had been crafted as a man who deeply missed his wife and children, who recently left him. He's the kind of guy who, seeing his daughter's pink hair comb in his fishing tackle box, has this reaction: "'My baby,' he says. 'My sweet girl.'"

What makes Nick's character consistent and believable? Despite Nick's genuine affection for his family, the intensity of his anger is apparent throughout the story. He talks about his wife and his resentment toward her. He drinks a great deal. Both of these indications of instability make Nick a volatile character and show the angry energy that simmers below the surface.

Some of his dialogue with his sister, Jill, betrays what he is capable of. For example, when his wife leaves, Nick calls Jill: "When Nick's wife told him she was leaving him, he called me up and was not my brother, suddenly. He said, 'Remember, I'm a hunter. Remember, I have a closet full of guns.'"

Later, he says of his wife: "She won't get away with this." He then quickly backtracks when Jill questions him: "'All I mean,' he says, the sweet tone in his voice back, 'is that she'll miss old Nick someday.'"

So these desperate ideas have been, in one way or another, roaming around in Nick's mind and the writer makes sure that the reader senses that. His motivations for his final, violent action are clear.

You do want a sense of surprise in your characterizations; it's part of what creates a satisfying sense of journey and discovery in a story. We see this kind of thing often in fiction: the humble and submissive Chief Bromden escapes from the oppressive ward at the end of *One Flew Over the Cuckoo's*

Nest; the hardened, bitter Joy in Flannery O'Connor's "Good Country People" removes her wooden leg, making herself feel completely vulnerable to the Bible salesman she at first disdains. You want your characters to be consistent, but you don't want characters who are completely straightforward and predictable, so much so that they are incapable of discrepancy or change.

THE ABILITY TO CHANGE

Characters should possess the ability to change, and the reader should see this potential. Change is particularly important for a story's main character. Just as the desire of a main character drives the story, the character's change is often the story's culmination. While a main character usually does change to some degree, either dramatically or in the more gentle form of a realization, this does not mean your character actually has to make a change at the end of the story or that the change has to be whole and complete. However, the reader should see that the character is capable of doing so throughout the story—the choice should be there. If you don't create the potential for change, the character will feel predictable and the reader will quickly lose interest. That puts you back on the couch with the character who has no desire, just hanging out and eating lemon squares.

In Anton Chekhov's "The Lady with the Dog," the main character, Dmitry, changes drastically. At the beginning of the story, his attitude toward women, who he deems "the inferior race," is dismal, although he recognizes his inability to spend more than two days without them. He finds his wife of "limited intelligence" but is fearful of her and has many fleeting affairs. The story centers around Dmitry's desire for Anna, a desire that starts out calmly, when he first hears about the buzz of the new woman in Yalta, "the lady with the pet dog," and builds in intensity through their affair. By the end of the story, Dmitry feels he is truly in love for the first time in his life. The story ends with Dmitry holding his head in frustration, wondering how he and Anna will be together. His attitude changes from women being expendable to finding this one woman absolutely necessary.

Going back to *Lolita,* the reader knows that Humbert Humbert is capable of not pursuing nymphets—not that it would be easy or desirable to him to change his ways. However, the reader sees that he is capable. He holds back and resists during times when he must, such as when Lolita's mother is around. He laments his own desire for nymphets and wishes that he could resist more often. In the end, he returns to Lolita when she is seventeen and pregnant, nowhere close to her former nymphet self, and he finds he is still in love with her. He's changed in that he loves Lolita beyond her nymphet status, but there's little doubt that, left alone with another young nymphet, he would likely try to quench his desire. So, Humbert Humbert does change, but not entirely.

> YOUR TURN:
> Return to the character for whom you have created a desire and contrasting traits. Time to bring this person to life. Write a passage where this character is pursuing his or her desire in some way. For example, perhaps the actress is traveling to an audition to which she was not invited. (Oh, yes, it'll help tremendously if you put some obstacles in the character's path.) You don't have to bring this "quest" to a conclusion, but have something happen that allows both contrasting traits to emerge and also try to include some hint that the character is capable of change. That's a lot of juggling, so don't worry if it comes out a little clumsy. Dimension doesn't always happen overnight.

WHERE CHARACTERS COME FROM

To craft fascinating and memorable characters, you will need a starting point. So where will your characters come from? Look around you, and into your memory and mind. Your characters will emerge from people you know and see and even imagine. Inspiration for characters is everywhere.

Writers often construct characters by beginning with interesting people or characteristics of people they know. Some writers even start with their own personality as a basis for a character and build from there. Nelson Algren immersed himself in the downtrodden of the Chicago he wrote about in *The Man with the Golden Arm*. He likely based the main character, Frankie Machine, on a man named Doc who dealt at the poker games Algren played in on Division Street. Parts of Algren went into Frankie too.

Like Frankie, Algren served in the army during World War II, and when he was discharged he came home with very little in his pockets. Starting with people you know, including yourself, lets you create characters that spring from a strong foundation of knowledge and intimacy.

However, keep in mind that when you deal with real people, you have to leave room for creative invention. I've worked with writers who say their character is based on someone they know, and then they spend all their time making sure the character's actions stick to fact. Instead of wondering *What would my character do in this situation?* they're wondering *What would my real-life brother (or aunt, or best friend) do in this situation?* You can drive yourself crazy trying to figure out if you're writing the story "right" or if the actual person would do what you have them doing. Much better to let yourself fictionalize these people, transform them into characters that suit the needs of your story.

You can also draw inspiration from people you don't know. People watching is a great activity for developing characters. Observe people in action and then take it a step further by imagining what kind of situation they are in. See that young girl on the bench at the bus stop wiping her eyes and trying to hold back her tears? Why might she be doing that? See the group at the bar, flight attendants on a layover? How do they get along? What is going on between the redheaded man who seems so self-conscious and the woman who's avoiding talking to him?

You can take this all a step further and introduce the question *What if?* What if someone tried to sit down by the weeping girl and console her? What would the girl do? What if one of the other men put his hand on the knee of the woman avoiding conversation with the redheaded man? How would each react?

Of course, you might find that characters people your imagination constantly. You don't need to investigate where they come from. Just pluck one out who seems particularly evocative to you and get to the task of getting acquainted.

GETTING TO KNOW THEM

Take the time to get to know your characters as if they were good friends, even the unpleasant characters whom you would probably not befriend in real life. Investing time during the developmental stages helps you understand your characters more intimately, which allows you to put them on the page with more authenticity.

Put your characters in different scenarios and imagine how they would get themselves out of or even deeper into those situations. For instance, what would your character do after accidentally walking out of a department store with an item she had tried on, like a bracelet or a hat, but didn't pay for? Characters do not exist in a vacuum, so imagine how they act and react in the world. Chris, born and raised in Brooklyn, is likely to react differently on a subway in New York City than on a bus in Atlanta, Georgia. In New York City, he's on his home turf, knows the stops by memory. In Atlanta, he might be watching out the window with anticipation, looking for street signs to see if he's reached his stop. He might be more inclined to put his bag on the seat next to him, something he'd never consider doing in the busy subways of the city.

While fleshing out your characters, you should consider the following categories:

Appearance: You can't judge a book by its cover, but a cover can be informative and set up expectations. How your character holds herself, what she chooses to wear, or what kind of expression she has when she walks down the street are meaningful. Think of your character in three dimensions, taking up space. The style and presence with which characters inhabit the world reveal a great deal about their attitude and personality.

Background: A woman who grew up in a family with seventeen kids is going to have a much different experience from a woman who grew up as an only child. While we certainly can't make sweeping value judgments about characters' backgrounds, the characters will undoubtedly be impacted by their previous experiences. How they grew up, how they loved, lost, learned . . . all these things will help to shape them.

Personality: This is shaped largely by the previous two categories, the end result of everything the person is and has been. What is your character really like? How does her mind work? What are his inclinations? Disposition? Outlook? Hopes? Fears? A character's personality contains the larger truths of the person, which will indicate how she will act and react in a story.

Primary Identity: What is your character's primary definition of herself? Ask several people to respond to this question: *Who are you?* Some will answer by occupation or ethnicity, others by gender or age. The answer to that question is usually what the person identifies with most strongly, how he defines himself. A person who answers "I am a lawyer" has a much different primary identity than the one who answers "I am Hindu." They may both be lawyers, they may both be Hindu, but they identify more strongly with different parts of their identity.

QUESTIONS

Ask yourself all sorts of questions about your characters to get a better idea of who they are. Many writers like to make lists of questions which they answer in writing. This type of "homework" helps you gain a wellspring of knowledge about your characters.

You might start with questions that address the basics about a character:

- What is your character's name? Does the character have a nickname?
- What is your character's hair color? Eye color?
- What kind of distinguishing facial features does your character have? Does your character have a birthmark? Where is it? What about scars? How did he get them?
- Who are your character's friends and family? Who does she surround herself with? Who are the people your character is closest to? Who does he wish he were closest to?
- Where was your character born? Where has she lived since then? Where does she call home?
- Where does your character go when he's angry?
- What is her biggest fear? Who has she told this to? Who would she never tell this to? Why?

- Does she have a secret?
- What makes your character laugh out loud?
- When has your character been in love? Had a broken heart?

Then dig deeper by asking more unconventional questions:
- What is in your character's refrigerator right now? On her bedroom floor? On her nightstand? In her garbage can?
- Look at your character's feet. Describe what you see there. Does he wear dress shoes, gym shoes, or none at all? Is he in socks that are ratty and full of holes? Or is he wearing a pair of blue-and-gold slippers knitted by his grandmother?
- When your character thinks of her childhood kitchen, what smell does she associate with it? Sauerkraut? Oatmeal cookies? Paint? Why is that smell so resonate for her?
- Your character is doing intense spring cleaning. What is easy for her to throw out? What is difficult for her to part with? Why?
- It's Saturday at noon. What is your character doing? Give details. If he's eating breakfast, what exactly does he eat? If she's stretching out in her backyard to sun, what kind of blanket or towel does she lie on?
- What is one strong memory that has stuck with your character from childhood? Why is it so powerful and lasting?
- Your character is getting ready for a night out. Where is she going? What does she wear? Who will she be with?

For a downloadable version of these and many other "character questions," go to the Writer's Toolbox area of the Gotham Writers' Workshop Web site—www.writingclasses.com.

You certainly won't end up using all the information you gather from these question—as a matter of fact, you shouldn't—but the more you know your characters, the better you will be able to draw them on the page in a believable way. The novelist E. M. Forster, in his classic book *Aspects of the Novel,* wrote that a character is real when the writer knows everything about him: "He may not choose to tell all he knows—many of the facts, even of the kind we call obvious, may be hidden. But he will give us the feeling that though the character has not been explained, it is explicable . . ."

YOUR TURN:
Go out into the world and find a character.
Observe someone you don't know, like a fellow

diner in a restaurant, or someone you know only a little, like the bank cashier you see once a week. Talk to him or her, if you like, though you don't have to. Make some notes, mental or written. Then fill in the unknown blanks of this person by answering all or most of the suggested questions on the preceding pages. You'll be making up most of the details, but that's okay. This *is* fiction.

KINDS OF CHARACTERS

Not all characters must be developed with the same depth. Your main concern with characterization falls on the most prominent characters in your story. They, of course, should be developed the most fully.

This is particularly vital for the main character of the story, often referred to as the protagonist. All of the dimensional aspects we've discussed—desire, complexity, contrast, consistency, change—invariably come into play with a story's protagonist. Stories tend to have one protagonist, although you will find that some novels have two or more protagonists. Jay Gatsby is the protagonist of *The Great Gatsby,* a man shrouded in mystery who devotes his life to winning back the elusive Daisy. The protagonist of Raymond Carver's "Cathedral" is an unnamed fellow who unexpectedly sees in a new way with the help of a blind man.

Stories sometimes include an antagonist, a person who poses a formidable obstacle to the protagonist's desire. Tom Buchanan, Daisy's husband, is the antagonist of *The Great Gatsby* because he actively stands in the way of Gatsby winning Daisy. Tom may be considered a "bad guy" because he is a philanderer and is sometimes rough with Daisy, but antagonists don't have to be "bad." Robert, the blind man who comes to visit in "Cathedral," is the story's antagonist but he's a perfectly nice fellow. Of course, there are often numerous major characters, aside from the protagonist and antagonist, especially in novels. In *The Great Gatsby,* for example, Daisy and Nick are certainly major and fully dimensional characters.

Secondary characters are the supporting cast. Some of the secondary characters will go through a bit of development, but not of the same intensity as the main characters. The trick with the lesser players in your story is to find a few defining details that really capture their essence. Jordan is a secondary character in *The Great Gatsby,* defined by her stature as a golf pro and her gossipy tendencies, as is Meyer Wolfsheim, who is defined as a shadowy figure of the business underworld. In "Cathedral," the wife is a secondary character, kind to Robert, irritated by her husband, but mostly in the background.

Extras are the characters who populate the fictional world but don't have a significant impact on the story. They appear but don't achieve any dimension beyond their limited role. The waitress who makes an appearance for one scene need not be thoroughly examined, nor the ex-husband who doesn't play a central role but occasionally takes the kids for a weekend. In *The Great Gatsby*, Gatsby's servants are extras, as are many of the lively attendees at his parties. "Cathedral," on the other hand, does not have any extras.

Often you'll hear the terms *round* and *flat* characters. Round characters are fully developed and lifelike, possessing the qualities we've discussed in this chapter. E. M. Forster notes that a round character is capable of surprising a reader in a convincing way, which echoes the need for contrast and consistency in characterization. Flat characters are those who are characterized only by their role or a minor action. Flat characters are not necessarily a bad thing; it's important to let very small characters be flat. Fleshing them out too much gives them an emotional weight that will mislead the readers or steal focus from the stars of the story.

SHOWING AND TELLING

A key question remains: how do we put seemingly real people on the page, conveying a sense of their total humanity using not blood, flesh, and muscle but merely words?

There are two basic methods of revealing a character in fiction: showing and telling. Sometimes it is most efficient for the narrator just to *tell* the reader about a character. For example, in *The Man with the Golden Arm*, the narrator simply tells the reader about Frankie Machine and his friend, Sparrow, as they sit in jail:

> *The tranquil, square-faced, shagheaded little buffalo-eyed blond called Frankie Machine and the ruffled, jittery punk called Sparrow felt they were about as sharp as the next pair of hustlers. These walls, that had held them both before, had never held either long.*

The characters aren't shown with specific actions that reveal their physical traits or their hustling. The writer just tells us what he wants us to know. Here telling is appropriate because it makes a quick distinction between Frankie and Sparrow and it introduces their racket as hustlers, in and out of jail.

But do not overrely on telling. Writing instructors frequently proclaim *Show don't tell* in the margins of student manuscripts, often adorning the advice with an exclamation point. For very good reason. Revealing information through showing is generally more interesting than telling about it, because showing gives the reader more with which to engage actively. The bulk of characterization should come through showing characters to the reader.

For example:

> *Greta is a twenty-three-year-old artist and interior designer who dislikes having a roommate.*

Now the basic information about Greta is out in the open and you can get on with things. In this *telling* example about Greta the reader learns her name, her age, her occupations, and her dislike of having a roommate. However, in most cases it would be stronger to *show* Greta's character rather than just tell about it.

The trick in showing instead of telling is to find the specific details that will convey the necessary information while the reader's attention stays on the character's emotion and actions—the interesting stuff. For example:

> *After a stressful week at Mr. Feinmen's, experimenting with materials that might transform their front foyer into a low-ceilinged cave, Greta sat at a secluded corner of the café, sipping tea. Maybe once her roommate left for the night, she could have a little time to experiement with molding the wire mesh into skeleton marionettes.*

The basic facts are still in this version—you get an idea of Greta's age, and learn about her job as an interior designer and her dislike of having a roommate. But in this version there's even more information. You get a sense of Greta's eccentric, even macabre, artistic taste. Also the nature of her roommate difficulty begins to appear: Greta doesn't feel like she has her own space to do her art at home. You also see how Greta handles stress: she chooses to hide in a café instead of confronting the problem. Interestingly, she seems to favor cavelike surroundings in both her artistic and her personal life. She drinks tea, which tells the reader something different than if she were drinking a beer. A martini would say something else.

And, best of all, the second version is much more interesting to read because it gives the reader an opportunity to interact more with the story. The reader's attention stays focused on the action and on Greta's desire, which creates momentum and tension while also conveying bits of characterization.

Showing also allows you to slow down and reveal the character's intricacies gradually. In real life you don't sit down and lay out all the beautiful and ugly things about yourself at once. You don't fess up to everything right away. Instead, those things about you that make you human and individual reveal themselves gradually over time to the people around you. This same thing happens in fiction, only it doesn't take a lifetime.

There are four ways to show a character's traits:

- Action
- Speech
- Appearance
- Thought

These four methods allow you to reveal characters in all their dimensional glory.

ACTION

You know the clichés: *Actions speak louder than words* and *I'll believe it when I see it.* Action is in demand in stories because it reveals so much to the reader. A character's personality comes through in the way she handles the next-door neighbor who leaves his garbage outside his apartment until someone else takes it out, the ways she spends her Tuesday nights, the way she copes with the screaming man on the train. Action is usually the strongest method of revealing a character.

In *The Great Gatsby,* Daisy is revealed very distinctly by her actions when she sees Nick, the narrator and Daisy's cousin, for the first time in years:

She laughed again, as if she said something very witty, and held my hand for a moment, looking up into my face, promising that there was no one in the world she so much wanted to see. That was the way she had.

Daisy treats Nick with earnest attention. She grabs hold of his hand and looks into his face, as if he's the only person in the world at that moment. This action helps to characterize Daisy's charm and her background as a Southern belle.

While all actions are revealing, the actions a character takes in the time of crisis often cut to the core of the character's true self and intentions. After Daisy admits to her husband, Tom, that she loves Gatsby and will be leaving Tom for him—showing her romantic longing—Daisy and Gatsby drive back from the city. Daisy, at the wheel, strikes and accidentally kills a woman (Tom's lover, no less) then drives away—showing her nervousness under pressure. Gatsby offers to say he was driving to protect Daisy and drops her off at home. He waits outside, thinking she's locked up in her room, as they had agreed to a code she could make with the lights should Tom give her any trouble. Nick, however, sees her downstairs with Tom:

Daisy and Tom were sitting opposite each other at the kitchen table with a plate of cold fried chicken between them and two bottles of ale. He was talking intently across the table at her and in his earnestness his hand had fallen upon and covered her own. Once in a while she looked up at him and nodded in agreement.

They weren't happy, and neither of them had touched the chicken or the ale—and yet they weren't unhappy either. There was an unmistakable air of natural intimacy about the picture and anybody would have said that they were conspiring together.

Here Daisy's true nature is revealed. In this moment, when she's pledged her love for Gatsby, then killed a woman with her reckless driving, she follows her husband and stays in the safety of her marriage, leaving Gatsby to take the fall. This reveals a great deal about Daisy: her duplicity, submissiveness, cowardice, and inability to withstand social pressure. She's come a long way from the charming belle we first meet in the beginning.

Flannery O'Connor, in her book *Mystery and Manners,* describes how she once gave a few of her early stories to a lady who lived down the street. The woman returned them saying, "Them stories just gone and shown you how some folks would do." To this, O'Connor commented: "I thought to myself that that was right; when you write stories, you have to be content to start exactly there—showing how some specific folks will do, will do in spite of everything." Place fourteen characters in the exact same circumstances and you should get fourteen very different courses of action and approaches to the situation—fourteen different illustrations of what each character *will do.*

SPEECH

Characters are also revealed through their speech. What people say, how they say it, and what they don't say are all very illuminating. If you want to get to know someone, what do you do? You talk to them.

In *The Great Gatsby,* Daisy talks with a childlike giddiness, as seen in these three snippets of dialogue:

> *"Do you always watch for the longest day of the year and then miss it? I always watch for the longest day in the year and then miss it."*

> *"I'll tell you a family secret," she whispered enthusiastically. "It's about the butler's nose. Do you want to hear about the butler's nose?"*

> *"You see I think everything's terrible anyhow," she went on in a convinced way. "Everybody thinks so—the most advanced people. And I know. I've been everywhere and seen everything and done everything."*

Daisy's questions and confidences and blanket statements show the reader her wide-eyed wonder and naïve nature. As the story progresses, however, we begin to glean that there is tension beneath the gaiety.

APPEARANCE

A glimpse of someone can give you a lot of information about his personality. You can draw conclusions from physical looks, clothing style, gait, and facial expression. The way a character appears gives the reader information about how this person presents himself and occupies space in the world.

In *The Great Gatsby,* the reader first meets Tom Buchanan, Daisy's husband, this way:

> *He had changed since his New Haven years. Now he was a sturdy, straw-haired man of thirty with a rather hard mouth and a supercilious*

manner. Two shining, arrogant eyes had established dominance over his face and gave him the appearance of always leaning aggressively forward. Not even the effeminate swank of his riding clothes could hide the enormous power of that body—he seemed to fill those glistening boots until he strained the top lacing and you could see a great pack of muscle shifting when his shoulder moved under his thin coat. It was a body capable of enormous leverage—a cruel body.

Tom's aggression and confidence are apparent in the way he stands with his legs apart on the front porch. The description of his mouth, his eyes, and the way he inhabits his clothing gives the impression of a strong and unrelenting man.

Don't just go for the obvious when focusing on your character's appearance. Sometimes oddball details, like the description of Meyer Wolfsheim's cufflinks made of human teeth and the "two fine growths of hair which luxuriated in either nostril," can be particularly revealing.

THOUGHT

Fiction has the pliancy to get inside characters' minds, often with more grace and depth than other forms of storytelling. In movies and plays thought is not as easily conveyed, but in fiction the character's thoughts can be bared directly to the reader.

In *The Great Gatsby,* the reader has direct access to Nick's thoughts since the story is told from his point of view. Here is a glimpse inside his mind:

I liked to walk up Fifth Avenue and pick out romantic women from the crowd and imagine that in a few minutes I was going to enter into their lives, and no one would ever know or disapprove. Sometimes, in my mind, I followed them to their apartments on the corners of hidden streets, and they turned and smiled back at me before they faded through a door into the warm darkness. At the enchanted metropolitan twilight, I felt a haunting loneliness sometimes, and felt it in the others—poor young clerks who loitered in front of windows waiting until it was time for a solitary restaurant dinner—young clerks in the dusk, wasting the poignant moments of night and life.

This moment of thought shows Nick's loneliness in the way he fantasizes about entering into women's lives, getting smiles from them before they move on, a moment of acknowledgment. The reader sees a very secret side of Nick, something he likely wouldn't share with anyone.

A SYMPHONY OF METHODS

Use these four methods—action, speech, appearance, thought—in concert to create a sense of depth in the moment-to-moment experience of the story. In real life, we experience people in a variety of ways, often simultaneously, and mixing the methods re-creates this sense of reality.

In "Cathedral," the narrator's wife is expecting a visitor: a blind man, Robert, whom she once worked for and continued to keep in touch with over the years. The narrator isn't thrilled about his visit and is uncomfortable about the fact that the man is blind. Here's what happens when the narrator first meets Robert:

> *This blind man, feature this, he was wearing a full beard! A beard on a blind man! Too much, I say. The blind man reached into the back seat and dragged out a suitcase. My wife took his arm, shut the car door, and, talking all the way, moved him down the drive and then up the steps to the front porch. I turned off the TV. I finished my drink, rinsed the glass, dried my hands. Then I went to the door.*
>
> *My wife said, "I want you to meet Robert. Robert, this is my husband. I've told you all about him." She was beaming. She had this blind man by his coat sleeve.*
>
> *The blind man let go of his suitcase and up came his hand.*
>
> *I took it. He squeezed hard, held my hand, and then he let it go.*
>
> *"I feel like we've already met," he boomed.*
>
> *"Likewise," I said. I didn't know what else to say. Then I said, "Welcome. I've heard a lot about you."*

Notice how the different methods of showing are used in combination to capture these three characters in this particular moment. With the narrator, we get his thoughts that the beard on the blind man is "too much" and his somewhat nervous actions of finishing up his drink and preparing to answer the door as well as his dialogue, which is mostly pleasantries he should say rather than genuine welcoming. The moment isn't limited to characterizing the narrator, either. The reader sees Robert's appearance, his speech, which is confident, and his actions, which are genial. The narrator's wife is also characterized through her attentive actions, her beaming face, and the excitement with which she introduces Robert to her husband. A tremendous amount of character information is portrayed in just this brief passage.

The four methods of showing can also work in opposition with one another to interesting effect. Do you always say exactly what you're thinking in an argument? Can you act like you're having a good time at your wife's important but stuffy work banquet when you would rather be out sailing on your cousin's keelboat? Might your body language give you away?

Often a truth is revealed about a person when there is a discrepancy between two or more of the four methods of showing: action, speech, appearance, and thought. For example, George may tell his sister over the phone that the Ye Haw Singles Sock Hop she's urging him to go to sounds ridiculous and desperate, but at the same time he might be writing down the date, time, and location of that very sock hop. George's speech (*"Are you crazy? What a stupid idea!"*) says something much different than his actions (*"Well, maybe I'll want to go."*)

In *The Great Gatsby,* Daisy shows a discrepancy shortly after we first meet her. Tom leaves the dinner table to take a phone call from his mistress and Daisy suddenly excuses herself and follows Tom. The dinner guests can hear their rising voices as they argue. When Daisy returns to the room with Tom, she says about the phone call, "It couldn't be helped," then she begins babbling blithely about a bird outside. However, her actions—abruptly leaving the dining room and having an argument with Tom—contradict her carefree speech. Even though Daisy acts as if everything is fine, her actions tell the reader, and the guests, otherwise.

Effective fiction makes use of all four methods of showing characters, whether the methods are supporting or contradicting each other. The idea is to blend them, rather like the balance of instruments in a symphony. Think of these four methods as the strings, winds, brass, and percussion of an orchestra, and yourself as the composer who must unite these sounds into a harmonious—or purposefully discordant—whole.

YOUR TURN:
Return to the character for whom you filled out the questionnaire. You're going to put this (now fictional) person into the world and let him reveal himself. Imagine this person

is entering the waiting room of a therapist's office for the first time. The type of therapy is up to you (it may even involve bringing a spouse or a pet), but chances are this person will be feeling a little stressed. Keeping the character in the waiting room, write a passage where he is revealed through all four of these "showing" methods—action, speech, appearance, and thought. For a bonus round, you can put this character in an even more stressful situation, like observing someone being held at gunpoint. What will your character do *then*?

ONLY RELEVANT DETAILS

Once you create fully realized characters, there is really no limit to how much you can know or show or tell about them. But when you shape your characters into the context of a story, make sure to pick and choose carefully what details you include. In other words, resist the urge to stuff in everything.

The fact that your character, Lance, spent a year and a half at Harvard might not be relevant in a story about Lance and Addie, a couple married for forty-three years who are now dealing with the recent death of their longtime pet, a Doberman pinscher named Eugene. However, the detail about Harvard might become important if, instead of being about the dog's death, the story is about how Lance is now regretting the decisions he made in the past to drop out of school and go to Paris with a woman he met at the student union. But do you need these details in the story about the dog's death? No, the Harvard education (or lack of it) likely isn't necessary. Every character detail included in your fiction should work to advance or enhance the story you are telling.

Don't let extraneous details sit around cluttering up your character-ization. In "Everything That Rises Must Converge" by Flannery O'Connor, Julian and his mother are about to leave for her Wednesday night weight-loss class at the Y:

> She was almost ready to go, standing before the hall mirror, putting on her hat, while he, his hands behind him, appeared pinned to the door frame, waiting like Saint Sebastian for the arrow to begin piercing him. The hat was new and had cost her seven dollars and a half. She kept

saying, "Maybe I shouldn't have paid that for it. No, I shouldn't have. I'll take it off and return it tomorrow. I shouldn't have bought it."

Julian raised his eyes to heaven. "Yes, you should have bought it," he said. "Put it on and let's go." It was a hideous hat. A purple velvet flap came down on one side of it and stood up on the other; the rest of it was green and looked like a cushion with the stuffing out. He decided it was less comical than jaunty and pathetic. Everything that gave her pleasure was small and depressed to him.

She lifted the hat one more time and set it down slowly on top of her head.

Julian's mother frets over this elaborate-looking hat—deciding to wear it, then deciding not to—regretting her decision to buy it and needing to hear from her son that it was fine for her to do so. These details show her insecurity, vanity, and slow pace. And perhaps most importantly we see that her behavior is a constant source of aggravation to her son. At first glance, this scene with the hat might not seem particularly important, but the hat, as well as the traits illustrated, plays an important role in the story's unfolding when they meet up with a woman on the bus who has the same hat!

WHAT'S IN A NAME?

Last, names are not trivial; they should feel right for the character. Granted, your parents likely named you before they even met you, and certainly before you developed a significant personality, but as an author, you have the opportunity to let the name of a character play a role in the characterization.

So avoid wishy-washy names that don't say much about the character, such as Joe Smith or Jane Jones. And avoid giving all of your characters similar names, like Mike, Mark, Mick, and Mary, as that only serves to confuse the reader. Instead, look for ways to reveal something about your characters through their names.

Some writers favor names that seem to make a literal statement about the character. Dickens used such pointed and colorful names, as in *Nicholas Nickleby* (a story largely about money), where you'll find such characters as Wackford Squeers, Sir Mulberry Hawk, and Miss Snevellicci. *Lolita's* narrator takes on the appropriately lumbering name of Humbert Humbert.

But names can also be revealing in more subtle ways. In Carson McCullers's *The Heart Is a Lonely Hunter,* the name Antonapoulos is appropriate for that character's fussy and persnickety nature, while his friend's name, Singer, echoes his more toned-down simplicity. And don't neglect nicknames. Frankie Machine's nickname comes from the sound of his real last name—Majcinek—and his ability to deal cards so flawlessly (his arm seemed like a machine).

> YOUR TURN:
> Go to the phone book. Open it up and point to a name, any name. That person is your character. Think about who that person might really be. Or what character would live well with that particular name. Let a picture form in your mind. If you like, jot down random details about this character. If you're so inspired, you may apply this character to any of the previous exercises in this chapter. And there's nothing stopping you from doing this exercise anytime you feel like finding a character. There are plenty of names in the phone book!

Sometimes characters go nameless, as is the case with the unnamed protagonist of "Cathedral." Some characters are known only by such names as "the man" or "the girl," as in Ernest Hemingway's "Hills Like White Elephants." In these instances the writers may have wanted the characters to have a certain anonymity, but you should be sparing with this device as it can run the risk of seeming pretentious and, worse, it can deprive you of a great way to characterize.

Indeed, in *The Great Gatsby*, Fitzgerald managed to characterize a whole group of people mostly by their names alone, as Nick recalls some of the guests at Gatsby's parties:

> . . . *I can remember that Faustina O'Brien came there at least once and the Baedecker girls and young Brewer who had his nose shot off in the way and Mr. Albrucksburger and Miss Haag, his fiancée, and Ardita Fitz-Peters, and Mr. P. Jewett, once head of the American Legion, and Miss Claudia Hip with a man reputed to be her chauffeur, and a prince of something whom we called Duke, and whose name, if I ever knew it, I have forgotten.*

Names are like the wrapping on a present, offering just a hint of what may be inside the person.

CHAPTER 3
PLOT: A QUESTION OF FOCUS

BY DAVID HARRIS EBENBACH

When I landed at Vermont College to enter a graduate program in writing, I had more than a hundred pages of my first novel in hand. I had been working on the thing for more than a few months already. Yet I'd also hit a wall—I wasn't exactly sure what to make of these pages I'd written. I handed off the partial draft to my adviser, Ellen Lesser. My secret hope, of course, was that she would declare it a work of true genius, giving me all the motivation I'd need to keep at it and write the rest of the book. What she actually said in response was less blindly positive, but much more helpful. What Ellen told me, in short form, was to cut fully half the pages I'd already written.

The first thing I decided, naturally, was that the novel was completely worthless garbage, and that I had to abandon it immediately, possibly shredding or burning the draft I had. But after I took a little time to calm down, I looked more closely at Ellen's comments, and more closely at the work itself. That's when I really began to learn.

She had actually liked many parts of the book—but she also pointed out the huge glut of exposition that was clogging up the first chapter while little was happening in the story. She highlighted a conversation between my main characters that looked like a real enough conversation, but wasn't accomplishing anything significant. She focused on scenes where characters engaged in the normal activities of life—brushing teeth, getting dressed, walking from here to there—even though those activities had little to do with the concerns at the heart of the novel.

In particular I remember a scene showcasing one of my two main characters pacing the length of the apartment with his cat draped over his shoulder. He had been reading and sleeping, on and off; now he fixed himself a peanut butter sandwich; now he looked out this window; now he looked out that one; it was hot. Nothing much was going on. As he paced he was thinking through the background of his life, details I was sure the reader would need and want to know. Meanwhile, the reader was falling asleep.

My adviser suggested that I had actually written these pages for myself—that I'd written them to get to know the people and places and situations in the book, so that I could write authentically about them. And that was well and good, probably even essential for me. But the reader didn't need to see all of that prep work. They needed the story, right then, right there.

In other words, I needed to think more about plot.

PLOT VERSUS REAL LIFE

Life may be interesting. Life is often moving and eventful. But rarely does life actually contain plot. I eat a sandwich because I'm vaguely hungry; I go to work and come home again, feeling pretty much the same as I did the day before; all sorts of people enter and exit the stage around me as I go through my day—but a lot of it seems more random and anticlimactic than what happens in good short stories and novels. Even death, probably the only true ending we have available to us as human beings, often happens right in the middle of things, leaving many things unfinished.

Now, I suppose you might say plot *is* like real life, if, as Elmore Leonard advises, you leave out all the boring parts. But that brings us back to my premise that plot is *not* exactly like real life. And so plot is one of the elements of craft that clearly separates the real world from the world of fiction. When people ask *What's it about?* in regard to their own existence, they're not sure they should even expect an answer. Yet they also, on some level, ask that question every time they approach a short story or novel—and this time, there had better be an answer. Successful fiction does have a point, does have a fascinating and meaningful sequence of events. The purpose of this chapter is to show how life can be brought to the page, by bringing plot to life.

Think for a moment about a story you really enjoyed—one of those stories that you just couldn't put down, that you had to keep reading because of all the suspense. Chances are this story had a magnificent plot. As you read, one event set into motion another one, more captivating than the last; the situation became more and more tense, with you wondering all the while how everything would turn out.

This is the most tangible benefit that plot brings to fiction. Although in some high-minded literary circles the term *page-turner* is less than a compliment, the fact is that some of our most celebrated novels—Toni Morrison's *Beloved,* for example, or Dickens's *David Copperfield,* or Richard Wright's *Native Son*—work as well as they do partly because they have plots that pull the reader irresistibly along, from beginning to end. We care about what's happening, and we're concerned about what might happen next. And if we don't care about these things, the stories in our hands may end up abandoned before we've even finished them, left to gather dust on an untouched shelf somewhere.

At the heart of most great fiction is the excitement created when we really feel that the work is after something specific—when it has plot.

The way all this happens is pretty simple, at least in theory. Plot makes fiction coherent by drawing together all the characters, settings, voice, and everything else around a single organizing force. That's right, *one* organizing force. After all, a short story, even though it might have a big impact on a reader, is actually a very small and focused world, and the same is surprisingly true of a novel. Works of fiction are not, and cannot be, about a million things—they are usually about just one thing. And that thing, the force that draws everything together in a successful piece of fiction, is a single, pressing question.

THE MAJOR DRAMATIC QUESTION

This question—often known as the major dramatic question—is generally a straightforward yes/no question, one that can be answered by the end of the story. *Will Brian find a job? Will Jamie and Ana move to separate apartments? Will Shira finally stop ignoring her inner child?*

If you stop to look around, you'll find major dramatic questions organizing things throughout the entire body of literature. Consider the following short stories. Bernard Malamud's "The Magic Barrel" is a busy piece, populated by fascinating characters and a memorable storytelling style, but the bottom-line concern is whether rabbinical student Leo Finkle will find himself a wife. In Peter Cameron's "Memorial Day," we wonder whether the little boy narrating the story can somehow get back his old life—with his parents still married. In "Sonny's Blues," by James Baldwin, our narrator asks whether Sonny can rise above his difficult life and his suffering, and, in the echoes of that, whether we all can.

The single major dramatic question remains the central organizing force even in the relatively complex world of novels. In *Pride and Prejudice*, by Jane Austen, the question is whether Elizabeth Bennet will end up with Mr. Darcy. The question in Ernest Hemingway's *For Whom the Bell Tolls* is whether Robert Jordan will escape his apparent fate by surviving his military mission. In John Steinbeck's *East of Eden* the question seems to be whether Cal is to be forgiven for who he's turned out to be. Hundreds of pages, but in all these cases, one dominant question is at the forefront. One of the major reasons why we keep reading is because of the suspense the major dramatic question creates. We need to find out what the answer will turn out to be.

Which naturally leads me to those all-important answers. It's obvious enough that you'll have to provide an answer, given that you've raised a question, but it's worth noting that your choice of possible answers is diverse—*yes, no,* and *maybe* are each fair game. That's right, it's okay if Brian finds a job, and it's okay if he doesn't, assuming that the events of the story and the nature of Brian's character justify the outcome. You're even allowed to say *maybe,* as long as you've convinced the reader that you've tried your best and that, in the end, neither *no* nor *yes* would really be honest.

One thing to bear in mind, though, is that readers tend to be unsatisfied if this answer, whatever it is, comes through some kind of *deus ex machina,* a Greek term that refers to a random act of God or luck that resolves everything. This is one reason why some readers shy away from Dickens now—the miracles that resolve many of his novels can seem a little too easy to the modern reader. Instead, the answer should come directly from the actions or thoughts of the protagonist.

The most important rule, however, is that your answer has to match your question. If you spend the whole story asking whether Brian will find a job, and you build tension around his repeated and increasingly urgent attempts to get a job, you can't end by concluding *Yes, he will learn to love again.* You must conclude with a decision about his employment future. This mismatch between question and answer is going to provoke the reader to say, with some irritation, *I can't tell what this story is about!* And that's the last thing you want.

The major dramatic question can seem strange to some writers, as though it's a foreign element that has to be forced into a piece where it might not belong, but it's an organic part of your fictional universe, connected to all the other elements of the piece. Most fundamentally, the question arises from the relationship among three elements: the protagonist, his or her goal, and the conflict blocking that goal.

> YOUR TURN:
> Think about one of your favorite works of fiction—*Gone with the Wind,* "Hills Like White Elephants," *Charlotte's Web* . . . Try to figure out what the major dramatic question might be. Remember, this is a question that can usually be answered with a *yes, no,* or *maybe.* Sometimes this question takes a little fishing around to find. You may even want to leaf through or reread the story you've picked.

PROTAGONIST

The protagonist is, simply enough, the main character in your work. He or she will be the most complex and dimensional character in the piece, the one illuminated most fully and followed most closely. The major dramatic question always centers around the protagonist, focusing above all on what will happen in his or her life.

Because of all this attention the protagonist gets, there's usually just one protagonist in a given work of fiction. Certainly there are novels with multiple protagonists—William Faulkner's *The Sound and the Fury,* Gabriel García Márquez's *One Hundred Years of Solitude,* and Rick Moody's *Purple America* are just a few examples—but for the most part even novels follow just one protagonist. Writers often use the added length in a novel not to explore a bunch of characters but to even more thoroughly explore *one.*

A classic example is J. D. Salinger's *The Catcher in the Rye,* which offers the reader the one and only Holden Caulfield. Holden, the tough-talking but ultrasensitive teenager, is smart and inept and world-weary and inexperienced and hopeful and miserable and lonely and young—all at once. He has become one of literature's favorite characters, in part because we get so deep into his mind that at times we almost become him.

Of course, as much as we might be drawn in by Holden's engaging and sympathetic personality, that personality alone won't be enough to keep us reading for the entire length of a book. In order to keep us turning those pages, Holden's got to have a story.

GOAL

Chapter 2 on Character suggests that desire lies at the heart of all characters. Here I suggest that the protagonist's desire is the key to the story's plot. Just as the story will be driven by *one* question, that question will come into play in the first place because of the *one thing* that the protagonist wants most. Call it the goal. Specifically, the protagonist's goal is going to be about getting a *yes* or *no* answer to the major dramatic question.

This goal may be conscious, with the protagonist knowing what he or she is after, or it may be unconscious, driving the protagonist's actions without ever making itself explicitly known to him or her. Either way, it pushes the question into the open for the reader.

Further, this goal may either be concrete, such as a job the character wants, or abstract, such as a desire for a sense of self-worth. It's important to note, however, that in practice abstract goals are associated with concrete ones, and vice versa; food can provide a feeling of comfort, power is often tied to money, and, of course, a job can provide a sense of self-worth. Generally, abstract goals need to be represented by something concrete in a story, or else the whole story is going to feel, well, abstract, and it will be harder to formulate the events of the plot.

In *The Catcher in the Rye* Holden's goal is to find a place where he belongs. He pursues this abstract idea in a concrete way, by going to New York City on a hunt for a person, any person, who is going to understand him and not turn out to be a "phony." From understanding our protagonist and his or her goal, we uncover the major dramatic question. The major dramatic question of *The Catcher in the Rye: Will Holden find a place where he belongs?*

Whether the character will get what he or she wants is another issue altogether.

YOUR TURN:
Imagine a protagonist who seems to have
it all—a home, financial security, a loving
spouse. Give this person a name and flesh out
some details. Then figure out an abstract goal
for this person. Then attach that abstract goal
to a concrete goal that might work in a story.
For example, if this person abstractly desires
adventure, then perhaps make his or her
concrete goal to sail around the world. Hint:
the goal should probably stem from something
that's missing in this person's seemingly
perfect life.

CONFLICT

The protagonist's goal may fly in the face of what other characters want, and the goal may even fly in the face of physical and social reality. In other words, there are obstacles in our main character's path. These obstacles create conflict. No, we can't make it easy for our characters, no matter how much we'd like to; making it easy makes for bad fiction. Plot depends on conflict.

And to keep things really interesting, the conflict should keep escalating. These forces—the ones pulling our main character toward the desired outcome and the ones pushing in the opposite direction—increase in equal measure across the fiction, like a pair of well-matched arm wrestlers, until one of them has to give out. The more fierce the fight, the better the story.

Conflict can take many forms. Some obstacles are external to the character, and can be found in other people (such as antagonists, characters who actively try to prevent the protagonist from meeting goals), or in societal structures, in nature, in acts of God, or in any number of other external possibilities. A woman seeking shelter may not have the money to get it, for example, or a man seeking love may not encounter anyone interested in providing it.

Other obstacles are internal. The same woman may not *feel worthy* of shelter, and the man may not *know how* to seek love. In these cases the struggle at hand takes place largely within the minds of our characters, between desires on the one hand and fears and personal inadequacies on the other. Stories that truly move us, stories with real depth, generally require that at least some of the conflict be internal.

Often there are many sources of conflict, both internal and external, within a given piece. Yet while all these obstacles are painful for the protagonist, they're good news for the story, and for the reader. After all, *A starving family goes out to beg for food but on their way out the front door they find food on their doorstep* isn't much of a story.

The Catcher in the Rye is rife with conflict. Holden Caulfield repeatedly attempts to find situations where he might find himself safe and understood—with authority figures like Mr. Spencer and Mr. Antolini, with peers like Stradlater or Carl Luce, with potential girlfriend-material Sally Hayes, with family, and even with a prostitute. But the attempts fail again and again; everywhere he goes he encounters external obstacles, meeting "morons" and "phonies" and people who abuse his trust. He also runs up against internal obstacles when he fails to express himself adequately to the people around himself, when he fails to be clear even with himself; he probably doesn't know he *has* a goal, and certainly doesn't know how to attain it. Yet he pursues this goal more and more intensely, by the end even considering a vague and desperate plan to run off to Colorado.

Does Holden ultimately find what he's looking for? Well, he does decide to abandon his Colorado plans and stay with the one person he really trusts—his sister Phoebe—but this positive move also gives his parents the chance to put him in a psychiatric institution, and then ship him off to yet another phony school. While Holden has not achieved his goal, he has not given up the hope of getting there one day. *The Catcher in the Rye* is one of those stories that ends with a *maybe*.

> YOUR TURN:
> Return to the protagonist you created for the previous exercise, the one with a concrete goal. Make a list of obstacles—internal and external—that might block the achievement of the goal. List as many obstacles as you can think of, more than you could possibly use in a story. Last, in one sentence, create a major dramatic question that you could employ for a story about this character. Remember, this is a question that can be answered with a *yes, no,* or *maybe*.

THE STRUCTURE OF PLOT

Now we'll take a close look at the structure that grows out of—and supports—the major dramatic question, and, thus, the plot. Structure, in fact,
is inseparable from plot. Plot is the sequence of events in a piece that drives
toward answering the major dramatic question; structure is the overarching
shape that keeps the sequence of events in good order. Luckily, we do not
have to reinvent structure every time we start writing a new fictional
work—we have a model readily available to us.

The model is certainly a tried-and-true one, having existed for more
than twenty-three hundred years, coming from Aristotle's *Poetics,* a dis-
course on how drama works. In fact, much of our thinking about storytelling
derives from *Poetics,* which itself was born from the thriving Greek theater
and from the surrounding mythology, both of which were rich with story and
plot. What Aristotle codified still plays itself out in story after story and novel
after novel written in our time.

The accepted model of plot offered by *Poetics* is more complex than it at
first seems. It says that fictional works have a beginning, a middle, and an
end. Well, maybe that's a *duh*—but more importantly it tells us that those
sections have distinct roles in the successful telling of a story.

Now we'll walk through these three sections, discussing the function
of each one, and illustrating those functions by looking closely at Raymond
Carver's "Cathedral," which is, at its simplest, about a man whose wife's old
friend—a blind man—has come to dinner.

THE BEGINNING

The beginning of a story has to get three things done: it has to drop
the reader right into the middle of the action, it has to provide all the
necessary background information to get the reader up to speed, and it
has to establish the major dramatic question. Let's discuss each of these
in turn.

The first job of a story's beginning is to start at the right time. It should
not start when things are quiet, when nothing's happening, when things are
much the same as they have always been. Think about how boring it would
be if your friend told a story about something really exciting but began the
anecdote two days before anything important actually got started. After all,

the whole reason we tell the story is because something about life is new and different, something's happening that stands out—and your responsibility, as the writer, is to begin the work at that point of change.

The first sentence of "Cathedral," for example, reads,

> *This blind man, an old friend of my wife's, he was on his way to spend the night.*

We do not begin the story a few weeks earlier, when nobody was coming to visit. We begin on the day that's the focus of the whole piece.

Yet starting at a point of change means that the reader will by necessity lack crucial background information that explains both the events at hand and the characters reacting to those events. The beginning of the story therefore also has to provide sufficient exposition so that readers will know what's going on and why. The most important issue here is to strike the right balance. The reader does not have to know everything, and certainly not right away; too much background slows the fiction down and can lead to boredom or confusion if the background contains the irrelevant, and some information should just be saved for later.

Exposition will certainly keep coming throughout the work. The key is to supply all the background needed for the time being—and not any more. Finding this balance, of course, is a matter of trial and error at first, but in the long run it will become a matter of instinct. With experience, you learn how to feed the reader information on a need-to-know basis only, and how to keep that information interesting and relevant by integrating it with ongoing action.

"Cathedral" is unusual in that it has a long beginning and does provide a lot of exposition at the outset. However, all of the exposition is useful. Primarily, we learn about the protagonist, who is also the narrator, and who is, interestingly enough, never named. We discover, for example, that the narrator has strange perceptions of the blind, derived from the movies, and that "A blind man in my house was not something I looked forward to." We are told that the blind man is coming to visit because his wife has died and he's going to be in the area, visiting in-laws. We also learn that the narrator's wife worked for the blind man (as the narrator continues to call him, even after learning that his guest's name is Robert) ten years ago, and that they've kept up a correspondence ever since, through her divorce to a first husband and through her marriage to the narrator.

More important, we learn that the protagonist isn't very interested in any of this. His wife, some time ago, showed him one of the poems she wrote about the blind man, his response being he "didn't think much of the poem." She played him one of the tapes sent by the blind man as part of their correspondence, and even though the narrator was mentioned on the tape (or perhaps because of that), he wasn't much curious about that, either. In fact, he seems to have little investment in life altogether. It seems he has no friends of his own. His disinterest in his wife's poetry is a disinterest in poetry in general. He has a job he doesn't like, but he has no plans to do anything about that. He describes drinking as a "pastime." The narrator is a lump.

This protagonist's goal is a strange one, especially if we're used to considering *goal* and *ambition* synonymous (which we shouldn't, in fiction), and it's one that he may not even consciously know about. Yet it's still a goal. He wants, more than anything, to give in to his own inertia, to avoid new experiences that would cause him to look too deeply at his own life. In the context of this story, his goal is to be unaffected, unchanged, by the arrival of his unwelcome guest.

The story begins with conflict, just because the narrator is so dreading the blind man's arrival, and that resistance becomes a serious issue as the time of his arrival draws nearer and husband and wife fight about it:

> *"If you love me," she said, "you can do this for me. If you don't love me, okay. But if you had a friend, any friend, and the friend came to visit, I'd make him feel comfortable."*

Already this visitor is disrupting our protagonist's stable, if unenviable, existence. And early on, we sense what the major dramatic question of the story will be—and it's essential that the story establishes this as close to the beginning as possible. The question is nicely illustrated in some of the protagonist's musings about the blind man:

> *[The blind man and his wife had] married, lived and worked together, slept together—had sex, sure—and then the blind man had to bury her. All this without his having ever seen what the goddamned woman looked like. It was beyond my understanding. Hearing this, I felt sorry for the blind man for a little bit. And then I found myself thinking what a*

pitiful life this woman must have led . . . A woman who could go on day after day and never receive the smallest compliment from her beloved. A woman whose husband could never read the expression on her face, be it misery or something better.

In this passage, the narrator could easily have been describing his relationship with his own wife, whom he doesn't understand, and the reader begins to see a parallel between the blind man and the narrator. This awareness, along with all the other background we've encountered, gives us our question: *Will the narrator, in the course of this story, come to change, so that he can truly "see" (or understand) himself and his life?* The reader probably hopes so; the narrator certainly hopes not. In any case, by this point we have our beginning, and we understand a great deal.

Now, despite these several responsibilities—starting with action, giving background, establishing the major dramatic question—typically the beginning is very short, often quite a bit shorter than the beginning of "Cathedral." The reader simply doesn't want to spend much time getting caught up, and so the exposition has to be limited. The reader wants to get to the interesting stuff, to the action—in other words, to the middle of the work.

THE MIDDLE

Although in practice the beginning and middle of a piece of fiction may overlap a bit, as they do in "Cathedral," they are quite different entities. First of all, the middle typically takes up the vast majority of space in the piece, more pages by far than the beginning or the end. No surprise—it has the most work to do. The story's middle usually contains additional exposition, further developing the characters and situations we've learned about in the beginning. It's also where the core action of the story happens, where everything but the opening and closing events takes place.

The middle section is, most importantly, where the protagonist's path toward his or her goal is blocked again and again by increasingly daunting obstacles, and where the forces arrayed against him or her become ever more powerful. In the middle, conflict increases and increases until it can increase no further. Some people picture a sort of "plot graph," where tension is represented by a line that rises as we move from left to right and then suddenly drops off at the end. However you visualize it, the bottom line is that tightly linked events must build in tension and conflict toward a crisis.

Of course, the events of the middle section are not by any means random happenings. It's worth emphasizing here that the fictional world is a cause-and-effect one; E. M. Forster once observed that *"The Queen died and then the King died"* is not a plot, but *"The Queen died and then the King died of grief"* is, because it contains cause and effect. In the fictional universe, things happen as a result of the actions of characters, and the actions of characters are a response to things that happen. Your story's middle shouldn't contain a jumbled pile of events in some arbitrary order—it should contain a chain of events, each one tightly linked to the event before.

In "Cathedral," the boundary between beginning and middle may be a bit blurry, but we can probably safely locate it at the point where the blind man arrives at our narrator's home. What follows is clearly a *chain* of events—every awkward move by the protagonist provokes a countermove on the part of the blind man, who is the antagonist (albeit a friendly one) of this story.

The tension and conflict increase when the guest actually shows up. From the very outset the narrator doesn't know what to say to this blind man, asking him what side of the train he sat on while traveling there because, irrelevantly, the scenery is better on one side of the train than the other. Because of his preconceived notions of the blind, the narrator is also caught off guard by just about every aspect of his guest—the fact that he doesn't wear dark glasses, that he's worked many jobs, that he smokes, even that he has a beard. If this protagonist wants more than anything to avoid new and eye-opening experiences, he's already in trouble.

All through drinks and dinner, the narrator is exposed to more and more information about this guest, as his wife focuses all conversation on the blind man and ignores the protagonist almost entirely. "I waited in vain to hear my name on my wife's sweet lips," he grumbles to us at one point. In one sense, he's glad to be left out, because he's able to keep to himself during the meal, but in another sense the scene is pretty awkward. The protagonist is even more clearly painted as a person who is quarantined in his own limited world. And he begins to grow a little jealous of all the attention the blind man is getting, calling him "a regular blind jack-of-all-trades" after hearing endless stories about the man's past.

The conflict further increases when the narrator's wife abandons them by falling asleep on the couch while the two men sit in front of the television. Now the protagonist is the guest's only company. He in fact pushes the blind man to go off to bed, but the guest would rather stay up and get to know the protagonist. The narrator quickly turns to methods to escape intimacy; he smokes a little pot with the blind man, and they sit in front of the television.

But then something interesting starts happening. Robert's relentless charm, finally, begins to affect the narrator just the least little bit. The narrator tries to fight it, struggling to find the right channel on TV, but, surprisingly, he also admits to himself that he's glad for the change of pace. Most evenings he watches TV and smokes pot by himself. After failing to find something better, they settle on a show about churches and cathedrals.

Around this time internal conflict is developing in the narrator. Although he's trying to fight it, our narrator is starting to recognize the emptiness of his own life as he feels growing curiosity and sympathy toward Robert. He asks the blind man,

> *"Do you have any idea what a cathedral is? . . . If somebody says cathedral to you, do you have any notion what they're talking about?"*

The blind man admits he knows very little about the subject, in fact, and asks our narrator to try to describe what he's seeing on TV. Our narrator does his best. Part of him now almost wants to do a good job, even though it flies in the face of his goal to stay mired in his own inertia. His own limitations, however, hold him back; he doesn't explain cathedrals very well.

After some prodding on the subject of religion by the blind man, the narrator goes further:

> *"I guess I don't believe in it. In anything. Sometimes it's hard. You know what I'm saying?"*

And:

> *"You'll have to forgive me," I said. "But I can't tell you what a cathedral looks like. It just isn't in me to do it. I can't do any more than I've done."*

The struggle inside the narrator is now growing to an almost titanic level. He is truly torn, in that he's still clinging to the status quo (his original goal), but in this moment part of him would actually like to become reconnected to the world and the higher meaning in life.

But this development doesn't serve as an answer to our major dramatic question. The question was not whether he would come to *want* that reconnection, that open-minded vision, but whether he would *get* it. Remember that it's crucial that your story answers not just any question but the question it's been pursuing all along. So, while our protagonist has changed a little, the story isn't over. In fact, he is now squarely facing the biggest conflict possible in his life, between his shut-down inertia on the one hand and his rusty interest in a meaningful life on the other.

The blind man forces him to face that conflict directly, by suggesting that the narrator get a pen and paper so that they can draw a cathedral together. This will force the narrator to take his guest's perspective, to feel the world through him, raising the tension to its highest point, and all this will lead to one of the more moving endings to be found in short fiction.

THE END

The end of the work is likely to be the shortest part of the piece, particularly in contemporary fiction. There tends not to be an extended dénouement, where we fully play out all the ultimate ramifications of what's taken place. Yet the end of a story does have significant responsibilities. This section of the story may be the shortest, but it's also the place where everything comes together.

The end generally follows a pattern that could be called "the three C's"—crisis, climax, and consequences. The crisis is the point where tension hits its maximum, and the climax is where the tension breaks, and where we get the answer to our major dramatic question. Then, the consequences, however briefly handled, are alluded to at the very end of the piece. "Cathedral," like most stories, follows this pattern.

We return to the narrator as he tries to draw a cathedral, with the blind man's hand over his own, so the blind man can follow the movement. This event produces the crisis, where the conflict between the protagonist's original goal and all the internal and external obstacles becomes too much to stand. He starts out simply:

> *First I drew a box that looked like a house. It could have been the house I lived in. Then I put a roof on it. At either end of the roof, I drew spires. Crazy.*

He's trying, but he hasn't yet broken through his limitations, and there's a real possibility that he'll drop the effort and sink back to his regular life at any moment. But the blind man is urging him on all the time, and he's gaining momentum.

I kept at it. I'm no artist. But I kept drawing just the same.

The narrator's wife wakes up to see this taking place, and recognizes it for the amazing event it is. "What's going on?" she asks desperately. The tension continues to hold at maximum while we keenly hope that our protagonist will really come to life, despite everything, right in front of us. And then the blind man pushes the story toward its climax:

"Close your eyes now," the blind man said to me.

This is asking everything of our narrator. If he can close his eyes to experience this moment in all earnestness, he will have actually *opened* his eyes, opened himself to the larger world around him. He closes his eyes—but what's happening inside him?

So we kept on with it. His fingers rode my fingers as my hand went over the paper. It was like nothing else in my life up to now.

And then the climax finally comes, the moment where we get the answer we've been waiting for. Remember that the major dramatic question was not whether our narrator will have a moment of insight—and he already has—but whether he will change, whether he will now be a person who truly *sees*. We get our answer in the story's final lines, when the blind man tells our narrator to open his eyes again:

But I had my eyes closed. I thought I'd keep them that way for a little longer. I thought it was something I ought to do.
"Well?" he said. "Are you looking?"
My eyes were still closed. I was in my house. I knew that. But I didn't feel like I was inside anything.
"It's really something," I said.

An ending like this can send a reader straight into tears—what an enormous release, getting our *yes* answer in the way that we get it. Our narrator is, for apparently the first time in a long while, completely open, seeing himself and the world in a whole new way, and we know it, ironically, because he's keeping his eyes *closed* here. He says he's no longer in his house, and we understand him to mean that he's no longer trapped in himself in the same way. In answer to the blind man's final question, our protagonist is, at last, looking and "seeing."

This climax, of course, contains the consequences, though they play out more in the reader's head than on the page itself. We don't know that we've got a turnaround as dramatic and permanent as with Ebenezer Scrooge in Dickens's *A Christmas Carol,* say, but we suspect that things will never be quite the same. All the things we noted at the beginning—the narrator's dread of new experiences, his preconceptions about people he hasn't met, his disinterest in his wife, in himself, and in his own existence—all these attitudes are now endangered species. Whether they'll outright disappear we can't be sure, but we know that, at least for the time being, he has risen above them, and we have reason to hope that the effects may be long-lasting. Of course, we are told none of these things directly. As in most contemporary stories, we are more likely to feel the consequences than to read about them.

It's been said that an ending should feel inevitable but unexpected—that, looking back, it is the only ending that really would have made sense, but that it still felt striking and surprising when it happened. Think of a good murder mystery. At the end, we realize all the clues were there, but we just hadn't put them together right. Now that we know what we know, in other words, it seems obvious.

In "Cathedral," for example, the ending is certainly unexpected—how could someone so stubbornly shut down ever open up again? But if we look back from the end, we see that there are also clues scattered throughout showing that he's more interested in changing than we might have first thought. There's his jealousy about the blind man's range of experience; his sympathy for the blind man's wife, who'd never even been seen by her husband; his shy and ambivalent pleasure at staying up alone with his guest. If we look back, we see how things have been leading, somewhat inevitably, to this unexpected conclusion.

YOUR TURN:
Return to the character you created in the previous exercises, the one with the seemingly perfect life. Now write an entire story centering around the major dramatic question you created. Your story should have a beginning, a middle with escalating conflict, and an ending that includes crisis, climax, and consequences. One more thing. This story can be no longer than five hundred words. Not five hundred pages. Five hundred *words*.

Afterward, if you're so inclined, you may turn
your idea into a longer work.

APPLYING STRUCTURE TO NOVELS

For the most part, what we've discussed in regards to "Cathedral" applies
just as well to novels as it does to short stories. Novels too need a beginning,
a middle, and an end, and the three sections serve the same functions here as
they do in shorter work. In Jane Austen's *Pride and Prejudice,* for example,
we begin in the midst of an exciting development—a wealthy and single Mr.
Bingley has moved into the area near the Bennets, and Mrs. Bennet already
has ideas about marrying off one of her daughters—and so we start to get
a sense of the major dramatic question: *Will Elizabeth get married?* Then
the novel moves through a middle, where her protagonist's desires become
more intense while being frustrated in ever more intense ways, and then in
the end we are treated to a happy ending where all these complications are
removed, and our central question is answered: Elizabeth gets her man.

Therefore, nothing radical changes about the basic structure of plot in
moving between the short and long forms of fiction. Yet there are, or at least
there can be, some differences worth talking about.

First of all, although the novel follows the same plot structure as a short
story, the great increase in size with the novel can bring some change to
the relative size and content of the three sections—beginning, middle, and
end. For example, the beginning of a novel might take up the entire opening
chapter, or possibly a bit longer, giving us an opportunity to take in more
background information, as long as it's integrated with important action.
Ultimately, in a novel, we'll know a lot more about our characters and their
world, and although we'll continue to encounter exposition throughout the
entire work, we can certainly get a good chunk of information at the start.
The reader, who already signed up for a long ride, will allow you the room
for more exposition up front.

The same size increase can hold true for the ending. In some cases,
and *Pride and Prejudice* is a good example, the end will actually allow
the consequences to play out for quite a while, telling us in a relaxed
way how things have really ultimately turned out. This is less common
in the contemporary novel—*East of Eden* isn't decided until the very last
sentence—but is still possible. In Russell Banks's *Rule of the Bone,* for

example, the final chapter is mostly devoted to consequences. The point, however, is that the extra room to be found in a novel allows extra room for the end to breathe, if needed.

But the main difference in the proportions allotted to these three sections is that where in a typical short story the middle takes up the vast majority of the work, in a typical novel the middle takes up the vast, vast majority of the work. That leaves hundreds of pages to develop your characters, raise and intensify your obstacles, relate numerous events. As with a short story, none of those pages should be wasted. Each page should move us farther along a linked chain of events, farther along that rising arc of conflict and tension toward the book's climax. If the release offered by a climax after ten pages can be powerful, imagine how much impact we can experience when it comes after 350 pages or so.

SUBPLOTS

Another difference between short stories and novels is that the length of a novel allows the plot to be more complex, containing more twists and turns and the like. This opens the door for the possibility of subplot. Subplot, when it exists, is a plotline that runs alongside the main plotline of the book. It may concern a character other than the main character, or it may focus on an issue that is not quite the main issue at hand, but it's not unrelated to the main plot. In fact, the subplot exists only because it's relevant to the main plot, commenting on it, exploring it. The connection between the two threads may not always be obvious, but it must always be there.

Sometimes the subplot serves as a lesser parallel to the main plot. In Chaim Potok's *The Chosen,* while the main character, Danny Saunders, struggles to come to terms with his religion and the future before him, his friend Reuven, the narrator, engages in a very similar struggle. We also see paralleling in Anne Lamott's *Rosie,* where both the title character and her mother learn to engage themselves with the real world, a world that is frequently intimidating and sometimes truly dangerous. In *Pride and Prejudice,* the marriage between Elizabeth and Mr. Darcy is not the only match to be made.

In other cases, the subplot is designed as a contrast with the main plot. In Salman Rushdie's *Midnight's Children,* for example, the focus is on the rise and fall of its main character, Saleem Sinai, but in the background is the fall and rise (and fall again) of the book's antagonist, Shiva. As the fortune of one character goes, so goes the other—but in the opposite direction. Although the fates of Saleem and Shiva are different, they are not unrelated; as opposites, they are bound together as tightly as possible. We see a similar contrast in Tolstoy's *Anna Karenina* between the destiny of Anna, on the one hand, and Levin, on the other. One is damned, and the other is saved. In Charles Dickens's *David Copperfield,* the downfall of the noxious Uriah Heep must be ensured before we can move forward to David's happy ending.

One of the natural consequences of subplot is that novels often have multiple climaxes rather than just one. For example, Uriah Heep loses before David Copperfield wins out, and both moments are climactic, though the second one is much more so. While the single major dramatic question must wait until the very end of the book for its ultimate answer, in novels lesser questions will be raised and answered along the way, whether there is subplot or not. In Harper Lee's *To Kill a Mockingbird,* Tom Robinson's guilty verdict is certainly climactic, and it answers the pressing question of his fate, but it does not give us the final answer we need from this book. In *East of Eden,* we experience a number of resolutions, some painful and some a relief: the villainous Kate dies, and then the naïve Aron runs away, and *then* the patriarch Adam suffers a stroke, and *only then* do we get the answer to the book's major dramatic question. Each climax resolves one concern but allows the main one to keep growing in intensity until it too finally breaks wide open.

Subplot is not, of course, necessary to a novel. In a book like *The Catcher in the Rye,* a subplot would disrupt the intensity of Salinger's focus on Holden Caulfield. The added length of the novel, though, does leave open the choice—how do you want to explore the main plotline and protagonist? By focusing tightly and directly on them, or by creating echoes for the main plot in other characters and their struggles?

HOW PLOT EMERGES

Perhaps by now you are in a state of panic. *Do you honestly expect,* you may be asking, *that I'll be able to figure out my major dramatic question, satisfy all the requirements of Aristotle's beginning-middle-end model, and work out all the myriad details of my plot before I even start writing?*

Luckily for all of us, the answer is *no.*

Sure, it's possible that you'll have firm ideas about all these issues before you begin. You may find, for example, that you're the kind of writer who likes to outline a piece thoroughly before starting to write it. However, if you're not that kind of writer, relax. You're in good company. For most writers, the first draft is the one where the inspiration runs wild, venting itself in thrilling and undisciplined fashion, and for most of us, there's no room for such careful plotting in that first explosion. Plot is instead something that emerges over time, over the course of a number of drafts. The issue of exactly when it emerges isn't so important. The only rule is that it must, at some point.

I'll return for a second to that overlong partial draft of a novel I brought with me to graduate school. Yes, I did need to cut out half the pages I'd written, but remember that my adviser didn't dismiss those pages as having been a waste of time. As she suggested, I'd needed to write all those go-nowhere scenes—to see how my characters acted in a variety of situations, and above all to see what they were like when they had the leisure to quietly be themselves. And of course it worked. A hundred pages deep into my novel, I showed every sign of knowing my characters well. Even when not writing, I thought about them constantly, empathized with their troubles enormously, and sometimes accidentally fell into their speech patterns when talking to my friends. Those extra pages had been valuable.

After all, plot is almost inseparable from character. In fact, they are so tightly intertwined that it often raises the chicken-or-the-egg question. Much of the time it's hard to say which of the two comes first in writing the work. But whichever comes first, it usually contains the other as well.

Maybe you have a fascinating protagonist in mind. Well, whatever fascinates you about that protagonist probably involves her or his big goal and therefore the major dramatic question (and therefore plot). On the other hand, you might have a really great question—but it can be good only if it's relevant to someone in particular. *Will some unspecified person have a religious experience?* is a much less interesting question than *Will this disaffected Buddhist monk from Muncie have a religious experience?*

Well, whether plot or character comes first, the point is that they both need to be compelling, and they should both inform one another. And if you're the kind of person who writes brilliant characters but can't seem to get plot jump-started, take a closer look at those characters of yours; they may know what the story is before you do.

And so, instead of imposing some abstract idea of plot from above, we turn to the story, to see what it has to say. After several rereads, you might decide that the primary issue in this piece seems to be whether the protagonist can assert his own needs in his love life. Or you might find that it's about whether your protagonist can regain a sense of innocence, or leave home, or get around to retiring. Whatever your major dramatic question is, it's probably already there to be found in your first draft, even if it's hidden so deep that you didn't notice writing it into the story.

> YOUR TURN:
> Take one of the characters you worked with in the exercises from chapter 2. Find a major dramatic question for that person. For clues, study whatever it is you wrote about that person. He or she is probably secretly holding the answer . . . or, we should say, the question.

One likely spot to look for the major dramatic question is the climax, the place where you'll often find your question is answered, even if you didn't know you had one. It's fairly common to base a story around a good climax, whether it's one you design in advance or one you produce while wandering through a first draft. But read the work as many times as it takes until you can see the question. It's the key to everything.

> YOUR TURN:
> Imagine this as a story climax: a person is rushing through a chaotic place—Times Square, Pamplona while the bulls are running, Mecca during a pilgrimage . . .

Decide where this character is going and why, bearing in mind that this is the story's climactic moment. Now start writing a story that is headed toward this climax. Feel free to steal a character from one of the previous exercises. Write as little or as much of the story as you like, but even if you write only one sentence, make sure it is approaching this peak.

Once you've unearthed a workable major dramatic question, you might want to think about the possibility of an outline. Yes, an outline. As much as it might seem like a potential killjoy, many writers at some point—before a first draft or after a draft or two—find outlines absolutely indispensable. This is especially true with novels, which are unwieldy creatures under the best circumstances, and can be downright unmanageable if you don't get a good grip on them early enough. Outlines work because they allow writers to distill their amorphous creations into their crucial parts, to find the places where tension will need to be increased and the place, or places, where crisis will set in and climax will result.

If the idea appeals to you, you might start by taking down some notes on how your story or novel could divide into a beginning, middle, and end, and think in detail about each section. As far as the beginning, where should it start, what exposition will you provide, and what's your major dramatic question? As for the middle, what additional exposition will be necessary and when will you reveal it? What conflict will the protagonist encounter—and how does the conflict *increase*? In considering the end, what's your crisis, your climax, and what are your consequences? Are they in the right order?

Another way to start is to write down all the events you want to include in your work, making sure each one offers some conflict between the protagonist and his or her goal, and then outline an order for those events, one that ensures that the conflict will, with each step, *increase*. In any case, the point is to boil the work down to its basics and see whether those basics are the right ones, and whether they're in the right order. You don't have to stick with the outline—your ideas will almost certainly change as you keep writing—but if you look at it as a tentative guideline, it can be helpful.

Whatever tools you use, be reassured that you don't have to have your plot nailed down before you begin to write. The story needs plot in the long run, but just like it took me so many pages to get to know my characters, it will take you time and writing and revising to get to know what your story is actually about. Have faith—you probably wouldn't have started writing the piece if it wasn't about something.

> YOUR TURN:
> Create an outline for a short story, novella, or novel that is structured as follows: the story should open with the protagonist setting out on a trip. The destination could be as close as the corner store or as far away as the other side of the universe, but the story should end when the character either arrives at the destination or returns to the starting point. Your outline should have a clear beginning, middle, and end, as well as crisis, climax, and consequences. Don't feel the need to make everything perfect, though. You can make different choices if and when you write the piece. On a journey, we don't always stick to the planned route.

FORM VERSUS FORMULA

Talking about plot like this really puts some writers off. Discussing structural models and plot graphs and outlines and the like can make the work of writing fiction seem like plugging numbers into a formula. And of course, although writing fiction is nothing whatsoever like plugging numbers into a formula, there is a great deal to be said for understanding the basic requirements of form. In the end, there is no real conflict between the requirements of form and the boundless nature of the creative impulse.

Take the analysis of E. M. Forster, who once said that there are only two plots in all of fiction: somebody goes on a journey, or a stranger comes to town. This (arguable) theory breaks down the vastness of literature to help us understand that stories are driven by the actions of characters, and that they must center around a time when something changes in the life of those characters.

Yet isn't it an oversimplification? Doesn't it imply that there are only two stories in all of literature? Hardly. In this chapter alone we've discussed many wildly different versions of the "somebody goes on a journey" plot—from "Sonny's Blues" to *David Copperfield, For Whom the Bell Tolls,* and *The Catcher in the Rye*—and we could certainly go back as far as *The Odyssey* or the biblical Exodus for other examples. As for "a stranger comes to town," we've mentioned *Beloved, Pride and Prejudice,* "The Magic Barrel," and, of course, "Cathedral."

The basic forms may be few, but the variations are infinite. Similarly, understanding that plot requires a protagonist, a central question, conflict, and a beginning, middle, and end doesn't limit us at all. Rather, it gives us something concrete to work with as we follow the urges of our imagination.

The possibilities are countless, and there are many examples where standard storytelling conventions have been successfully flouted. Nontraditional works are one of the great traditions of literature and from them we learn that there are many ways to tell a good story.

First of all, we don't have to present the events of a story in chronological order. Morrison's *Beloved,* for example, moves in two time frames that unfold side by side, following the protagonist both as a slave and in her life afterward, during Reconstruction. In *The Sound and the Fury,* Faulkner uses linear time only when it suits him. In the first chapter, where Benjy's mind is a continuous stream of free associations, we experience events in the present time as essentially simultaneous with events from weeks or months or years ago.

Writers are continually experimenting with story structure. For example, Tim O'Brien's story "The Things They Carried" is structured around long lists of things carried by a group of soldiers in Vietnam. The novel *The Mezzanine* by Nicholson Baker is similarly irreverent, the plot covering the length of time it takes to ride a single escalator between two floors, and the text is regularly broken up with footnotes!

Yet while all of these are nontraditional in terms of specific form, all of them follow the general demands of structure, plot, and beginnings, middles, and ends. All of them succeed partly because they pay attention to plot; even Jean-Paul Sartre, whose existentialist philosophy seems to reject any kind of conventional form, can't resist having the protagonist of *Nausea* struggle and then change, by book's end. In regard to plot, while the specifics change, the general rules, for the most part, hold. Even if we try to *avoid* plot, in telling a story we often end up creating it anyway. And that's probably a very good thing.

CHAPTER 4
POINT OF VIEW:
THE COMPLETE MENU

BY VALERIE VOGRIN

When I consider a photograph of myself taken from several feet away I see a caricature—comically high eyebrows and a crooked chin. When my mother looks at me she sees herself as a younger woman, sort of. When my husband gazes at me he sees a big smile and bright eyes and a mop of tousle-ready hair and twelve years' worth of complicated history. From a traffic helicopter I am one of many toy-size drivers inching my way up Interstate 5. What makes me in turn humorous, poignant, beautiful, and insignificant is point of view. Point of view (also referred to as POV) is equally influential in fiction writing.

Consider the story of a lovers' triangle. Imagine how you might respond to that story presented primarily from the point of view of the husband, left at home with his young son over Thanksgiving weekend while his wife slips away for a ski trip with her lover in Vermont. Now how would you respond if the same story was presented from the point of view of the unfaithful wife, whose husband hasn't made love to her, or spoken a kind word to her, in four years, since she was six months' pregnant; or from the point of view of the lover himself, recently flunked out of law school, adrift in the world, desperate for someone to tell him what to do next? Or what if this story's events are observed by some fourth party, such as the young son or a private detective hired by the husband to spy on his wife?

There you have it—more than anything else, the point of view you choose for your story or novel will affect the way readers respond emotionally to your characters and their actions. Your choice of point of view will also influence other elements of your piece, such as tone and theme. Depending on who is narrating the lovers' triangle story, the tone of the story could be repentant, cruel, caustically funny, wistful, or bitter. The story's theme could be the improbability of marriage, the slippery slope of fidelity, the sacred nature of vows, the tenuousness of love, the fickleness of women, the perfidy of men, etc. And all of this depends on the point of view the writer chooses for the story. As I was saying, pretty darn powerful, this POV business.

Point of view is my favorite topic to teach. I like that there are so many variations to consider. Yet I also appreciate that POV is based on a very basic concept: things look different depending on who is doing the looking and what their vantage point is. Point of view, like microscopes and telescopes, can reveal things ordinarily unseen. But point of view is something of an underdog, in that many writers, inexperienced and experienced, don't give it a second thought. Poor, misguided fools.

When it comes right down to it, POV deals with the following issues:

- Who is speaking: a narrator or a character?
- Whose eyes are seeing the events of the story unfold?
- Whose thoughts does the reader have access to?
- From what distance are the events being viewed?

There are a multitude of ways to handle these issues, and this makes POV a rather complex topic. It's like you've just walked into a restaurant for the first time. You're hungry, unfamiliar with the cuisine, and the host hands you a three-pound menu, twenty laminated pages of culinary possibilities. To a novice fiction writer, the array of point-of-view choices may appear just as overwhelming. There, under entrées, is something called "third-person multiple-vision point of view." *Huh? Does that come in a red sauce?*

This is one reason why some writers just shrug and point to something on the menu that sounds familiar. A better bet might be to spend some time with someone who has your best interests at heart, such as me. Thus I will perform the duties of a shrewd, seasoned waiter, walking you through the menu, helping you make informed choices.

FIRST PERSON

A story told from the first-person POV is narrated by a character in the story, usually the story's protagonist. The narrator tells the story of what *I* did. If the story is about a crime, the narrator is at the scene of the crime. As the police cars pull up, lights flashing, the narrator might be standing in a pool of blood holding a switchblade, or watching from the backseat of the getaway car, or peering out the window of a second-story apartment across the street. The narrator is the story's eyewitness, the reader's means of perception. The reader experiences the fictional world through the narrator's eyes and ears and nose and skin.

> *I saw my wife laughing as she parked the car. I saw her get out of the car and shut the door. She was still wearing a smile. Just amazing. She went around to the other side of the car to where the blind man was already starting to get out. This blind man, feature this, he was wearing a full beard! A beard on a blind man! Too much, I say.*

As demonstrated in this example from "Cathedral," the narrator does more than simply observe. Here we are getting the narrator's take on what he sees.

Now watch how the first-person narrator in Margaret Atwood's story "Weight" tells us what she thinks and how she feels.

> *I am gaining weight. I'm not getting bigger, only heavier. This doesn't show up on the scales: technically, I'm the same. My clothes still fit, so it isn't size, whatever they tell you about fat taking up more space than muscle. The heaviness I feel is the energy I burn up getting myself around: along the sidewalks, up the stairs, through the day. It's the pressure on my feet. It's a density of the cells, as if I've been drinking heavy metals.*

There's nothing standing between this character's consciousness and the reader.

When writing in the first person, you are also writing in the voice—the words and tone—of the character. Writers often create memorable voices for their first-person narrators. Here's Richard, the narrator of Thom Jones's "Cold Snap":

> *Son of a bitch, there's a cold snap and I do this number where I leave all the faucets running because my house, and most houses out here on the*

> *West Coast, aren't "real"—they don't have windows that go up and down,*
> *or basements (which protect the pipes in a way that a crawl space can't), or*
> *sidewalks out in the front with a nice pair of towering oak trees or a couple*
> *of elms, which a real house will have, one of those good old Midwest houses.*
> *Out here the windows go side to side. You get no basement. No sidewalk*
> *and no real trees, just evergreens, and when it gets cold and snows, nobody*
> *knows what to do.*

Jones convinces us that we're hearing Richard's voice for ourselves. Richard might be sitting two stools down from yours at the local tavern, close enough that you can smell his whiskey breath.

The first-person narrator may even use the reader as a confidante, perhaps addressing the reader directly. I chose to do this in my story "Who Can Say Otherwise?" in which a teenage girl narrates the unlikely story of her love affair with a middle-aged rock star:

> *I'm telling you this so you know, so I can try to explain how it is. You'll see*
> *the pictures in the tabloids and say, "But she's no one special!" and of him,*
> *looking a little less dissipated, but with that same famous, wasted face, you*
> *might ask, "What's wrong with that man?" I'm writing against all that.*

Sometimes a narrator addresses a specific someone. For example, Philip Roth's narrator in *Portnoy's Complaint,* Alexander Portnoy, relates his story to his psychoanalyst. The narrator may tell her story to herself in the form of a diary, as in Helen Fielding's *Bridget Jones's Diary.* J. M. Coetzee's *Age of Iron* consists of a single book-length letter written by a mother to her daughter. Though this kind of thing isn't necessary, you might find it helpful in choosing your narrator's words if you imagine what kind of person the narrator is speaking to.

The main advantage of first person is intimacy. The writer can eliminate almost all distance between the reader and the story by placing the reader into the narrator's skin. Also, the narrator's voice can reveal a lot to the reader about the kind of person he is. When we hear Richard speak in "Cold Snap" a picture forms in our minds. We would be surprised to see this guy show up wearing Italian loafers or a pinkie ring.

But the first-person POV does offer some challenges. The writer is stuck in the narrator's skin, along with the reader. All you have to work with is that one character's observations and thoughts. You're not free to wander anywhere, physically or mentally, unless your narrator comes along.

You're also limited by the intelligence and vocabulary of the first-person narrator. Say your story is about an eleven-year-old girl who wants to spend the summer with her ballet-teacher mother in New Orleans despite the fact that her father, an uptight D.C. lawyer, refuses even to consider it. Is the girl up to the job of telling her own story? How mature is she? Does she understand enough about her divorced parents' relationship to make it clear to the reader? Will her observations be interesting enough to keep the reader involved in the story? After all, some eleven-year-olds would make splendid, entertaining companions on a long train trip and others you'd want to shove off the train at the first stop.

> YOUR TURN:
> Get inside someone's skin. Write a passage from the first-person POV of a person walking to a mailbox to send a difficult letter—breaking up with someone, confessing something unpleasant . . . Then pick another character also walking to a mailbox to deliver a difficult letter and write from that character's first-person POV. These characters can be anyone you like, but make them the opposite sex from each other and quite different in age. Remember, this is first person, so you should inhabit these characters and tell things the way they would tell them.

FIRST PERSON: MULTIPLE VISION

Most often first person uses just one first-person narrator, but occasionally there are multiple narrators. A short story writer is confined by space, and more than one narrator will usually play havoc with the writer's ability to create a tight, coherent story. But a novelist, working with plenty of elbow room, may decide that a story will be strongest if more than one witness describes the story's events.

In the novel *The Sweet Hereafter,* Russell Banks uses four first-person narrators to tell and retell the same basic story of a tragic school bus crash: the bus driver, a man whose two small children were killed in the crash, a New York City negligence attorney hoping to make some big bucks off the bereaved, and a teenage girl who will never walk again as a result of the accident. Each character gets a shot at telling his or her own story. The book is divided into discrete sections in which each character presents his or her own version of the truth. The reader hears from Billy Ansel, the young father:

> *And then there were the folks who wanted to believe that the accident was not really an accident, that it was somehow caused, and that therefore, someone was to* blame . . . *Naturally, the lawyers fed off this need and cultivated among people who should have known better. They swam north like sharks from Albany and New York City . . . slipping their cards into pockets of mourners as they departed from the graveyard, and before long that segment of the story had begun—the lawsuits and all the anger and nastiness and greed that people at their worst are capable of.*

The reader may consider Mitchell Stephens, Esq., to be a vulture, but perhaps there is more to him than that:

> *People immediately assume we're greedy, that it's money we're after, people call us ambulance chasers and so on, like we're the proctologists of the profession, and, yes, there's lots of those. But the truth is, the good ones, we'd make the same moves for a single shekel as for a ten-million-dollar settlement. Because it's anger that drives and delivers us.*

But Nichole Burnell, the girl who is now paralyzed, someone who can reasonably be assumed to have reason to be angry, has a different take on it:

> *It just wasn't right—to be alive, to have what people assured you was a close call, and then go out and hire a lawyer, it wasn't right . . . Not if I was, like they said, truly lucky . . . There was no stopping Mom and Daddy, though. They had their minds made up. This Mr. Stephens had convinced them that they were going to get a million dollars from the State of New York and maybe another million from the town of Sam Dent. Daddy said they all have insurance for this sort of thing; it won't come out of anybody's pocket, he kept saying; but even so, it made me nervous.*

Banks actually *forces* the reader to participate in making the story's meaning by deciphering the similarities and differences among the versions. Who is telling the truth about the accident? Whose motives are noble and whose are not?

One variation on the multiple first-person narrator POV uses the epistolary technique—the story is presented as a series of letters exchanged between characters. Though this technique was more common in centuries past, appearing in novels such as *Pamela* and *Les Liaisons Dangereuses,* it still turns up in contemporary fiction. An extremely popular recent example is the *Griffin & Sabine* trilogy by Nick Bantock.

On rare occasions, such as in William Faulkner's "A Rose for Emily," you'll see the first-person plural, where *we* is used instead of *I* even though one person is usually speaking for the *we*.

One of the chief strengths of first-person multiple-vision POV is the reader's intellectual involvement in the story. It doesn't allow the reader to sit back and be told what to think and feel. The reader must piece things together for himself, which can make for an interesting reading experience.

You might choose this point of view for your own novel if your characters have strikingly different perspectives and you want readers to hear each character's voice directly and to draw their own conclusions. Of course, many writers find it's not that easy to create a single strong convincing voice, much less a handful of them. And you will almost certainly lose some of the focus of first-person singular as the reader slips in and out of several characters' skins.

FIRST PERSON: PERIPHERAL

Although the first-person narrator is usually the protagonist, you may choose to have your first-person narrator be another character in the story. A famous example of a peripheral narrator is found in F. Scott Fitzgerald's *The Great Gatsby.* Most of the events narrator Nick Carraway describes in the novel concern the misadventures of the protagonist, Jay Gatsby. Nick's primary job is to observe and relate the story, as he does here:

> And as I sat there, brooding on the old unknown world, I thought of Gatsby's wonder when he first picked out the green light at the end of Daisy's dock. He had come a long way to this blue lawn and his dreams must have seemed so close that he could hardly fail to grasp it.

The peripheral point of view is effective when the story's protagonist is blind to his or her own actions and when that blindness or its consequences are significant enough to strongly affect someone who stands outside the action, as in *The Great Gatsby.*

Say you want to write the story of a failing marriage in which both spouses believe themselves to be the injured party. The point of the story is that they're trapped, blind to the wider sense of the truth. So a better choice for a narrator than either the husband or the wife might be someone who is capable of observing things fully, such as the couple's adolescent son. There's nothing he can do to help his parents. He can only watch and learn—that's what makes him peripheral.

But there's a real challenge with this POV as the narrator must report on the protagonist while stuck in the body of a bystander. Nick isn't Gatsby's shadow. He has to go home sometimes. And he's only just met Gatsby. A writer often has to get creative to work around a problem like this, as when Fitzgerald has Nick's (sort of) girlfriend, Jordan, relate the history of the romance between Daisy and Gatsby.

THE UNRELIABLE FIRST PERSON

In a sense, all first-person narrators are somewhat unreliable. Even the most scrupulous characters may, unconsciously perhaps, shade the truth or emphasize one fact over another to make themselves look ever-so-slightly better. A boy telling the story of his sister running away from home might not want to own up to his role in her unhappiness. Even an honest fellow like Nick Carraway may distort the truth a bit.

However, if the answer to the question *Who is speaking*, for example, is an autistic person, a very young child, a psychopath, a cat, a jealous lover, or a habitual liar, the reader understands that the ordinary skepticism does not apply. This narrator has extraordinary limitations and her version of the facts is not to be trusted.

The reader understands after only a few sentences that the narrator of Edgar Allan Poe's "The Tell-Tale Heart" is insane, although he tries to convince us otherwise:

> *True!—nervous—very, very dreadfully nervous I had been and am; but why will you say that I am mad? The disease has sharpened my senses—not destroyed—not dulled them. Above all was the sense of hearing acute. I heard all things in the heaven and of the earth. I heard many things in hell.*

In Poe's story the narrator's madness leaves the reader off balance, unable to distinguish between the narrator's delusions and reality. The narrator's unreliability adds to the story's unsettling effect. Contemporary writers have used unreliable narrators to underscore my point—that there's no such thing as a reliable narrator. The unreliable narrator emphasizes the philosophical view that there is no such thing as a single, static, knowable reality.

Using an unreliable narrator forces the writer to create two versions of the truth, a steep challenge. But if the POV is handled well, the results can be quite intriguing.

> YOUR TURN:
> Write a passage from the POV of an unreliable narrator who skews the facts, intentionally or unintentionally. For example, what might a child at a boisterous cocktail party hosted by her parents confide about the guests? What erroneous conclusions might she draw from their behavior and their jokes? Might her false equations add up to cold, hard truths? Of course, if you favor a deluded or deceitful character, go for it. Whomever you pick, see if you can make a reader understand the narrator's unreliability.

THIRD PERSON: SINGLE VISION

With the third-person point of view the narrator is *not* a character in the story. The narrator is a voice created by the author to tell the story. The narrator tells the story of what *he* did or what *she* said. Third person has numerous variations with unwieldy names. Never fear. These variations are quite manageable when broken down into their parts.

Perhaps the most prevalent version of the third person is the third-person single vision. With this POV, the narrator has access to only one character's mind. Thus, single vision refers to the way the narrator views a story's events—through the eyes of a single character. The story is told *by* the narrator, *from* the perspective of a single participant in the action. The character whose point of view is being recognized by the author is called the point-of-view character. (This term really applies in any type of POV.) The entire story is filtered through the point-of-view character's consciousness.

In the short story "Earth to Molly," Elizabeth Tallent intends for the reader to understand that the opinions the narrator expresses are Molly's:

> At the hotel, really a shabby bed-and-breakfast, the landlady, pinching her upper lip in displeasure at having to hoist herself from her chair, let Molly into her room and left her with the key. The landlady was a long time retreating down the hall. The dolor of her tread, with its brooding pauses, was not eavesdropping but arthritis. Molly was sorry for having needed her to climb the stairs, but of course the old woman complained her stiff-legged way up them all the time, showing lodgers to their rooms. Why, oh why, would anyone spend the night here? A prickly gray carpet ran tightly from wall to wall. It was the color of static, and seemed as hateful.

Notice that it's Molly who is thinking, "Why, oh why, would anyone spend the night here?" just as the details concerning the carpet are filtered through Molly's consciousness.

While this narrator seems to stand just behind Molly's shoulder, or perhaps even lurk in her mind, the third-person narrator may also stand back at a little distance. This may create an ironic or comic effect, as in this description in Kingsley Amis's *Lucky Jim* of an aspiring academic reacting to a tiresome joke by his superior:

> [Dixon] tried to flail his features into some sort of response to humour. Mentally, however, he was making a different face and promising himself he'd make it actually when next alone. He'd draw his lower lip in under his top teeth and by degrees retract his chin as far as possible, all this while dilating his eyes and nostrils. By these means he would, he was confident, cause a deep and dangerous flush to suffuse his face.

With many of the advantages of first person (the reader empathizes with the point-of-view character much as she does with a first-person narrator), employing an "outside" narrator allows the writer to craft the language in ways that may be implausible coming from the mouth of a first-person narrator. Also, if your narrator is a fictionalized version of yourself, allowing the third-person narrator to tell the story avoids the appearance of self-indulgence.

The third-person single vision is an excellent POV if your point-of-view character is someone with limited intellectual powers or verbal skills. For example, what if the girl who wants to spend her summer vacation with her mother in New Orleans is autistic? Even though she may be quite perceptive, she can't tell her own story if she doesn't have the words to describe what her world is like. The situation would be similar with a character who has little formal education. No matter that he's the smartest person in the story, you'll probably find that a narrator with a greater facility with language will be more successful in conveying the character's shrewdness than the character himself.

The disadvantage of this POV—perhaps the only one—is that the point-of-view character must be present for everything that takes place in the story, just as with a first-person narrator. If your point-of-view character overhears a conversation, she may report that to the reader. However, if the conversation takes place in a health-food store across town, the discussion is off-limits.

> YOUR TURN:
> Imagine an incident in a department store in which a salesperson and a customer clash over something—shoplifting, rudeness, racial misunderstanding . . . Using the third-person single-vision POV, write a passage detailing this clash through the eyes of the customer. As is customary with third-person single vision, include the character's thoughts.

THIRD PERSON: MULTIPLE VISION

As with first-person POV, a writer using the third-person POV may decide that two or more heads are better than one. The multiple-vision POV allows the writer to show a story's events from different angles.

This point of view is most often used in longer pieces of fiction—novellas and novels. In a shorter piece you might find that you don't have the room to develop numerous point-of-view characters. After all, the reader needs to know fully who these people are in order to make sense of what they're thinking and feeling. Indeed, writers often arrange the perspectives of the point-of-view characters to emphasize their differences.

In *The Watch*, a novella by Rick Bass, the three point-of-view characters are Hollingsworth, the middle-aged proprietor of a country story in Mississippi, his seventy-seven-year-old father, Buzbee, who has run away to live in a tree in the woods, and Jesse, a cyclist-in-training. The following paragraphs represent two of these characters:

> *Hollingsworth would sit on his heels on the steps and tremble whenever Jesse and the others rode past, and on the times when Jesse turned in and came up to the store, so great was Hollingsworth's hurry to light his cigarette . . . that he spilled two cigarettes, and had barely gotten the third lit and drawn one puff when Jesse finished his Coke and then stood back up, and put the wet empty bottle back on the wire rack, waved, and rode off, the great backs of his calves and hamstrings working up and down in swallowing shapes, like things trapped in a sack.*

> *The first thing Jesse did in the mornings when he woke up was to check the sky, and then, stepping out onto the back porch, naked, the wind. If there wasn't any, he would be relaxed and happy with his life. If it was windy—even the faintest stir against his shaved ankles, up and over his round legs—he would scowl, a grimace of concentration, and go in and fix his coffee.*

Both characters have active inner lives, but Hollingsworth directs his thoughts outward. He craves companionship; in an earlier section we see that he invents names for the other riders in Jesse's group. Jesse is self-absorbed. The wind has no existence for him except as a condition affecting his ride each day. These are my conclusions as a reader, conclusions Bass intends for me to draw.

As a general rule you should make distinct transitions between point-of-view characters. You do not want your reader to be unsure of whose eyes are witnessing the events of the story. Rick Bass never switches point-of-view characters mid-paragraph, and he uses white space on the page to mark the transition for the reader. Novelists often make this switch at a chapter break; that is, each chapter belongs to a single point-of-view character.

Many fine novels use this technique of alternating points of view. Sometimes each point-of-view character gets equal time. But a book may be dominated by one point-of-view character, with only occasional switches to a secondary character's viewpoint. Sometimes the points of view alternate in a pattern and the reader becomes less conscious of the switches as she reads on. In *Happenstance: Two Novels in One About a Marriage in Transition*, Carol Shields's switcheroo between the husband's and wife's point of view is impossible to ignore—the reader must turn the book over to begin the second half. And in another POV twist, Shields gives no instructions or even hints as to which half should be read first. The reader's experience of the book is literally in his own hands.

No matter what variation or twist you choose, if you elect to use more than one point-of-view character make sure you have good reason. There's no sense in it if the characters view the world in nearly identical terms. As with first-person multiple-vision stories, much of the interest is generated by the disparities and similarities that emerge between the points of view.

Third-person multiple vision also provides a wider view, often creating an effect like a collage. In *The End of Vandalism,* Tom Drury, the writer, has different episodes seen through the eyes of multiple characters, with the result being a picture of an entire made-up world—Grouse County. The focus is on the community.

With access to more than one character's thoughts the writer gains flexibility. Your story may seem roomier once you leave the confines of a single character's head. In a third-person multiple-vision POV, each character's experience is interesting, but the writer highlights what's most interesting by juxtaposing the various viewpoints.

As occurs with first person, the flexibility you gain with multiple viewpoints costs you focus. The reader's attention and concern are spread more thinly. But this can just as easily be seen as an advantage. With the addition of just one more consciousness the reader is immediately engaged in a more complex way. The reader must observe and draw conclusions based on how the different characters' beliefs contradict or confirm each other. The reader's divided sympathy may be the point of the story.

You might show, for instance, how disastrous it would be for one sympathetic character if another sympathetic character's desires are fulfilled. First you introduce Lily, a young widow, as a point-of-view character, showing the reader how desperate she is and how hard she's trying to be a good mother, and what awful luck has brought her to this place, alone and broke and applying for a job as an attendant at a Laundromat, a job that would allow her to keep her toddler son with her while she worked. (Did I mention that the boy has a rare degenerative disease for which the only promising treatment centers are two thousand miles away?) Then in the next chapter you introduce a second point-of-view character, Jack, who recently lost his hand in a farming accident. He's behind on his car payments and his thoughts are on his beloved dogs, four retired seeing-eye dogs, and the few pieces of dog food rattling in the bottom of the twenty-pound bag. And inevitably, in the way of stories, Jack applies for the same job as Lily because he wants to stay in town and try to get his bearings while he decides what to do next. This is a job he can perform one-handed while he learns to use his prosthetic hand. Now you've engaged the reader by putting him in a very thorny spot. Who should he root for? Which of these wretched souls is more deserving? Multiple-vision points of view can add the desirable kind of complexity to a story, the kind that honors the way our lives are entwined and our sympathies are divided.

> YOUR TURN:
> Return to the previous exercise, the one with the clash at the department store. Write a passage about the exact same incident through the POV of the salesperson. Then write again about the same incident, this time from the POV of an innocent bystander. You will then have viewed this department-store clash through the eyes of three different characters. Who has the most interesting point of view on this incident?

THIRD PERSON: OMNISCIENT

Think "god's-eye view." Think Zeus enthroned at the top of Mount Olympus, the archetypal deity peering down from heaven. Omniscient means all knowing, and thus the writer is always omniscient; the writer should always know everything there is to know about each character and the setting, and every event related to the story, past, present, and future. What distinguishes the omniscient point of view is that the writer who employs it is free to share directly some, or all, of this vast amount of information with the reader.

In each of the points of view I covered earlier, essential information is filtered through the consciousness of one or more of the characters. In the third-person omniscient point of view, the story's information is filtered through the narrator's all-knowing consciousness. Through the omniscient narrator you have the ability to do any of the following: enter the mind of any or all of the characters, interpret the story's events, describe incidents unobserved by any of the story's characters, provide historical context for the story, and inform the reader of future events.

Prior to the twentieth century, most fiction employed omniscient narrators, including many of the big names in literature such as Fielding, Dickens, Tolstoy, Flaubert, and Austen. Their omniscient narrators often had authoritative, opinionated voices, like the one we hear in Washington Irving's *Rip Van Winkle:*

> *Whoever has made a voyage up the Hudson must remember the Kaatskill Mountains. They are a dismembered branch of the great Appalachian family, and are seen away to the west of the river, swelling up to a noble height and lording it over the surrounding country. Every change of season, every change of weather, indeed every hour of the day, produces some change in the magical hues and shapes of these mountains, and they are regarded by all the good wives, far and near, as perfect barometers.*

Soon thereafter a variety of social changes occurred related to the rise of democracy (and the decline of empires), Freud, religious skepticism, feminism, and so forth which over time resulted in the (now seemingly paternal, heavy-handed, one-sided, bigheaded) omniscient point of view falling out of favor with contemporary writers. Once enough writers traded in omniscience for more limited points of view, this kind of omniscience seemed old-fashioned and fell out of favor. Yet it is still an effective device.

Here's a twentieth-century example of omniscience from Eudora Welty's "No Place for You, My Love":

> *They were strangers to each other, both fairly well strangers to the place, now seated side by side at luncheon—a party combined in a free-and-easy way when the friends he and she were with recognized each other across Galatoire's. The time was a Sunday in summer—those hours of afternoon that seem Time Out in New Orleans.*
>
> *The moment he saw her little blunt, fair face, he thought that here was a woman who was having an affair. It was one of those odd meetings when such an impact is felt that it has to be translated at once into some sort of speculation.*
>
> *With a married man, most likely, he supposed, slipping quickly into a groove—he was long married—and feeling more conventional, then, in his curiosity as she sat there, leaning her cheek on her hand, looking no further before her than the flowers on the table, and wearing that hat.*
>
> *He did not like her hat, any more than he liked tropical flowers. It*

was the wrong hat for her, thought this Eastern businessman who had no interest whatsoever in women's clothes and no eye for them; he thought the unaccustomed thing crossly.

It must stick out all over me, she thought, so people think they can love me or hate me just by looking at me. How did it leave us—the old, safe, slow way people used to know of learning how one another feels, and the privilege that went with it of shying away if it seemed best? People in love like me, I suppose, give away the short cuts to everybody's secrets.

Welty's narrator enters the minds of both characters. She also interprets the characters' reactions and draws definite conclusions. Yet she is gentle, not insistent. There's room for the reader to draw his own conclusions.

As some contemporary writers have discovered, omniscience doesn't require adopting a biblical tone or throwing the literary equivalent of thunderbolts. A modern and more subtle form of omniscience appears in works by Andre Dubus, Michael Ondaatje, Nicola Barker, Ellen Gilchrist, and Alice Munro, to name a few.

Postmodern writers, such as Milan Kundera, have adopted a conspicuous form of omniscience, eschewing verisimilitude. They call attention to the novel as a *made* thing. They flaunt their godlike powers. For example, in *The Unbearable Lightness of Being,* Kundera often interrupts the flow of the story to comment on the story, its themes, or fiction itself:

It would be senseless for the author to try to convince the reader that his characters once lived. They were not born of a mother's womb; they were born of a stimulating phrase or two from a basic situation. Tomas was born of the saying "Einmal ist keinmal." Tereza was born of a rumbling of a stomach.

The first time she went to Tomas's flat, her insides began to rumble. And no wonder: she had had nothing to eat since breakfast but a quick sandwich on the platform before boarding the train . . .

Once Kundera has made his point, reminding us of the fictional nature of his characters, he returns to their story.

When you think about it, omniscience represents freedom. And freedom is good, yes? Instead of being limited by the intelligence and maturity and sanity of your characters, omniscience provides you with a way to take charge, to make sense of your characters' bizarre behavior or the customs of the planet you just invented.

You can use omniscience to create suspense by supplying the reader with information unknown to the characters. The narrator might inform the reader that even as Sue and Harry prepare for their wedding a giant wave is approaching their town and that when the tsunami strikes in one hour only one of them will survive. Or the narrator might tip off the reader that Miss Harriet Wood, beloved by her first-grade students and their parents and school administrators and stray dogs everywhere, is entertaining a dangerous criminal in her home, and not a representative from an educational book company as she believes. The narrator can make Miss Harriet's story downright painful for the reader, as he anxiously turns the page, hoping against hope that Harriet will get a clue before this villain can harm her.

However, there are reasons why omniscience is used rarely now. Omniscience usually calls attention to the presence of the writer—an undesirable thing for writers who want their readers to suspend their disbelief willingly. Omniscience may seem impersonal to the reader, who is used to being asked to care for a particular character or characters. Omniscience is not for the faint of heart; most writers find it's easier to manage POV when they're limited to revealing the thoughts of just one or two characters. Too much freedom makes them dizzy, like riding a unicycle across the high wire without a net.

> YOUR TURN:
> Using the omniscient POV, write a scene in which something gets broken at a wedding reception. A gift, a bottle of champagne, somebody's heart . . . Demonstrate at least three of the five omniscient powers—entering the mind of any character, interpreting events, describing unobserved incidents, providing historical context, revealing future events. There is plenty of opportunity here, as there are bound to be many people in attendance. Relish your godlike ability to know and see everything.

THIRD PERSON: OBJECTIVE

This is the ultimate POV challenge, a real test of your abilities to reveal information in scenes. The narrator in the third-person objective point of view is denied access to even a single character's mind. The writer must reveal *everything* about the story (background, characterization, conflict, theme, etc.) through dialogue and action. The effect is a bit like reading a journalist's account of events, getting only the hard facts.

In his story "Little Things," master short story writer Raymond Carver demonstrates that he's up to the challenge of this point of view:

> *He was in the bedroom pushing clothes into a suitcase when she came to the door.*
>
> *I'm glad you're leaving! I'm glad you're leaving! She began to cry. You can't even look me in the face, can you?*
>
> *Then she noticed the baby's picture on the bed and picked it up.*
>
> *He looked at her and she wiped her eyes and stared at him before turning and going back to the living room.*
>
> *Bring that back, he said.*
>
> *Just get your things and get out, she said.*
>
> *He did not answer. He fastened the suitcase, put on his coat, looked around the bedroom before turning off the light. Then he went out to the living room.*
>
> *She stood in the doorway of the little kitchen, holding the baby.*
>
> *I want the baby, he said.*
>
> *Are you crazy?*
>
> *No, but I want the baby. I'll get someone to come by for his things.*
>
> *You're not touching this baby, she said.*

This unnamed couple goes back and forth, arguing about who gets the baby. Ultimately, gruesomely, each grabs hold of the child and, Carver deadpans, "in this way the matter was decided." This isn't the kind of thing most people want to believe they're capable of. How could Carver ever convince us of the thoughts a mother or father might have that would allow them to act so atrociously? The objective POV solves the problem for Carver. By reporting the events rather than trying to explain them, he makes what occurs credible.

The primary strength of the objective point of view is that it offers a sense of integrity and impartiality. Objective POV prevents a writer from overexplaining because the writer can't really *explain* anything at all.

Here's the downside. One of fiction's major attractions is that we, as readers, are allowed insight into the murky minds of others—unlike in real life, where we are left guessing at what's behind a boss's costly dentistry, a child's smirk, a lover's raised eyebrow. The opacity of the objective POV denies us these insights. A story told in objective POV is like a flower minus its scent and vivid colors, a vaguely interesting oddity perhaps, but not likely to attract much attention.

> YOUR TURN:
> Take the wedding reception passage from your omniscient POV exercise, and revise it using the objective POV. Employ your powers of observation and describe what takes place, as though you are a journalist writing a news account. Remember, this time you can't enter anyone's head. But, what does the behavior of the characters reveal about their thoughts?

SECOND PERSON

As with the third-person points of view, second-person POV stories are told in the voice of a narrator. In second person, however, the narrator tells what *you* did or said.

When Jay McInerney published his novel *Bright Lights, Big City* in 1987, his use of the second-person point of view created quite a stir in literary circles. His choice of POV was denigrated by some critics as a gimmick. Readers couldn't remember seeing this done before, and they certainly weren't accustomed to being addressed like this by a narrator:

> *You are at a nightclub talking to a girl with a shaved head. The club is either Heartbreak or the Lizard Lounge. All might come clear if you could just slip into the bathroom and do a little more Bolivian Marching Powder . . . Your brain at this moment is composed of brigades of tiny Bolivian soldiers. They are tired and muddy from their long march through the night. There are holes in their boots and they are hungry. They need to be fed. They need the Bolivian Marching Powder.*

The novel's POV caused many readers to get the sensation that they were the protagonist, the barhopping, late-night snorter of cocaine. Though the book was a best-seller, other novelists didn't rush to follow suit. The POV choice felt like a novelty act—a how-many-times-do-you-need-to-watch-a-man-eat-a-car type thing.

Lorrie Moore employed the second-person POV quite differently in her collection of short stories *Self-Help*. The narrators of many of the book's stories (i.e., "How to Be an Other Woman" and "How to Become a Writer") mimic the advice-giving voice of self-help writers. This is from the story "How":

> *Begin by meeting him in a class, in a bar, at a rummage sale. Maybe he teaches sixth grade. Manages a hardware store. Foreman at a carton factory. He will be a good dancer. He will have perfectly cut hair. He will laugh at your jokes.*
>
> *A week, a month, a year. Feel discovered, comforted, needed, loved, and start sometimes, somehow, to feel bored. When sad or confused, walk uptown to the movies. Buy popcorn. These things come and go. A week, a month, a year.*
>
> *Make attempts at a less restrictive arrangement. Watch them sputter and deflate like balloons. He will ask you to move in. Do so hesitantly, with ambivalence. Clarify: rents are high, nothing long-range, love and all that, hon, but it's footloose. Lay out the rules with much elocution. Stress openness, non-exclusivity. Make room in his closet, but don't rearrange the furniture.*

Imagine what you could do with this. What would be the title of your "self-help" short story?

I must tell you, however, that the second person is closely associated with McInerney and Moore. Second person has possibilities and it's quite fun to use, but if their goal is publication, it's up to other writers to make it their own—to make it fresh—by using it to create a different effect.

One writer who has done so recently is Helen Dunmore in her novel *With Your Crooked Heart:*

> *You lie down on the warm stone, and wriggle your body until it fits. Then you relax, and the terrace bears you up as if you are floating out to sea. Sun has been pouring onto it since seven o'clock, and every grain of stone is packed with heat. Sun pours on to the glistening mound of your belly, on to your parted thighs, your arms, your fingers, your face. No part*

of you resists, no part does not shine. The moist lips of your vulva are caught in a shining tangle of hair.

Though I do feel the odd sensation, at first, of being addressed, I don't think Dunmore's motives for using second person have much to do with directly addressing the reader. Instead, I hear the voice to be narrating a particular character's experience, putting words to a set of feelings and sensations that would otherwise be unexpressed. I find the voice to be quite intimate, as if the narrator is whispering in the character's ear as she lies in the hot sun.

If you can find a compelling way to use the second-person POV, go forth and conquer. Otherwise, proceed with caution.

> YOUR TURN:
> Rewrite one of your first-person POV passages using the second-person POV. Though you may do little more than switch the pronoun *I* to *you*, the effect may be profound. And feel free to change anything you like to fit this new POV. Compare the two versions and consider the different emotional impact of each.

DISTANCE

Early on I stated that one of the questions POV answers is *From what distance are the events being viewed?* And yes, it's one more thing to factor into your point-of-view decision-making.

EMOTIONAL DISTANCE

This is the distance that we sense between the narrator and the characters, a distance that affects how close the reader feels to the characters. We usually think of emotional distance as an abstract idea, like asking someone, *How close do you feel to your sister?* But with POV this distance can actually be measured, if we think about it in terms of camera distance:

Long shot: *The man hurried through the cold night.*
Medium shot: *The man hurried through the night, squinting against the cold.*

Close-up: *As the man hurried through the night, he felt the bitter cold air on his lips.*

If the narrator is close enough to feel the cold on the character's lips, we presume the narrator's empathy for the character—very little emotional distance.

Often a writer will pick a camera distance, so to speak, and stick with it for the entire story. But sometimes the camera distance will change during the course of the story.

Jane Smiley opens her novel *A Thousand Acres* with a panoramic shot:

> *At sixty miles per hour, you could pass our farm in a minute, on County Road 686, which ran due north into the T intersection at Cabot Street Road . . . Because the intersection was on this tiny rise, you could see our buildings, a mile distant, at the southern edge of the farm. A mile to the east, you could see three silos that marked the northeastern corner, and if you raked your gaze from the silos to the house and barn, then back again, you would take in the immensity of the piece of land my father owned, six hundred forty acres, a whole section, paid for, no encumbrances, as flat and fertile, black, friable, and exposed as any piece of land on the face of the earth.*

Because this land is at the center of the novel's conflict, it is important that Smiley establishes it as a physical, known presence. Yet we wouldn't choose this distance for an entire story or book if we wanted the reader to care about the characters. At this distance the characters would be specks. That distance changes in the next chapter. Smiley zooms the camera in on her narrator, so close the lens could touch her skin:

> *Linda was just born when I had my first miscarriage, and for a while, six months maybe, the sight of those two babies [her nieces], whom I had loved and cared for with real interest and satisfaction, affected me like a poison. All my tissues hurt when I saw them, when I saw Rose with them, as if my capillaries were carrying acid into the furthest reaches of my system.*

TIME DISTANCE

If it isn't specified, we normally presume that the events in the stories we read occurred relatively recently. In this case we might say there is very little distance in time between the narrator and the story. Though the story is written in past tense (as most are) a writer often creates the effect of immediacy—of the story occurring just now, as we read:

> *A young man said he wanted to go to bed with Alexandra because she had an interesting mind. He was a cabdriver and she had admired the curly back of his head. Still, she was surprised. He said he would pick her up again in about an hour and a half. Because she was fair and a reasonable person, she placed between them a barrier of truthful information.*

In this, the opening passage of Grace Paley's story "Enormous Changes at the Last Minute," we are meant to be drawn into the present of the story—Alexandra's thinking about how to react to the cabdriver and the hospital visit to her father that the cabbie is driving her to.

Writers occasionally try to narrow this time distance by telling the story in the present tense, as Margaret Atwood did in her novel *Surfacing:*

> *He feels me watching him and lets go of my hand. Then he takes his gum out, bundling it in the silver wrapper, and sticks it in the ashtray and crosses his arms. This means I'm not supposed to observe him; I face front.*

Does this sound more immediate to you than the previous passage? Well, yes, and that's the intent. But because past tense has been a convention of fiction for so long, most readers now find its use invisible. Formerly quite unusual, present tense doesn't upset many soup bowls anymore.

Sometimes a writer specifies that the events of the story took place long ago, creating a substantial time distance. When this occurs, the reader may feel that the story is tinged with nostalgia or that the account may be in some other way suspect, memory having been eroded over time. The distance is striking in George Eliot's story "The Lifted Veil," which begins:

> *The time of my end approaches. I have lately been subject to attacks of angina pectoris; and in the ordinary course of things, my physician tells me, I may fairly hope that my life will not be protracted many months.*

The narrator goes on to reflect on the span of his lifetime. He tells us, "my childhood perhaps seems happier to me than it really was, in contrast with all the after-years." Several pages later he's leaped ahead to describe his young adulthood: "At Basle we were joined by my brother Alfred, now a handsome self-confident man of six-and-twenty, a thorough contrast to my fragile nervous ineffectual self."

In an instance like this, when the reader is aware that the story's events occurred long ago, the emotional urgency and suspense of the story may be diminished. In Eliot's story we know the narrator is about to die—there's no hope of a different outcome to the story's events. But this kind of time distance allows the narrator to tell the story with an interesting perspective, often fusing emotions of both the past and the present.

THE POV CONTRACT

What you must never forget is that point of view establishes a contract with the reader. POV tells the reader what kind of story he is reading. Break this contract and you risk losing the reader's trust in you. Thereafter the story will never feel quite "real" to the reader. You will distract the reader from the smooth red-carpet-like unfolding of your story.

Novice writers sometimes break the POV contract with a careless slip. One of my fiction students chose a third-person limited single-vision POV for her story, the point-of-view character being Barbara, the CEO of a cosmetics company. Thus, the contract is this: all the events should be filtered through Barbara's consciousness.

My student's story was moving right along, with competent handling of character development and conflict. Then, *bang!* The narrator entered the head of a minor character and the story stumbled, like so:

> *Barbara spent the next ten minutes listening to her accountant. She couldn't focus on the papers Ted waved in front of her or his words. All she could think of was of the message John had left on her answering machine.* I'm heading to Montana. I know this is sudden and I feel like a jackass, a cliché, but I've really got to get away and figure some things out.
>
> *She pushed back from her desk and grabbed her jacket from the chair. She thanked Ted for his attention to detail.* "And as soon as I finish with today's meetings I'll look over these ledger sheets."
>
> *Once again feeling dismissed and belittled, and wondering why he*

kept working for such an ungrateful boss, Ted began to gather up the papers from her desk.

"You can leave those papers where they are, Ted. I said I'd get to them later."

No offense to administrative assistants, but in this story Ted has a walk-on role. His only reason for existence in the story is to inform Barbara that one of her trusted employees has been embezzling. My student confessed she hadn't even noticed the lapse. To adhere to the POV contract while still revealing Ted's attitude, my student can simply describe Ted's actions. She might rewrite the offending paragraph to read:

Ted sighed and started to gather up the papers from her desk. "Fine, just fine," he muttered, "I'll just go sit in my corner and wait meekly for the madam to summon me."

As a safeguard against POV abuses, you might write down your point-of-view rules regarding omniscience, reliability, and distance. When you finish a draft you can check every paragraph against these rules.

But as many a recording artist knows, contracts are made to be broken. Occasionally a very daring writer will break the POV contract deliberately, to achieve a special effect—when that is what the story needs.

In Richard Russo's *Empire Falls,* the preface is presented by an omniscient narrator. Then a third-person narrator follows the protagonist, Miles Roby, for two chapters; we get a chapter told from the POV of Miles's estranged wife and one (suddenly switching from past to present tense) from the POV of Miles's daughter. Thereafter Russo establishes a pattern of third-person multiple vision, the vision shifting with chapter breaks. But, wait, in chapter 7, we're in a tavern and the POV suddenly starts shifting back and forth between the tavern's owner and the only two customers in a way that looks suspiciously like omniscience. However, none of this feels careless. The author wants us to view the inhabitants of this town in a slightly unpredictable manner and we trust that he knows what he's doing.

HOW TO CHOOSE

As I warned you, the POV menu is complicated, but I hope you're beginning to feel comfortable with it. And I'm betting that by now you're convinced that your choice of POV is one of the biggest choices you will make with a piece of fiction. As stated earlier, it affects everything. As with all significant and complex decisions, your task will be easier if you're able to narrow your choices.

I suggest asking yourself, *Whose story is this?* Many times you'll be able to answer immediately. Stories written in the first person usually do belong to the narrator, just as stories written in third-person single-vision POV usually belong to the point-of-view character. That character most often has the most at stake. Whether the reader thinks the story has a happy ending depends on whether the point-of-view character thinks it does. If your story clearly belongs to a single dominant character, then first person or third-person limited is the obvious choice. Then it's just a matter of deciding if you want the story told in the character's voice or not.

Stories populated by extended families, blended families, marriages, soccer teams, submarine crews, and people linked by a situation (as in *The Sweet Hereafter*) often have more than one protagonist. Many times each and every character has a goal, and frequently the goals conflict with one another. In this case you must ask yourself, *What's most interesting to me about this story?* Say your story is about a prestigious jazz quintet in which the trumpet player, after a dozen years with the group, wants out. As you consider this scenario, are you most interested in how the trumpet player struggles with his feelings of obligation and the obstacles the other four musicians create? If so, use one of the single-vision POVs. Maybe, however, you are most intrigued by what happens to the group as a whole. Does a leader emerge? Do any of the other members secretly work to help the trumpet player? Will the group be able to stay together if the trumpet player succeeds in leaving? Your interest in the group's story doesn't necessitate a multiple-vision or omniscient point of view; perhaps there is one character who can act as the spokesperson, providing the eyes and ears for the whole group—but you will at least want to consider them because of the flexibility they offer.

Another question you can ask yourself is as basic as it gets. *What kinds of stories do I like to read?* If you had a whole glorious weekend to read—if by some miracle you weren't going to be allowed to do anything but read—what would you pick up first, a multigenerational epic or an intense story with a memorable protagonist? Are you most interested in psychological dynamics—what happens to one person as she faces adversity or social dynamics—or in how individuals react and play off one another as they struggle to achieve their individual goals? Which movie better suits your tastes, *Rocky* or *A League of Their Own*?

You can't, however, be confident you've found the best POV for your story when it's just an abstract idea. You need to taste that POV. Just as the wine connoisseur holds a sip of wine in her mouth and swirls it across her tongue and cheeks to get the full effect, you need to discover how the POV feels on the page. Does it sound like you expected it to? Does it have the complexity of flavor your story needs?

You may be able to learn all you need with only a page or two of a draft. You may reach a bull's-eye certainty after considering only a couple of points of view. Then again, maybe not.

I wrote half a novel in first person because my inspiration came in the form of a sentence landing in my head on my morning walk. The voice said, "My name is Eleanor Sweetleaf and I've lived in this house since I was three days old." Who was I to argue with inspiration? But a year or so later I was stuck. Eleanor Sweetleaf was a good soul, but not quite the right voice for the story after all. She took her story a little too seriously. After grinding my teeth for a while, I began rewriting in the third-person single-vision POV— a better choice, I quickly realized. The revised story was funnier and I felt freer to play with language. Once I let go of my death grip on first person I found I was also willing to change other aspects of my story. My husband was horrified at first; he didn't understand how I had failed to realize sooner that I was writing in the wrong point of view. He felt bad about all that "wasted" work. But what he didn't know (yet) was that writing is all about trial and error. And he also didn't know that it's the writer's duty to fully exercise the enormous power of point of view.

CHAPTER 5
DESCRIPTION: TO PICTURE IN WORDS

BY CHRIS LOMBARDI

About twelve years ago, my best friend was reading a draft of a story I'd written about a woman recently returned from years in a far-off country, grieving the lover she had left behind. In one scene Ruth, the protagonist, is insomniac and considers calling her lover four time zones away. Or rather, she gets up at two A.M. and stares at the telephone, an old, black instrument with a battered dial, even though it's the late 1980s:

The light from the street made the phone a ghost.

My friend, reading this, looked up from the page and cried out: "Where do you get such descriptions? You never notice anything!"

And she's right. When walking down the street together, she was always the one to point things out, while I remained absorbed in my thoughts. But it seems that even back then I noticed details from my peripheral vision and filed them for later use. I learned, in the back of my brain somewhere, the heft of a hammer in the palm, the way a set of keys feels like home. Somewhere I noticed the weird shadows cast by city lights that turned familiar objects eerie. When I was imagining Ruth contemplating the telephone, she (and I) saw a ghost.

My first teacher of fiction was the novelist and much-heralded writing teacher John Gardner, who taught that any good writer is creating, with words on paper, "a vivid and continuous dream." By *vivid* he meant a dream that feels as sharp and focused as real life. By *continuous* he meant a dream that remains vivid, not allowing the reader's mind to wander out of the fictional world.

When I think of description, I think of film, which is quite similar to a dream state. Think about it. You enter a darkened theater and for a couple of hours you are enveloped by an alternate reality that leaves you blinking as you emerge. With the movie, it's the filmmaking that keeps you engrossed. With fiction, more than anything else perhaps, it's the description that envelops you because really everything in a work of fiction, except for the dialogue, is a description of some sort. When writing this description you want to make sure the reader experiences the story as vividly and continuously as if he or she is watching a spellbinding film. You don't want the story fading out in the middle like an old Super 8 home movie shown on a bad projector. You want to ensure that your movie is written in full color, even if the colors are gentle, muted, not blazing at all.

Webster's New World Dictionary offers two definitions for the verb *describe:*

1. to tell or write about; give a detailed account of
2. to picture in words

To give a detailed account. To picture in words. That particular *Webster's* scribe is a poet.

For the purposes of storytelling, description is anything that creates a picture in a reader's mind. If the descriptions are good enough, the reader will forget about the rain outside his window, the fact that her chair is a little uncomfortable, the fact that the rent is due. The reader will be swept along by the words, believing every moment of the story, as if it's a dream or a movie, or as if it were actually happening.

THE FIVE SENSES

You write and read with your brain, but you live your life most definably in your body. To convey that experience, you need the *physicality* of it. Your morning trek to work consists of a series of aggravations, or so my writing students have told me repeatedly. But at bottom, it consists of your feet on the carpet, the feel of your jacket on your skin, the noise of the street, and so on. That's how we learn the world.

To bring a reader into your fictional world, you need to offer data for all the senses. You want to make your readers see the rain's shadow, taste the bitterness of bad soup, feel the roughness of unshaved skin, smell the spoiled pizza after an all-night party, hear the tires screech during the accident. Note that I've referred to all five senses. Don't be tempted to focus only on sight, as many beginning writers do. It may be the sound after the party that your character really remembers. You may find that the feel of the fabric of a character's dress tells more about her upbringing than her hairstyle does.

In Anna Quindlen's spellbinding novel *Black and Blue*, the protagonist—a battered woman fleeing her attacker—meets her first new friend in a suburban Florida town:

> *She was wearing pink linen shorts and a matching blouse, white sunglasses, and pink nail polish. She sounded like an actress playing Blanche du Bois in summer stock, and looked and smelled as if she'd groomed herself as painstakingly for that morning as I had the morning I got married. A drawl and Diorissimo, or something that smelled a whole lot like it.*

We get a strong sense of this character because we are experiencing her through our senses, in this case sight (her clothing), sound (the way she talks), and smell (her perfume).

You need these kinds of sensory details to support more general statements or abstract descriptive phrases. You may write poetic, sweeping statements, in sentences whose music makes the reader smile. But giving too many of those without sensory detail is kind of like serving the aperitif without the meal. I might get drunk, but I'll fall asleep during the movie.

William Faulkner, in his story "Barn Burning," begins with smell and expands to include other senses:

> *The store in which the Justice of the Peace's court was sitting smelled of cheese. The boy, crouched on his nail keg at the back of the crowded room, knew he smelled cheese and more: from where he sat he could see the ranked shelves close-packed with the solid, squat, dynamic shapes of tin cans whose labels his stomach read, not from the lettering which meant nothing to his mind but from the scarlet devils and the silver curve of fish—this, the cheese which he believed he smelled and the hermetic meat which his intestines believed he smelled coming in intermittent gusts momentary and brief beneath the other constant one, the smell and sense just a little of fear because mostly of despair and grief, the old fierce pull of blood.*

Here Faulkner weaves in smell, sight, taste (even if vicarious), and the physical sensations attached to emotion—all pretty compact within this rather robust passage.

Or how about this brief passage from Amy Tan's "Rules of the Game" that utilizes all five senses:

> *We lived on Waverly Place, in a warm, clean, two-bedroom flat that sat above a small Chinese bakery, specializing in steamed pastries and dim sum. In the early morning, when the alley was still quiet, I could smell fragrant red beans as they were cooked down to a pasty sweetness. By daybreak, our flat was heavy with the odor of fried sesame balls and sweet curried chicken crescents. From my bed, I would listen as my father got ready for work, then locked the door behind him, one-two-three clicks.*

We see, hear, smell, feel, and even taste this world. We are physically *there*. The most powerful method for luring readers into the fictional world is through sensory experience.

> YOUR TURN:
> Pick a character and imagine he or she has gone spelunking (cave exploring) with a group of friends. Unfortunately, your character has become separated from the group and now he or she is groping through a pitch-dark passage (without a flashlight), searching for either a way out or the missing companions. Write a passage bringing this scene to life through sensory description. Since vision is limited, you'll have to rely on hearing, smell, touch, and taste. Let the reader physically experience this place through these senses.

SPECIFICITY

Your descriptions can't just offer sensory details, though; the details also have to be specific. The cumulative effect of specific sensory details is verisimilitude—the sense that these events have really happened.

Many years ago a high school writer friend of mine, who's now a professor, asked about my use of *his intense gray eyes.* "What does that mean?" he asked. I've never forgotten it. Vagueness is often our first impulse when we're getting something down. When I wrote *intense gray eyes,* what did I mean? I meant, first, that the eyes were slate gray, and second, that they glittered a little, like he had extra tear ducts. But that is not what I conveyed with my vague description.

Specificity also prevents a sort of writer's laziness. *She was a beautiful blonde.* That's vague enough not to give us a picture at all, and it smells like it was easy to write. Give us specific details about this blond beauty, like so:

> *Her nose was dusted ever so lightly with freckles, as softly colored as the skin below.*

Paint a picture with your words. For example, Jeannette Winterson offers this sweeping description in her novel *The Passion,* a fable of eighteenth-century Venice:

> *There are exiles too. Men and women driven out of their gleaming palaces that open so elegantly to shining canals.*

It sounds powerful, with adjectives like *gleaming* and *shining* suggesting the glamour of what's been lost. But we're not actually in the picture until the author follows it up with:

> *One woman who kept a fleet of boats and a string of cats and dealt in spices is here now, in the silent city. I cannot tell how old she may be, her hair is green with slime from the walls of the nook she lives in. She feeds on vegetable matter that snags against the stones when the tide is sluggish. She has no teeth. She has no need of teeth. She still wears the curtains that she dragged from her drawing-room window as she left.*

Note the stones, the green hair, the lack of teeth, the curtains. With these specific details, Winterson brings this mythical woman alive as a macabre figure in her near-noir romance. Specifics can make the reader believe anything, including that an aristocrat fleeing the French Revolution ended up feeding in Venice's canals while she played in its casinos. Or that all Venetian boatmen, like Villanelle, the book's narrator, have webbed feet. The specific details weave a world, and the reader is willing to stay in it—to watch Villanelle fall in love with an aristocrat's wife, and later to watch her pair up with one of Napoleon's cooks.

Specific descriptions make true more homespun locations as well. Louis B. Jones's *Ordinary Money* shows the reader its location in working-class northern California by simply directing the reader there:

There is a stop sign at the 7-Eleven, and you go left onto Robin Song Lane, then right onto Sparrow Court, and Wayne and Laura Paschke's house is the third on the left, the same model as the neighbor's, but painted an out-of-date sherbert green, with a big chicken-wire thing on the side, left there by the previous tenant—and the hard lawn and the oil-stained driveway which always provide a landlord with a reason for keeping the damage deposit.

The author is so specific in conjuring this place that it's almost impossible not to believe it truly exists.

If, say, a character drives a car, consider telling us what kind of car. Earl, the car thief in Richard Ford's "Rock Springs," drives a cranberry-colored Mercedes. Not only can we picture that particular car, but it also tells us a few things about Earl and his taste in stolen vehicles.

Think of yourself as a collector—of sensations, of objects, of names. Especially names. Don't be like one of my favorite poets, John Berryman, who famously said: "I don't know one damned butterfly from another." I'm as guilty as many in this; urban chick that I am, the names of trees and such send me scurrying to books. But I go to those books to learn the names of trees and colors and everything else because I know those names will notch up the clarity of my fiction.

You should do this too. Name exact colors, for example—not that you should rattle off every gradation in the Crayola 64 box, but learn and use the names of some: ocher, cornflower, or even something like "pale pink shading to white." Name fabrics, tastes, musical instruments. Even brand names can be useful, though if overused they come off as a cheap thrill, and distract the reader. (Of course, Bret Easton Ellis disagrees with me, as readers of his novel *American Psycho* can attest. But there the brand names support the theme of American greed.)

And sometimes a list of names itself becomes accomplished description. Students of Homer call them "heroic catalogs," after those breathless recitations of a hero's armor, a goddess's boudoir, an army's food supply, that march through Homer's *Iliad*.

Watch how Barbara Kingsolver, in *The Poisonwood Bible*, paints the Congo with little more than this list:

All God's creatures have names, whether they slither across our path or show up for sale at our front stoop: bushbuck, mongoose, tarantula, cobra, the red-and-black monkey called ngonndo, *geckos scurrying up the walls. Nile perch and* nkyende *and electric eel dragged from the river.* Akala, nkento, a-ana: *man, woman, and child. And everything that grows: frangipani, jacaranda,* mangwansi *beans, sugarcane, breadfruit, bird of paradise.*

> YOUR TURN:
> Think of a place well known to you from your youth—a street, park, school . . . Write a passage where you describe this place with great specificity. What color were the bricks? Was the slide straight or curving? How far was the pond from the house? If you can't remember key details, fill them in with your imagination. For a bonus round, do the same for a person you knew from this place.

THE BEST WORDS

What is description made of? Words, of course. If you're bringing the movie in your head to the page, words are the strands of light that determine the colors, and shadows, and clear shapes.

Mark Twain once noted that the difference between the right word and the almost right word is the difference between lightning and a lightning bug. Always challenge yourself to find the best possible word to convey the picture in your mind. Quite often the perfect word comes to you instinctually and, no, you shouldn't agonize over every word as you fly through a first draft. But at some point, find the words that best sustain the magical illusion of your story.

Let's return to this line from *The Passion:*

> *One woman who kept a fleet of boats and a string of cats and dealt in spices is here now, in the silent city.*

Everything is pretty straightforward in that sentence except for the phrase *a string of cats.* Why did the author choose *string*? She could have used any number of other words—*collection, group, family, pack, litter, entourage, coterie,* to name just a few. But obviously she felt there was a particular meaning in the word *string* that made it feel just right. Perhaps she liked the sense of the cats following in single file or the sense that the cats were somehow attached to the woman. Regardless of whether the author found this word instantly or spent half a day worrying over it, the word *string* makes a strong and specific impact.

How big is your vocabulary? Though you don't want to show off by using elaborate words all the time, you should always seek to widen your choice of word possibilities. Keep a dictionary around. An old, old language, English has absorbed words from Latin, French, Spanish, Asian languages, and many others, giving us a range of choices that rivals the spectrum of the rainbow. If you're at a loss for a word, the dictionary and its cousin, the thesaurus, could be your best friends.

Just watch out for adjectives and adverbs. Like sirens, they can lure you into the perilous waters of weak description.

When many people think description, they often think adjectives and adverbs. As you know, adjectives describe nouns, as in *her light hair,* and adverbs describe verbs, as in *she walked lightly.* Think of the pattern of speech: *The word I'd use to describe Alan is fulsome.* But the truth is that adjectives and adverbs can be very lazy words. They deceive you into thinking they're doing their job when really they're not doing much at all. Remember my *intense gray eyes.* That's two adjectives pretending to really describe those eyes. But they haven't done much at all—a hint of sensory, a hint of specificity, but nothing that brings those eyes, or their owner, to life.

And a sentence with too many adjectives and adverbs is like an unpicked apple tree, the boughs sagging from the weight. Like so:

> She walked gracefully into the spacious room, swiftly removing a letter from her designer-label purse and regarding us all with her intense gray eyes.

Despite all those adjectives and adverbs, we're getting little more than the bare facts. This tree needs picking.

If you look carefully at good description, you'll notice that writers are often quite sparing in their use of adjectives and adverbs. In "Cathedral," the narrator relates his first impression of the blind man's eyes:

> At first glance, his eyes looked like anyone else's eyes. But if you looked close, there was something different about them. Too much white in the iris, for one thing, and the pupils seemed to move around in the sockets without his knowing it or being able to stop it. Creepy. As I stared at his face, I saw the left pupil turn in toward his nose while the other made an effort to keep in one place. But it was only an

effort, for that eye was on the roam without his knowing it or wanting it to be.

How many adjectives do you pick out of that passage? Three: *different, creepy,* and *left* (*white* is being used as a noun). And Carver isn't depending on those adjectives to do the real work.

However, when used sparingly and well, adjectives and adverbs can be quite effective. Let's return once more to that sentence (with the cats) from *The Passion:*

> *One woman who kept a fleet of boats and a string of cats and dealt in spices is here now, in the silent city.*

This sentence contains one well-placed adjective—*silent*—and it works magnificently, adding a perfect and necessary final touch to this sentence.

Adjectives and adverbs are helper words, what the grammarians call "modifiers." They help refine the impression cast by your true building blocks: nouns and verbs. At a writers' conference a few years ago, a supposedly clever expression was circulating: *Are your verbs working hard enough?* Granted, the expression isn't all that clever, but it points to a truth. The stronger your nouns and verbs are, the better they can support your carefully chosen modifiers.

Look at this passage from F. Scott Fitzgerald's *The Great Gatsby.* As one of Gatsby's famous parties begins:

> *Suddenly one of these gypsies in trembling opal seizes a cocktail out of the air, dumps it down for courage, and moving her hands like Frisco dances out alone on the canvas platform.*

Look carefully at this sentence. It features only two adjectives (or three, if you count *alone*), but its nouns and verbs carry maximum impact. Not *a woman* but *one of these gypsies,* not *takes* but *seizes.* Notice how the strong verb phrases alleviate the need for modifiers, as in *dumps it down for courage* and *moving her hands like Frisco.* (The last phrase refers to a jazz dancer of the 1920s.) I'm fascinated by the fact that I can draw such sparing use of modifiers from one of our more florid writers.

For a more contemporary example, let's look at the following portrait of the narrator's mother from Melanie Rae Thon's story "Nobody's Daughters":

> *Past noon, Adele still fogged. I knew everything from the sound of*

her voice, too low, knew she must be on night shift again: nursing home or bar, bringing bedpans or beers—it didn't matter which. I saw the stumps of cigarettes in the ashtray beside her bed. I saw her red hair matted flat, creases on her cheek, the way she'd slept. I smelled her, smelled the smoke in her clothes, the smoke on her breath.

You'll find very few modifiers in here. But notice the strength of the nouns: *stumps of cigarettes, creases on her cheek.* And notice such strong verbs as *fogged* and *matted.* The nouns and verbs paint a picture.

As previously noted, strong verbs can even alleviate the need for adverbs. For example, *she walked lightly* can be effectively transformed into *she glided* or *she floated,* each more evocative than the version leaning on the adverb.

Look at this example from Arundhati Roy's *The God of Small Things:*

By early June the southwest monsoon breaks and there are three months of wind and water with short spells of sharp, glittering sunshine that thrilled children snatch to play with. The countryside turns an immodest green. Boundaries blur as tapioca fences take root and bloom. Brick walls turn mossgreen. Pepper vines snake up electric poles. Wild creepers burst through laterite banks and spill across the flooded roads. Boats ply in the bazaars. And small fish appear in the puddles that fill the PWD potholes on the highways.

Note how vibrant this place is made through such dynamic verbs as: *breaks, snatch, blur, root, bloom, snake, burst, spill, ply.* No adverbs needed. Though a few adjectives are sprinkled in, they are invariably linked to strong nouns that don't get overshadowed by them.

I'm not telling you to avoid adjectives and adverbs entirely. But first focus on the best possible nouns and verbs, then find the modifiers that enhance these words, adding subtle touches to the foundation.

> YOUR TURN:
> Pick a person you know. Fictionalize the name, which will also give you license to alter other characteristics, if you so desire. Now describe this person as vividly as you can. Here's the catch: you *cannot* use a single adjective or adverb. This will force you to use strong nouns and verbs and employ

some of the other techniques you've picked up in this chapter. Though challenging, you will probably end up with a very well-drawn picture of this person.

TRICKS OF THE TRADE

Now that we've covered some of the brass tacks of good description, it's time to look at some ways to further expand your palette of descriptive options.

First, learn to embrace figurative language, a fancy expression for figures of speech, as in similes and metaphors. These are scary-sounding words out of an English class, but they're really shorthand for the way we think, the way we process information and emotions.

A *simile* is defined (by the *American Heritage Dictionary*) as "A figure of speech in which two essentially unlike things are compared, the comparison being made explicit typically by the use of the introductory 'like' or 'as' . . ." A *metaphor* (according to *Chambers's Twentieth Century Dictionary*) is "a figure of speech by which a thing is spoken of as being that which it only resembles, as when a ferocious man is called a 'tiger.'"

We use these every day. When you tell a friend, *I was like a house on fire!* or *He's such a wet blanket!* you're doing it—taking an image or idea from the universe of common memory and yoking it to a person or experience. Of course, the examples I've given are hackneyed—that's one reason why they work well on the phone or on the street. Everyone understands them.

But in fiction, your task is to use similes and metaphors that are too fresh, too surprising, to be something you've heard on the phone. Why should you bother? Because figures of speech are a stealthy way of reaching into your reader's subconscious. You're pulling up visual images, remembered experiences, bits of their own dreams, and showing them anew. Your descriptions now have double the power.

Here are two arresting similes from Mary Gaitskill's "A Romantic Weekend":

She felt like an object unraveling in every direction.

His gaze penetrated her so thoroughly, it was as though he had thrust his hand into her chest and begun feeling her ribs one by one.

In Calvin Baker's novel *Naming the New World,* a metaphor appears when a man sees the rising sun as

> *a beautiful almond with honey edges.*

Now, you would never say on a street corner, *Wow, look at that sunrise! A beautiful almond. Yeah, with honey edges.* But this jazzy metaphor used in description feels just right, especially as it takes a little bow toward the Deep South, where the novel takes place.

My partner, a poet, told me when we met, "I hate similes; I like metaphors better." I agree that metaphors feel more powerful, but I think similes are a far suppler instrument. You can do anything with them—stick them in dialogue, give them to a first-person narrator, embed them in news headlines or gossip. Metaphors lend themselves to a heavier narrative style, which may or may not work for your story, depending on its tone. And an extended metaphor can dominate a story entirely, as when the protagonist of Franz Kafka's *The Metamorphosis* finds himself transformed in his bed into a giant insect. That's when you find yourself at the level of allegory where a whole story stands for something else.

Are you one of those people whose writing prompts comments like *That's very poetic* or *Wow, it's almost poetry*? If so, count yourself among the lucky few who already know a few things about lyricism. By lyricism, I mean prose that plays with sound and rhythm in the way that poetry does.

Feel the lyricism in the final line of James Joyce's "The Dead":

> *His soul swooned slowly as he heard the snow falling faintly through the universe and faintly falling, like the descent of their last end, upon all the living and the dead.*

How do you know if you've got any lyricism? It helps to read your work aloud and hear the ebb and flow of the rhythm and hear how the words slide and sing. You'll also hear where things start to *clunk*.

What does all this lyrical effect do for fiction? Just like figures of speech, lyricism sinks your story deeper inside the subconscious of the reader. If music says things words can't express, text that feels like music also carries those nonverbal meanings, immersing the reader in the experience in a rather primal way. And just because I say *lyrical,* this doesn't mean you must use long, elaborate sentences.

Ernest Hemingway knew how to make beautiful music of simple words and short sentences, as in the following descriptive passage from "True at First Light":

> *Then I looked through the trees at the Mountain showing very big and near this morning with the new snow shining in the first sunlight.*

Notice the almost iconic power of the image, rendered through the chantlike rhythm.

In "Cathedral," the narrator, who doesn't even *like* poetry, manages a simple lyricism when he asks the reader to

> *Imagine a woman who could never see herself as she was seen in the eyes of her loved one. A woman who could go on day after day and never receive the smallest compliment from her beloved. A woman whose husband could never read the expression on her face, be it misery or something better. Someone who could wear make-up or not—what difference to him?*

To further deepen your descriptions, consider onomatopoeia, achieved when words sound like what they are. I just did it earlier, when I mentioned prose going *clunk*. If people in your stories *murmur*, if crowds *buzz*, if the tea kettle *hisses*, you're employing onomatopoeia.

In this passage from Barry Hannah's "Testimony of a Pilot," check out the effectiveness of the onomatopoeia *whistling* at the very end:

> *It was a grand cannon, set up on a stack of bricks at the back of my dad's property, which was the free place to play. When it shot, it would back up violently with thick smoke and you could hear the flashlight battery whistling off.*

Also consider alliteration, where two or more words have a common initial sound. Alliterations comes naturally to us; it's a game we've played since we were three. *Meet Bobby Bumblebee!* Alliteration can be overused, but when used judiciously it introduces a wonderful grace note to a description.

Notice how alliteration helps conjure the sense of quietly falling snow in that passage from "The Dead":

> *His soul swooned slowly as he heard the snow falling faintly through the universe and faintly falling, like the descent of their last end, upon all the living and the dead.*

When done well, these creative elements can blend together in an effortless flow. Note Bharati Mukherjee's description, in *Leave It to Me,* of the place where her narrator was born:

> *I have no clear memory of my birthplace, only of the whiteness of its sun, the harshness of its hills, the raspy moan of its desert winds, the desperate suddenness of its twilight: these I see like the pattern of veins on the insides of my eyelids.*

In addition to alliteration ("harshness of its hills"), note how Mukherjee also uses simile (those veins) and onomatopoeia ("raspy moan"). Her rhythm's not bad, either. Try reading that paragraph aloud. Hear the music.

Finally, I'm going to pass on one of my own trade secrets, a way of conjuring fresh images that's often got me out of a description jam: use an image or adjective usually associated with one sense unexpectedly with another. It's a poet's trick, known as synesthesia. John Keats used it here:

> *Taste the music of the vision pale . . .*

A couple that I've used in my own work:

> *the sound that washed your senses*
> *his dark chocolate voice*

Try it. At the very least, synesthesia is fun to play with; at best, your description will jump to life in a startling way.

> YOUR TURN:
> Take one of the previous exercises from this chapter and revise it by leaning on such devices as simile, metaphor, lyricism, alliteration, onomatopoeia, and perhaps even synesthesia. Run wild, using as many of these devices as you can. The results may be a bit overripe, but you will have cultivated your inner poet.

TELLING DETAILS

You've picked up a lot of techniques to energize and excite your descriptions. You may be tempted to run free with them, alliterating here and bursting with high-flung metaphors there, layering on smells and tastes and sounds, until your readers feel gorged with sensations.

But it's important, ultimately, to choose your descriptive details. As readers, we know what it's like to slog through a thicket of description—to lose track of a story in the avalanche of detail about the lush tropical stream, the cold Manhattan apartment, the overview of a village at the top of a mountain. All I wanted to know, you want to say to the author, is what she looks like, and you gave me three rambling pages describing her every detail.

There's a fine line between lush description and the kind that chokes the reader. Such description is easy to fall into when you're describing a place you think may be foreign to your readers, or even working to get the details of someone's clothing or gestures. Be particularly careful of language that's so beautiful you notice it just for that. Always ask yourself: *Does the description interrupt the flow of the story?*

Anton Chekhov, one of the pioneers of the contemporary short story, gave us the classic definition of what a story does: "the casual telling of a nuclear experience in an ordinary life, rendered with immediate and telling detail." What did he mean by the *telling* detail?

A telling detail does what it says: it tells the essence of what it's describing. Telling details are the Scotch tape holding up Susie's hemline in the back, the tiny piece of ice that never seemed to melt in the bottom of Mom's martini, the street sign on the corner that still says, to this day, SCHOOL CROSSING, though the school is long gone. A telling detail can speak volumes in a very short amount of time. They help you achieve a golden mean—enough description to paint the picture, but not so much as to weigh it down.

Look at the opening of Anna Quindlen's *Black and Blue:*

> *That butterscotch-syrup voice that made goose bumps rise on my arms when I was young, that turned all of my skin warm and alive with a sibilant S, the drawling vowels, its shocking fricatives. It always sounded like a whisper, the way he talked, the intimacy of it, the way the words seemed to go into your guts, your head, your heart.*

The telling detail of the character being described is his voice. The author gets the most out of her description of the voice by using synesthesia ("butterscotch-syrup" to evoke the voice's smoothness and sweetness), simile ("like a whisper"), and a precise catalog of detail: "sibilant *S*, the drawling vowels, its shocking fricatives." For the character's response to the voice we get a quick hit that tells all—"made goose bumps rise on my arms when I was young" and "the words seemed to go into your guts, your head, your heart."

Soon enough this man will be described visually, his actions named. But the voice is how he is introduced and his voice is what we'll remember. Just as many people, if they remember nothing else about *The Great Gatsby,* remember that Jay Gatsby felt the voice of his beloved, Daisy, was "full of money."

In Toni Morrison's *Beloved,* the eyes of Sethe, the protagonist, are certainly a telling detail. (Handled so much better than my *intense gray eyes.*) Here is how Sethe's eyes are seen by her old friend Paul D:

> *irises the same color of her skin, which, in that still face, made him think of mercifully punched-out eyes.*

Later, another character sees Sethe's eyes this way:

> *Since the whites in them had disappeared and since they were as black as her skin, she looked blind . . .*

Such telling details stick with us and define the place, character, or atmosphere. And they stay in the reader's mind with an almost hypnotic force.

You may not know which of your details, at first, are the telling ones. It's only when all of them have made it out of your head and onto the page, only when you've gotten to the end of your first or second draft, that you'll notice which have borne repeating. What does your protagonist remember about his childhood home years later? What feature of Vietnam's spectacular sunsets represents the whole, years later? I ended up having to answer the latter question in one of my novels, when too much detail about Asia threatened to choke. What remains now are colors associated with tastes, "watermelon colors," "rose ice cream skies," repeated through three Asian countries and my character's dreams. The combination of color and taste and sunsets seemed to be the telling detail that most reflected the emotional response to the place. You'll know when you've found the telling detail: it's the detail that sticks with you the most.

Until you find that telling detail, however, be generous. As the story in your head starts to move and your hands follow it, try to write it all down, everything that comes to you, especially any sensory detail.

I can't tell you how many times I've looked at a student's work and asked for more detail about this or that—a place, a person—only to be told,

"I didn't want to overdo it." Novice writers, just getting their chops, need to worry more about saying *enough*. You're so familiar with the scene in your head that you may think just a few words are needed to bring it alive. And it's possible that you're right—but it's unlikely that you know, right away, which few words those are. Get it all on the page first, and then cut back as needed. Even if your preferred style is on the minimalist side, if you like Raymond Carver more than Arundhati Roy, I encourage you to be generous on the page.

A brilliant young writer, whom I knew in graduate school, favors a stripped-down, economical delivery. His stories, from draft to draft, undergo constant unfolding and compression, compression and unfolding. One draft may be four pages, the next eleven, the next five, and so on, as he fills out the scene and then pares the excess.

For right now, give it all you've got. Eventually you'll find the right time to pick and choose the most telling details.

> YOUR TURN:
> Return to the previous exercise, where you let your poetic impulses run wild. Pick a telling detail—one particular thing that most embodies the thing you described. Revise the passage, this time focusing only on that one telling detail. And while you're in there, this time try to keep the description from being too long or overwrought. You should end up with a description that is both economical and effective.

DESCRIPTION TRAPS

I've spent this whole chapter encouraging you to utilize many different descriptive methods, to bring your movie ever more vividly and continuously to the reader's mind. Now I need to point my usher's flashlight at some examples of what you *don't* want to do with description. Bad description stops readers cold, yanking them from the spell of your story, the last thing you want to do.

First and foremost, avoid clichés. I know there's nothing new under the sun. But anything you can do to loosen the grip of overly familiar language is a plus:

Bone-chilling cold
He smiled daggers
Her cascading hair
Sleeping like the dead
Turning on one's heel
Feet planted firm on the ground

Such expressions have been used so many times that they're meaningless now. They leave the reader unengaged, painting almost nothing in the mind's eye.

A student in my class a few summers ago was a sweet and voluble retiree with white hair and a big laugh. I was surprised, therefore, when he stood up to protest during my lecture on description. "What if she really did have 'legs that don't quit'?" he demanded. He raised his chin and looked at me, his lips pursed, either a defiant schoolboy or a guy calling for his lawyer.

I told him that the phrase had meaning to him because of the layers of movies, books, and TV shows that used the phrase. And that the same things that made the phrase work for him have dimmed it for the purposes of improving and strengthening any story he might tell.

Also watch out for being imprecise or even sloppy with your description. Take this example:

He felt like a punching bag without air.

We'll give some credit here for using a simile. But not much. Punching bags don't have air, and anyone who knows this will immediately stop believing in this story and this writer. Make it *a balloon without air* or *a punching bag without stuffing* and we're back inside the fictional illusion.

How about this one:

She tossed her head at me.

Here we assume the writer means something like *she tossed her hair* or *she tilted her head,* rather than that she actually took off her head and tossed it. But with writing this sloppy, it's hard to be sure.

Also problematic are mixed metaphors. You can't have Joanne metaphorically swimming against a tide in one sentence and climbing a tall mountain a few lines later, or, worse, in the same sentence. The reader doesn't know if she's on land or water, and the power of either image is lost. If you want your mother to be a fish, fine, just don't turn her into an elephant three chapters later.

Sometimes, of course, we just need to get the story down, that first mad time, and we put down bad description—clichés, imprecise phrases, and such. That's quite all right. Think of those phrases as markers, as *blah blah blah* written down. You can then tinker in your revision phase, replacing the bad descriptions with specific, precise, and interesting language. It's part of the fun of revision, even if you find yourself going *ouch!* when you notice the cliché or ridiculously mixed metaphor.

DESCRIPTION OF INNER LIFE

Most of what we've been discussing has dealt with the externals: what places and people look like, how they sound, how they make themselves available to the senses. All of which is central to how we use description. But description is also used to portray the inner life of characters—their thoughts and emotions.

Essentially, the same rules of description apply to emotions and thoughts as to anything else. For example, you could write:

Susanna was angry that Max didn't understand.

This sentence does the job, I suppose, but it actually conveys very little. *Angry* is an idea, an abstract concept, a pointer to an emotion. Emotions are physical. They're expressed and felt in sensation or action or both. As with any kind of description, emotions are rendered more vividly when dealt with specifically, through the senses.

If you want Susanna to be angry, there are many good ways to get this across. Perhaps her chest feels tight and hollow or she can't breathe or her jaw tightened or she speaks in a gutteral voice. Any of these things will convey her emotion more descriptively than simply saying she was angry. For example:

The second Max said the words, Susanna felt her skin flush hot. Rage closed her throat.

The poet T. S. Eliot said, when discussing Shakespeare's *Hamlet:*

The only way of expressing emotion in the form of art is by finding an "objective correlative"; in other words, a set of objects, a situation, a chain of events which shall be the formula of that particular emotion; such that when the external facts, which must terminate in sensory experience, are given, the emotion is immediately evoked.

Eliot is asking you, in other words, to make the reader feel the same emotion as the person you're describing, by naming enough familiar details to evoke empathy.

Lynne Sharon Schwartz's narrator in her novel *Disturbances in the Field* doesn't write:

I was depressed after Althea was born.

Instead she writes:

When she sucked at my breasts she was sucking the life out of me, and when she was done I swayed on my feet . . . I was cut off from the subtleties of common language and, like a non-native speaker, from idioms.

We are made to actually feel the emotion alongside her.

On a related note, the emotions and thoughts of characters may actually color all of the description in a work of fiction. As you learned in chapter 4, often the narration is filtered through the consciousness of a character, or perhaps several characters. Bear in mind that anything from a character's viewpoint will be somewhat subjective, and that this subjectivity will affect the way something is described.

John Gardner liked to have his students write a description of a barn from the point of view of a man who had just murdered someone. The idea was that the description of the barn would somehow take on the man's feelings or thoughts about the murder. Perhaps the claustrophobia of the enclosed barn would remind him of his emotions while killing, or perhaps the red color of the barn's door would remind him of blood. To some degree, this effect should occur anytime you're writing through the filter of a character's consciousness.

For example, Mary Gordon's novel *Men and Angels* is told partly from the point of view of a young, disturbed live-in baby-sitter named Laura, who becomes infatuated with her employer's best friend. Here's what she thinks of him:

She knew Adrian really liked her. He said she was a good listener. He was the handsomest man she had ever seen, with his thick gray curly hair, his open shirts, his shoulders. But really she wanted to be in the room with him without Anne there. If she went on and listened to Adrian, looked into his eyes when he told her things, praised whatever he said, someday he would like her more than he liked Anne.

Is Adrian really handsome? Maybe, maybe not. But he is to this character. Will Adrian someday like her? Perhaps not, but Laura thinks so. This third-person narrator is giving us Laura's perceptions, not objective fact.

In Frederic Tuten's *Tallien: A Romance*, a first-person narrator reflects on his father, the charismatic union organizer:

Nobleman that he was, riding down the fields of wrath, his terrible swift sword cutting a swath of fat pinky-ringed capitalists, defunct leases and eviction notices still clutched in their pudgy fists, Rex, the radical prince of the Confederacy, under whose ceaseless guard none would suffer except his periodically abandoned family, unpaid bills rolling up like waves against the door, his decade-old son staring up at the light bulbs, waiting for them, like stars blinking off into cold cinders, to go dead for failure of payment . . .

This man's memories of his father are certainly tinged with rage, and the depiction may or may not be objectively true.

> YOUR TURN:
> Describe a character who is going about the mundane job of cleaning his or her home. Write from the POV of this character (either first, second, or third person), which means the character's consciousness will inform the description. Here's the twist: the character has just recently fallen in love, and you should let this emotion color the description without being directly stated. Then rewrite the passage, but this time the character has just had a painful romantic breakup. You'll see how different the world looks depending on how people feel.

With his groundbreaking *Ulysses*, James Joyce attempted to merge his descriptions as completely as possible with the minds of his characters. In the following passage, notice how the description follows a young woman's free flow of thought, where a sight of the sea unleashes barely related memories of chalk drawings and church incense:

> *She gazed out towards the distant sea. It was like the paintings that man used to do on the pavement with the coloured chalks and such a pity too leaving them there to be all blotted out, the evening and the clouds coming out and the Bailey light on the Howth and to hear the music like that and the perfume of those incense they burned in the church like a kind of waft.*

There really is no limit as to how deep inward description may reach.

CHAPTER 6
DIALOGUE: TALKING IT UP
BY ALLISON AMEND

I've been on a lot of bad dates. A lot. Some were blind dates; some I wish I had been blind for. But what amazes me is that the more I learn about fiction, and the more I learn about dating, the more they seem eerily parallel. Why? Because dialogue is the key to a successful date, and, I would argue, to successful fiction. There is nothing worse than sitting over a plate of cooling penne with nothing to say, and there is no substitute for the heady feeling you leave with when you just seem to "get each other." That connection hinges on dialogue.

Fiction can go without dialogue, and I've certainly been on a couple of great dates that didn't involve a lot of conversation, but, in general, dialogue is what keeps you coming back for more. The characters' interactions provide the scintillation that brings the reader to the story, and more often than not dialogue is a key part of this interaction. What makes the *War* part of *War and Peace* so boring (sorry, Tolstoy) is the fact that it's just the author droning on and on like a college lecture on geology. What's exciting is hearing Natasha speak with Andrei (*Peace*), not reading dry re-creations of military maneuvers (*War*).

The characters are the ones in the story interacting with each other, so they are the people, not the author, who have the power to affect other characters. Perhaps the best way to let the reader really see the characters interacting with each other is to let them talk to each other. If it's done well, the readers will forget that the people they are reading about are the writer's creation. The characters will assume a life of their own. And isn't that the real purpose of fiction?

DIALOGUE EXPLAINED

Dialogue is everything in fiction that isn't narration. In other words, it's the stuff between the quotation marks—what the characters "say."

There is no official rule for how much dialogue to use in fiction. Some stories are dialogue-heavy, others dialogue-light. For example, Ernest Hemingway's "Hills Like White Elephants" is almost all dialogue, while *The Metamorphosis* by Franz Kafka has practically no dialogue. Most stories find a balance between dialogue and narration. Switching between the two gives a work of fiction a nice diversity. Narration tends to have a dense feel, whereas dialogue—which reads quickly and offers lots of white space—has a zippier feel, making it like a cleansing dish of sherbet between courses. Again, I reference the theoretical "perfect date." You neither talk too much nor have to prod the conversation. It should be an exchange, a give-and-take.

There are two fundamental ways a writer can reveal any moment in a story—summary or scene. Summary is where the action is summarized, or "told." In contrast, a scene depicts the moment in real time, showing us exactly what transpires. Scenes are where dialogue makes its appearance. The effect is similar to that of watching a scene in a play or film, where the actors are speaking to and interacting with each other. Both scene and summary are frequently used techniques, and both have their place in fiction. But just as showing is more powerful than telling, scene is more powerful than summary. In fact, scene is the primary means by which a fiction writer "shows."

Save summary for moments when you want to relay information quickly and efficiently or when you want the narrator to revel in the pure telling of something. For the most important moments in your story, you'll want to switch to scene.

In Lorrie Moore's "People Like That Are the Only People Here," a mother brings her seriously ill baby to the doctor for some tests. Moore could have given the reader a summarized account, something like this:

> As the doctor explained that the baby had a tumor, the baby practiced his new pastime by switching the light on and off, on and off, increasing the Mother's nervousness and fear. When the doctor pronounced the words Wilm's tumor, *the room went dark.*

This summary is fine. But notice how much more lifelike and dramatic the moment is when translated into scene. Here is what actually appears in the story:

> *The baby wants to get up and play with the light switch. He fidgets, fusses, and points.*
>
> *"He's big on lights these days," explains the Mother.*
>
> *"That's okay," says the surgeon, nodding toward the light switch. "Let him play with it." The Mother goes and stands by it, and the Baby begins turning the lights off and on, off and on.*
>
> *"What we have here is a Wilm's tumor," says the Surgeon, suddenly plunged into darkness. He says "tumor" as if it were the most normal thing in the world.*
>
> *"Wilms?" repeats the Mother. The room is quickly on fire again with light, then wiped dark again. Among the three of them here, there is a long silence, as if it were suddenly the middle of the night. "Is that apostrophe s or s apostrophe?"*

We see and hear the scene with enough detail that it feels as if we're really there in the hospital witnessing it. Notice how effectively the on/off of the light plays against the dialogue. Also pay attention to the contrast between the surgeon's calm and the mother's nervousness, beautifully illustrated with her irrelevant question about the apostrophe. The summarized version gets the point across; the scene immerses us in the moment.

It's entirely possible to have a scene with no dialogue, where the thrust is conveyed just through physical action, but more often than not, dialogue will play a central role in a scene.

How do you know if a moment should be translated into dialogue or not? Well, dialogue tends to draw lots of attention to itself so you want to make sure you are dialoguing moments of real significance, be it character development, plot advancement, or a moment of extreme drama. A six-page scene of dialogue in which characters discuss carpool arrangements followed by a six-page scene in which the same characters reveal past infidelities serves the purpose of both inflating the importance of the first scene and diminishing the power of the second—if the reader even got to the second scene after slogging through the first six pages about the traffic on Main Street. The wise writer would relate only what was necessary about the carpool, perhaps not even using dialogue, then save the dialogue for the good part.

Key moments in a story lend themselves to being portrayed in dialogue.

If a moment is of real significance, the reader likes to be there, sitting front and center, watching and hearing. Often, authors choose dialogue to portray a confrontation scene, for example, when Patricia accuses her sister of stealing her boyfriend, or when Richard finally summons the nerve to ask his father if he lied about his military record. The dialogue doesn't have to show a cataclysmic moment for the characters, but the reader should come away from the dialogue scene with an increased understanding of the story.

In Charles Baxter's "Gryphon," a boy's boring suburban existence is exponentially expanded by the arrival of a mysterious substitute teacher who awakens his imagination. To get a sense of the teacher's unorthodox views, Baxter lets us hear her speak:

> *"Did you know," she asked, walking to the side of the room so that she was standing by the coat closet, "that George Washington had Egyptian blood from his grandmother? Certain features of the Constitution of the United States are notable for their Egyptian ideas."*

One of the kids at school is skeptical about the teacher, so it's important that we hear his reaction to her:

> *"I didn't believe that stuff about the bird," Carl said, "and what she told us about the pyramids? I didn't believe that either. She didn't know what she was talking about."*

When the teacher reads the class's tarot cards and foretells a death, one of the students reports her to the principal, and she is dismissed. The climax of the story is when the protagonist explodes in anger at the snitch. This important moment is portrayed, of course, through dialogue.

> *"You told," I shouted at him. "She was just kidding."*
> *"She shouldn't have," he shouted back. "We were supposed to be doing arithmetic."*
> *"She just scared you," I said. "You're a chicken. You're a chicken, Wayne. You are. Scared of a little card," I sing-songed.*
> *Wayne fell at me, his two fists hammering down on my nose. I gave him a good one in the stomach and then I tried for his head. Aiming my fist, I saw that he was crying. I slugged him.*

Throughout the story Baxter alternates scene with summary, using ample portions of each, but he knows exactly which moments are worth letting the characters speak for themselves.

THE ILLUSION OF REALITY

Everybody talks. Well, practically everybody. One would think that dialogue would be one of the easiest aspects of fiction to pull off. After all, we use it every day. But good dialogue is deceptively difficult to write.

Your first task is to ensure that your dialogue sounds real. In past centuries, fictional dialogue had a certain theatricality, as in this line from Emily Brontë's *Wuthering Heights:*

> *"Why, Master Heathcliff, you are not fit for enjoying a ramble, this morning. How ill you do look!"*

But nowadays dialogue tends to sound like actual people conversing with one another. What they say shouldn't seem rehearsed or robotic. And yet it's all too easy to write something along these lines:

> *Upon spying the Grand Canyon for the first time, Jeannie-Lynn and Billy-Joe exclaimed, "What a splendid vista!"*
> *"See?" Their mother pointed. "The scrub brush creates a harmonious palate of green-tinted lushness in the vastness of the canyon."*
> *"I'll have to relate this to my fourth-grade class!" Jeannie-Lynn said.*

Few people talk like that. They talk more like this:

> *When they finally reached the edge of the Grand Canyon, Jeannie-Lynn and Billy-Joe opened their eyes wide in amazement. "Wow," said Billy-Joe.*
> *"That's so awesome," Jeannie-Lynn whispered.*
> *"See the scrub brush like we saw in Grandma's backyard?" Their mother pointed. The children nodded.*
> *"I'm going to talk about this in show-and-tell," Jeannie-Lynn said. "Can we take a picture?"*

The best way to get a feel for realistic dialogue is by listening to people talk. Listen to people on the bus, in the elevator, on the radio; pay attention to their speech patterns and the content of their conversations. Imagine writing their words down. Maybe even try writing them down. This will help develop your ear for dialogue. Being able to listen and mimic is the best preparation for writing realistic dialogue.

Two little tips for realistic dialogue. Contractions are good. Only a very formal person will say: *I do not think this is the best idea.* Most folks would say: *I don't think this is the best idea.* And though writers are instructed to avoid clichés, characters often use hackneyed phrasing. As a description, *hot as hell* doesn't do very much. But it would be perfectly acceptable for certain characters to use this phrase in dialogue.

But simply capturing the sound of lifelike dialogue isn't enough. Actually, the realism of good dialogue is something of an illusion. Readers of fiction have a higher expectation for dialogue than the conversations of real life. Fictional dialogue needs to have more impact, focus, relevance, than ordinary conversation. The truth is most real-life conversations are dull, or at least they would come off as dull on paper. Try transcribing a conversation that you overhear. Or tape one and then type it onto the computer. It probably won't make any sense. If it does, it will most likely be tedious. The dialogue will probably take a long time to get to the point.

Let's look at a clip of lifelike conversation:

> *"Hey. Um, hey."*
> *"Oh, hey."*
> *"Hey, Dana. It's Gina."*
> *"Oh, hi. Wait, can you hold on? Okay, hi."*
> *"Hey. What's up?"*
> *"Good. I mean, nothing. How're you doing?"*
> *"Good. Where are you?"*
> *"On my cell."*
> *"I mean, where."*
> *"Oh, on my way after work, like, in the street."*
> *"Yeah?"*
> *"Um, yeah."*

The above selection is dull and would do absolutely nothing for a story, because it mimics real speech too closely. Now, were it fictionalized, it might sound more like this:

> *"Hey, Dana. It's Gina."*
> *"Hi. What's up?"*
> *"Good. I mean, nothing. How're you doing?"*

Here we get to the point much more quickly. But this still isn't quality dialogue because there's no real significance to the conversation. Take a look at what happens when the dialogue is transformed to this:

> *"Hey, Dana, it's Gina."*
> *"Hi. Was I supposed to call you?"*
> *"Yeah, it's Wednesday. Are you still up for seeing a movie?"*
> *"I have to wait to see what Matt is doing."*

In this dialogue, you get a real sense of the characters and the tension between them. Gina's tone is a little challenging, as if she's used to Dana blowing her off. And we see that Dana has an avoidance of making concrete plans, due to her reliance on Matt. With just a few lines, this dialogue gives us a wealth of valuable information.

So, you see, dialogue has to seem real and yet not be too real and also do something important.

> YOUR TURN:
> Recall a dialogue exchange you had in the past few days. Do your best to write it down being faithful to what was actually said. Don't airbrush out the boring parts or make the dialogue snappy. Pretend you're transcribing a conversation from a tape recorder. Just write each character's name, then put the dialogue beside the name. (Jack: Hey, what's going on, man?) Then rewrite the dialogue exchange, this time making it concise and dramatically interesting. Why don't you fictionalize the names this time and feel free to embellish a bit.

DIALOGUE CONVENTION

Convention is the fulfillment of an established expectation. There are certain things our society has grown to expect because that's the way certain things are usually done. We expect a bride to wear white; we expect to be given a speech about wearing seat belts low and tight across our laps on airplanes. Dialogue too follows convention. The reader is used to dialogue looking and performing a certain way. Let's examine some of the conventions of dialogue.

Double quotation marks signal to the reader that someone is speaking:

> *"Dude, you seen my left shoe?"*
> *"Dude, check your right foot."*

Occasionally, authors break with convention, foregoing double quotation marks for single ones, dashes, brackets, or even nothing:

> *—Dude, you seen my left shoe?*
> *—Dude, check your right foot.*

But unless you have a compelling reason to do otherwise, stick with double quotes.

Usually dialogue dedicates one paragraph per speaker, no matter how short the speech:

> *I sidled up to the bars of the drunk tank, resting my forehead on the cool steel. The keys to the jail dangled from the guard's belt.*
> *"Hot enough for you, mate?" I asked the guard.*
> *"Shut up," he said.*
> *"Okay, okay." I sat back down on the wooden bench and tried to close my eyes.*

The fact that each line of dialogue gets its own paragraph highlights the importance and makes it easier to follow the flow of the conversation. Sometimes writers put different speakers in the same paragraph. While it's not wrong do to so, it can look confusing or intimidate the reader.

One of the major conventions of dialogue is the use of tags. In dialogue, most writers add speech tags, also known as attributions, so that the reader can follow who's saying what. *Said* is the most frequently used tag. In fact, you could use nothing but *said* and probably no one would notice. It may feel tedious to you to keep writing *he said, she said, the dog said,* but the reader is trained to look at speech tags only to gather his bearings, the way commas signal pauses. Readers don't even notice that you've used the word *said* 507 times. *Said* becomes invisible:

> *"You gonna drink that?" she said.*
> *"Yes, I am," he said.*

You can use verbs other than *said,* but you want to make sure they don't seem forced or get distracting.

> *"You gonna drink that?" she asked.*
> *"Yes, I am," he replied.*

However, it can be dangerous to veer too far from the *said* paradigm. It's tempting to get out the thesaurus and have your characters *utter, express, state, announce, articulate, voice*, etc., but overuse will provide a trampoline effect, making it seem as though all of your characters are springing five feet in the air when they speak:

> *"You gonna drink that?" she sputtered.*
> *"Yes, I am," he proclaimed.*

These tags are a little strong for such a banal statement. You *proclaim* emancipation from tyranny, but you *say* that you had a good night's sleep.

Similarly, adverbs in speech tags tend to make the author seem amateurish. Let what the character is saying tell the reader the tone of voice; don't have your characters speak *coquettishly* or *snidely* or *sarcastically*. Occasionally, adverbs are useful, but use them sparingly; they can draw attention to themselves in the wrong way, like an eighties hairdo. And more often than not they are just plain unnecessary, as seen here:

> *"DON'T YELL AT ME!!!!" she screamed stridently.*

Also, exclamation points in dialogue tend to make statements sound like lovesick teenage e-mail. Try at all costs to avoid using them!

When you attribute speech, make sure you place the tags in a logical or effective place. The following is jerky and awkward:

> *"I don't," she said, "love you anymore."*

While this is appropriately devastating:

> *"I don't love you anymore," she said.*

But if the phrase is long, you might want to put the tag in the middle, so that the reader knows who is speaking. Tags in the middle should follow a natural "breath," or break, in the sentence. Like so:

> *"I don't love you anymore," she said, "even though you still write me poems every day and shower me with gifts and tell me that I'm the most beautiful woman alive."*

Tags aren't the only way of indicating who is speaking. You can let the reader know who is talking to whom by having a character say someone's name, like so:

> *"Hey, Pete, you got a light?"*

Be aware, though, that people don't usually call others by their names when they speak to them. Use this technique sparingly, as it can sound forced:

> *"Bonnie Marie McGee, please pass the carrots."*
> *"I'd be glad to, Aunt Fiona."*

Another effective way to attribute speech is to link an action with the dialogue, like so:

> *"I don't think I believe in God." Bert put down his coffee cup to stare out the window.*

Or a thought:

> *"Get me a half-pound of that salami." Marsha wondered if she'd been a little harsh. "Please," she added.*

Attribution for every single line of dialogue is not strictly necessary, as long as it's perfectly clear who is speaking when. Here's a passage from Hemingway's "Hills Like White Elephants," where a man and a girl are sitting in a bar in Spain:

> *The girl looked at the bead curtain. "They've painted something on it," she said. "What does it say?"*
> *"Anis del Toro. It's a drink."*
> *"Could we try it?"*
> *The man called "Listen" through the curtain. The woman came out from the bar.*
> *"Four reales."*
> *"We want two Anis del Toro."*
> *"With water?"*
> *"Do you want it with water?"*
> *"I don't know," the girl said. "Is it good with water?"*
> *"It's all right."*
> *"You want them with water?" asked the woman.*
> *"Yes, with water."*

With a sparing but skillful use of tags, we have no trouble knowing who is speaking when, despite the fact that there are three characters and none of these characters seems to have a name.

STAGE DIRECTIONS

Adding physical action to dialogue can help bring a scene to life. Take a look around you the next time you're at a party. You can tell someone's personality by how they interact with others. Gregarious people talk with their hands; seductive people run their fingers through their hair. Anal people gather all the toothpicks from the ashtrays and throw them away. Nervous people laugh too loud; attention seekers act outrageously to try to get others to notice them. All of these gestures, interspersed with dialogue, give a much more subtle and imaginative idea of the character than just *She tried to seduce him*, or *Aiden was nervous*.

If the author gives the reader no clue as to whether the characters are sitting or standing, eating lunch or driving a car, the scene can sound like floating heads reciting words. By mixing in narration details with your dialogue, you can shed light on your characters and give the scene a real physical presence. In a play or film, we have the actors to interpret the dialogue, through their gestures, movements, expressions, and tone of voice. This extra dimension can be achieved in fiction too with the skillful use of "stage directions."

Notice how physical action enlivens this scene from Denis Johnson's "Emergency." The drifter main character is talking to his friend and fellow orderly from the hospital, Georgie, who "often stole pills from the cabinets."

> He was running over the tiled floor of the operating room with a mop.
> "Are you still doing that?" I said.
> "Jesus, there's a lot of blood here," he complained.
> "Where?" The floor looked clean enough to me.
> "What the hell were they doing in here?" he asked me.
> "They were performing surgery, Georgie," I told him.
> "There's so much goop inside of us, man," he said, "and it all wants to get out." He leaned his mop against a cabinet.
> "What are you crying for?" I didn't understand.
> He stood still, raised both arms slowly behind his head, and tightened his ponytail. Then he grabbed the mop and started making broad random

arcs with it, trembling and weeping and moving all around the place really fast. "What am I crying for?" he said. "Jesus. Wow, oh boy, perfect."

The actions are important in that they show the drug-induced insanity of the characters, an integral element of the book's bizarre tone.

Similarly, thoughts can be used in stage directions, giving us an extra dimension, as in this clip from "Emergency":

> *Georgie opened his arms and cried out, "It's the drive-in, man!"*
> *"The drive-in . . ." I wasn't sure what these words meant.*

Stage directions are especially useful when there is a conflict between what a character says and what a character feels or thinks. If a character says she's not hurt and yet starts to cry, the reader knows that really she does feel injured. Like so:

> *"Nothing you say can hurt me," she said, fighting back tears.*

Also add action or thought if the tone of the words spoken needs to be explained. *"I hate you," she said slamming the front door* is a very different sentence from *"I hate you," she said, hitting him playfully on the arm.*

On the flip side, there is such a thing as too many stage directions. The reader doesn't really need to know every single time the character shifts his weight or scratches behind his ears or thinks about doing the laundry. The scene can sound "overacted." Like so:

> *She took the Brita pitcher out of the refrigerator.* Did I drink that much, *she wondered,* or did I forget to refill it? *She tilted the pitcher, pouring the clear, cold liquid into the glass. The condensation immediately began to bead down the sides. She returned the pitcher to the refrigerator, placing it next to the kiwi and an unopened jar of olives.* "Oh," she said, "did you want a glass of water, too, Mom?"

In this instance, the reader probably wouldn't even *get* to the dialogue.

> YOUR TURN:
> Take the second version of the dialogue
> exchange you did for the previous exercise
> (the fictionalized one). Using the same
> dialogue that you wrote, rewrite the exchange,
> this time adding in tags and stage directions.
> Your tags should make it clear who is

speaking and your stage directions should offer an added dash of nuance or meaning. Hint: it may help if one or both of the characters are engaged in a physical action. Then marvel at how well you've transformed real life into an interesting clip of fictional dialogue.

INDIRECT DIALOGUE

So far, we've been discussing direct dialogue—where the actual lines spoken are given. But there's another option and that's indirect dialogue—where the dialogue is summarized rather than quoted, appearing in summary rather than scene. Indirect dialogue can come in handy when the gist of what was said is more important than the actual dialogue.

Look at this passage from Tobias Wolff's "Smokers." Here the narrator is accosted by an annoying boy traveling by train to the same boarding school:

> *He started to talk almost the moment he sat down, and he didn't stop until we reached Wallingford. Was I going to Choate? What a coincidence—so was he. My first year? His too. Where was I from? Oregon? No shit? Way the hell and gone up in the boondocks, eh? He was from Indiana—Gary, Indiana. I knew the song, didn't I? I did, but he sang it for me anyway, all the way through, including the tricky ending.*

By just summarizing the annoying boy's questions, we are spared a monotonous conversation but get the most important information—the boy's desperate appeal for friendship and the narrator's annoyance at him—and we get it in a most economical fashion. In this instance, the reader doesn't really need the back-and-forth of the actual conversation.

Let's look at another example from "Smokers," where Wolff mixes both direct and indirect dialogue:

> *As it happened, the courts were full. Talbot and I sat on the grass and I asked him questions I already knew the answers to, like where was he from and where had he been going to school the year before and who did he have for English. At this question he came to life. "English? Parker, the bald one. I got A's all through school and now Parker tells me I can't write."*

Here we get the gist of the conversation, but then, on an especially significant line, we get the actual quote.

So, in addition to asking yourself if a moment should be dialogued or not, you can also ask yourself if direct or indirect dialogue is the best choice for that particular moment.

> YOUR TURN:
> Return to the dialogue exchange you wrote in the previous exercise. This time convey the gist of it with just a few sentences of *summarized* dialogue. In addition to conveying the facts, hint at the character personalities and/or tension in the exchange. If you wish to include a line or two of the actual words spoken, do so. The determine if this particular exchange would be better served by dialogue or summarized dialogue in a work of fiction—a choice you will always have.

DIALOGUE AND CHARACTER

Perhaps the best thing about dialogue is that it allows characters to speak for themselves. You don't really know someone in real life until you've talked to them and heard them talk to you; the same principle applies to fiction. Unless you're superficial, a person's outside appearance doesn't matter nearly as much as what he has to say. It's on the basis of what comes out of his mouth that you decide whether you like the person and want to spend more time with him. Okay, sometimes on dates we get superficial at first, but you know what I mean.

For example, rather than being told that Mr. Jackson is a highly educated and rather stuffy man who has an interest in German opera, let's hear him speak:

> *"I am emotionally attracted to Ms. Mason. She has a Wagnerian formality that begs to be breeched."*

We get it, quite effectively.

Every person in life speaks in a somewhat unique fashion, and the same should be true for fictional characters. Just as you look for unique traits in your characters, look for the uniqueness in how they speak. Avoid having all your characters talk exactly the same way, or even having all of them talk just like you. Seek out the distinctive ways that characters express themselves when they open their mouths.

You should think about the plentitude of a character's speech. You might create characters who speak in never-ending segments that travel over hill and dale and try the patience of everyone in the room or characters who only grunt monosyllabic responses, which could be equally trying to those in the conversation. If you find yourself on a date with either of these habits, you're in trouble, but, fortunately, there are many variations in between.

People often have pet expressions that they use over and over again in dialogue. *Oh, my head!* instead of *Oh, my God!* or *Don't piss in my Cheerios* instead of *Don't rain on my parade.* Jay Gatsby, for example, is fond of the term "ol' sport," and Bartleby in Herman Melville's "Bartleby, the Scrivener" would utter the phrase "I prefer not to" in response to just about anything, even when his employer insists he leave his job.

Ask yourself questions about how your characters might talk. Do they use incorrect grammar and colloquialisms, or do they speak "perfectly"? Does their background and social status affect the way they talk? Do they tend to beat around the bush or get to the point quickly?

Here's an example from J. D. Salinger's *The Catcher in the Rye,* where Holden Caulfield is conversing with a New York City cab driver:

> "Hey, Horwitz," I said. "You ever pass by the lagoon in Central Park? Down by Central Park South?"
> "The *what?*"
> "The lagoon. That little lake, like, there. Where the ducks are. You know."
> "Yeah, what about it?"
> "Well, you know the ducks that swim around in it? In the springtime and all? Do you happen to know where they go in the wintertime, by any chance?"
> "Where *who* goes?"

These two characters clearly have different backgrounds and we hear it in the way they speak. We also hear the difference in their personalities. Holden is chatty, curious, even a bit nervous. The cabbie just wants to drive in peace without worrying about the damn ducks.

In Ethan Canin's "The Accountant," an accountant is at an adult baseball fantasy camp chatting with the legendary Willie Mays:

Willie Mays said, "Shoot, you hit the ball, brother."
I ventured, "Shoot, yes."
Willie Mays said, "You creamed that sucker."
I said, "Say, I bet they sock you at tax time."

Here it's humorous watching the accountant trying to sound loose and cool talking to Willie Mays. Though the two men are speaking a similar lingo, it's clear that the accountant is much less at home with it. Perhaps it's because he says "Shoot, yes," instead of the more natural "Shoot, yeah." When it comes to dialogue, such minute nuances make a world of difference.

Here's an example from Philip Roth's *Portnoy's Complaint,* where a Jewish mother is conversing with her adolescent son:

"I don't believe in God."
"Get out of those dungarees, Alex, and put on some decent clothes."
"They're not dungarees, they're Levi's."
"It's Rosh Hashanah, Alex, and to me you're wearing overalls! Get in there and put a tie on and a jacket on and a pair of trousers and a clean shirt, and come out looking like a human being. And shoes, Mister, hard shoes."
"My shirt is clean."
"Oh, you're riding for a fall, Mr. Big. You're fourteen years old, and believe me, you don't know everything there is to know. Get out of those moccasins! What the hell are you supposed to be, some kind of Indian?"

Here both characters are from the same family but they clearly have different methods of expressing themselves. Notice that no tags are used, although the mother calls the boy by his name a few times. When characters speak this distinctively, tags become superfluous.

Now notice how different all the characters above sound from these two servants in an English manor in Kazuo Ishiguro's *Remains of the Day:*

Miss Kenton had entered and said from the door:
"Mr. Stevens, I have just noticed something outside which puzzles me."
"What is that, Miss Kenton?"
"Was it his lordship's wish that the Chinaman on the upstairs landing should be exchanged with the one outside this door?"
"The Chinaman, Miss Kenton?"
"Yes, Mr. Stevens. The Chinaman normally on the landing you will now find outside this door."

> *"I fear, Miss Kenton, that you are a little confused."*
>
> *"I do not believe I am confused at all, Mr. Stevens. I make it my business to acquaint myself with where the objects properly belong in a house. The Chinamen, I would suppose, were polished by someone then replaced incorrectly. If you are skeptical, Mr. Stevens, perhaps you will care to step out here and observe for yourself."*
>
> *"Miss Kenton, I am occupied at present."*
>
> *"But, Mr. Stevens, you do not appear to believe what I am saying. I am thus asking you to step outside this door and see for yourself."*
>
> *"Miss Kenton, I am busy just now and will attend to the matter shortly. It is hardly one of urgency."*
>
> *"You accept then, Mr. Stevens, that I am not in error on this point."*
>
> *"I will accept nothing of the sort, Miss Kenton, until I have had a chance to deal with the matter. However, I am occupied at present."*

Not only do these characters speak in a formalized manner, but they become disturbed in a formalized manner. And though Mr. Stevens and Miss Kenton both strive for the propriety demanded by their setting, Miss Kenton has more trouble than Mr. Stevens with keeping her emotions in check. The interesting thing about Mr. Stevens is that, in the manner of the perfect English butler, he almost blends into the polished woodwork, and this is certainly reflected in his dialogue.

In addition to getting a sense of who characters are, dialogue can also convey a strong sense of the interaction between characters. Let's return to the man and girl in Hemingway's "Hills Like White Elephants." Here's what they say right after they get the Anis del Toro that they ordered:

> *"It tastes like licorice," the girl said and put the glass down.*
>
> *"That's the way with everything."*
>
> *"Yes," said the girl. "Everything tastes of licorice. Especially all the things you've waited so long for, like absinthe."*
>
> *"Oh, cut it out."*
>
> *"You started it," the girl said. "I was being amused. I was having a fine time."*
>
> *"Well, let's try and have a fine time."*

We don't have to be told there's tension between this couple. We can *hear* it. Almost as though we are sitting at the neighboring table. Here's a tip: tension between characters will almost always notch up the interest level of your dialogue.

In "Cathedral," look at the dialogue shortly after the blind man arrives.

> *"Did you have a good train ride?" I said. "Which side of the train did you sit on, by the way?"*
>
> *"What a question, which side!" my wife said. "What's it matter which side?" she said.*
>
> *"I just asked," I said.*
>
> *"Right side," the blind man said. "I hadn't been on a train in nearly forty years. Not since I was a kid. With my folks. That's been a long time. I'd nearly forgotten the sensation. I have winter in my beard now," he said. "So I've been told, anyway. Do I look distinguished, my dear?" the blind man said to my wife.*

Here we clearly see the tension between the narrator and his wife, a continuation of an earlier argument about the narrator's unwillingness to welcome the blind man into their home. Despite the marital unrest before him, Robert, the blind man, seems remarkably at ease. We also see each character thrown into sharp relief through the words spoken. The narrator is being flip, even ornery, by asking the blind man on which side of the train he sat. The wife, poor woman, is trying to curtail her errant husband. And right off the bat Robert is demonstrating his relaxed friendliness and social ease. He even shows a touch of the poet by referring to "winter in my beard," a significant point considering poetry is something shared by the wife and blind man and disliked by the narrator. A rather complex character triangle is revealed quite specifically in just this short passage.

YOUR TURN:
Jessica, a somewhat stuffy university professor (you pick her field), stops at a gas station in some backwater place. As she fills her tank, Alvin, the attendant, approaches her. He is an uneducated sort (though not necessarily dim) and, being both bored and friendly, he wants to chat. Jessica would rather not chat but she also doesn't want to alienate Alvin because she would like directions to a nearby restaurant that won't be too greasy or ghastly. Write a scene between Jessica and Alvin, using dialogue, tags, and stage directions. Your main goal is to capture the flavor of these two people through how they speak.

SUBTEXT

Check out the relationship section of a bookstore. There are thousands of books on communication between partners. Our society may be excellent at talking, but we have trouble communicating. People often don't say what they mean. Sometimes they say the opposite of what they mean. They hide insults in sugary language (or sugary feelings in insults). They don't listen. They mishear. They don't answer. They remain silent.

Capitalizing on miscommunication improves fictional dialogue because it makes it more true to life. Misunderstandings can also add tension to the dialogue exchange. This tension results from the gap between what's being said and the subtext—the meaning beneath the surface meaning. Dialogue with subtext has two levels of meaning.

A great illustration of subtext occurs in the film *Annie Hall*. Woody Allen and Diane Keaton, who have recently met, are standing on a terrace carrying on a nervous conversation. She says: "Well, I-I-I would—I would like to take a serious photography course soon." But what she's really thinking appears in a subtitle: "He probably thinks I'm a yo-yo." Then he says: "Photography's interesting, 'cause, you know, it's-it's a new art form, and a, uh, a set of aesthetic criteria have not emerged yet." But his subtitle says: "I wonder what she looks like naked?" How much does this mirror real-life conversation? Probably more than any of us would like to admit.

Though you are unlikely to use subtitles with your dialogue, subtext can be enormously effective in fiction.

In *The Good People of New York* by Thisbe Nissen, Edwin, long divorced, asks his daughter about her mother's live-in boyfriend.

> Edwin is silent for a time. "You didn't like Steven much, did you?" he finally asks.
> Miranda shrugs. "He was my orthodontist."

Miranda's evasive answer contains much meaning. In the sullen manner of a teenager, she's explaining how embarrassing it is to have her mother date the man who tightens her braces, and her further embarrassment at discussing it with her father. But her response wouldn't be nearly as interesting or relevatory (or concise) if she were able to articulate her complicated feelings.

In *The Great Gatsby,* when Gatsby shows Daisy his exquisite collection of monogrammed shirts, this is how she reacts:

"They're such beautiful shirts," she sobbed, her voice muffled in the thick folds. "It makes me sad because I've never seen such—such beautiful shirts before."

Daisy is sobbing for many painful reasons but the shirts aren't one of them. Her inability to express her feelings adds tremendous poignancy to the moment.

Finally, let's look at another dialogue exchange from "Cathedral." The narrator and his wife are arguing as they prepare for the blind man's visit. As you read this, try to determine if the characters are speaking in subtext or not:

"Maybe I could take him bowling," I said to my wife. She was at the draining board doing scalloped potatoes. She put down the knife she was using and turned around.

"If you love me," she said, "you can do this for me. If you don't love me, okay. But if you had a friend, any friend, and the friend came to visit, I'd make him feel comfortable." She wiped her hands with the dish towel.

"I don't have any blind friends," I said.

"You don't have any friends," she said. "Period. Besides," she said, "goddamn it, his wife's just died! Don't you understand that? The man's lost his wife!"

If you answered *yes,* you're right. If you answered *no,* you're also right. The narrator *is* speaking in subtext. When he says, "I could take him bowling," he's really saying how ridiculous it is to be entertaining a blind man. When he says, "I don't have any blind friends," he's really saying that a blind friend is worse than no friend. The wife, on the other hand, is saying exactly what's on her mind. This is a very lifelike situation, where one person is more inclined to speak sideways than another.

Having thus emphasized that dialogue should not just be a representation of everyday speech, I should add that there is real pleasure to be had in the way people actually talk, their confusion, their circumlocution, their mistakes, misunderstandings, repetitions, and their small talk. There exists a fine line between actual and fictionalized dialogue. But in fictional dialogue you want to make sure the poor communication serves a dramatic purpose that is understood by the reader. When you achieve this, your dialogue will take on layers of realism and depth.

As the old Yiddish proverb goes, "A man hears one word but understands two." Good advice for writing dialogue. A layered conversation is the difference between what seems to be a stage-set version of a house and a genuine lived-in home.

> YOUR TURN:
> Envision a husband and wife or any other kind of romantic pair. Give them names and think about who they are. One of these characters suspects the other of being unfaithful (in some way), and let's say the other character is (in some way) guilty. Write a dialogue exchange between these two where the sore topic is never referred to directly but instead simmers beneath the words spoken. Don't enter the thoughts of either character. And keep the conversation focused on tuna steak, which they are having for dinner at the moment. If you exhaust tuna steak, you can move on to politics or movies. Silly as this sounds, see if the finished product doesn't have a ring of truth to it.

BAD DIALOGUE

Bad dialogue makes characters seem like puppets, mere creations of the author. Of course they are, but the reader will conveniently forget that if the dialogue is well rendered. Bad dialogue exposes the author, in much the same way that Toto exposes the Great and Powerful Oz when he tugs back the curtain in *The Wizard of Oz*. When you can see the machinations behind the writing, the entire illusion is lost.

You remember Mulder and Scully from the TV show *The X-Files*? They worked together for nine years and still, each week, Scully patronizingly explained simple medical terms to poor, brilliant Mulder. Why? So that the audience could figure it out. Lesson: dialogue is often *not* a good venue for exposition:

> Scully: *He's exsanguinating from a laceration in his jugular.*
> Mulder: *You mean he's bleeding to death from his neck?*

There's no way that Mulder, expert in all things paranormal and disgusting, wouldn't know what *exsanguinating* means. Find some other way to impart the information (the dying man's wife wants to know what's going on; or show us the gaping, bloody wound). I made up that exchange, but it could very well have been in one of the episodes. While these exchanges had a certain charm on the TV show, they would ring phony in fiction.

Though you're not likely to be using the word *exsanguinating,* you may find yourself trying to sneak in some exposition through your dialogue, like so:

> *"Troy, you were six years old when your mother left you and your sister to join the circus as a high-wire acrobat."*

Presumably Troy hasn't forgotten this odd fact, so why is he being told? Read your dialogue over. If it sounds forced in places, or unrealistic, see if you can turn the dialogue around so it's not so obvious:

> *"Troy, grow up. It's been twenty years since your mother left, and you're still harping about how much you hate aerialists. Don't you think it's time you let go?"*

Now there is a credible reason why the information is introduced. The speaker is making a point about "letting go," and the exposition just happens to be included. If you can't find a plausible way to get the exposition in the dialogue, then you're better off just putting the exposition in the narration:

> *At the age of six, Troy and his sister had the misfortune to be abandoned by their mother, who fled to fulfill her lifelong ambition of performing as a circus acrobat.*

Another thing to watch out for is preaching in dialogue. Some writers, once they gain your attention, use their stories as political platforms. Their characters expound the writer's views on various social issues or prejudices. Don't give your characters a podium from which to harangue the reader. If you want to write about the evils of corporate greed, draft a letter to the editor, but don't make poor fictional Johnny argue at length with his basketball buddy about the pitfalls of capitalism:

> *"You may think the raffle is a good idea but I'm telling you it's merely a capitalistic ploy to get rich. Capitalism, my friend, is the root of all evil. Today it's a raffle. Tomorrow you'll be paying Guatamalan families a penny a week to produce your goods so you can travel first-class and keep a summer house in East Hampton."*

If the reader feels that the author is making the character's voice the author's own opinion, the reader might feel manipulated and bored. That said, there are some authors who made a career of exactly this—Ayn Rand, Jean-Paul Sartre, George Orwell, to name a few—but it's extremely hard to pull off.

One last thing on bad dialogue. For reasons as yet undetermined by modern science, profanity on the page is much more alarming and vulgar than spoken profanity. Even foul-mouthed characters appear to overuse swear words when they are written down. If you don't believe me, write a dialogue between rampant cussers, truck drivers or socialites, and you'll see what I mean. A couple of well-chosen profanities work much better than a string of four-letter wonders, bringing all the flavor of X-rated speech without overdoing it.

DIALECT

Dialect is like walking on eggshells—tread carefully. It's tough to do well, and even if it is done well it can be distracting.

If rendered carelessly, dialect runs the risk of sounding hackneyed, exaggerated, or even offensive, as in:

> Moishe tripped over a piece of gefilte fish that was lying on the kitchen floor.
> "Oy gevalt!" cried Sadie. "Bubbela, the scare you gave me."
> "What, are you meshugana, leaving this fish on the floor?"

We're being clobbered on the head with Yiddishisms. Less is more, as in:

> Moishe tripped over a piece of gefilte fish that was lying on the kitchen floor.
> "Oy gevalt!" Sadie said. "The scare you gave me."
> "Well, I didn't expect there should be fish on the floor," Moishe said.

Here we get the flavor of the ethnicity without having it shoved down our throat.

Mark Twain is considered a master of dialect, but it's important to remember how difficult it is to read the character of Jim, the escaped slave, in *The Adventures of Huckleberry Finn* because the dialect is executed so faithfully:

> "Well, you see, it 'uz dis way. Ole missus—dat's Miss Watson—she

pecks on me all de time, en treats me potty rough, but she awluz said she
wouldn't sell me down to Orleans."

But it is possible to make dialect work smoothly if you focus on just giving a flavor of it—with key words and speech patterns and rhythms. In *Beloved*—which deals with black characters living around the time of the Civil War, contemporaries of Twain's Jim—Toni Morrison manages to capture the essence of her characters' dialect without throwing it in the reader's face:

> *"Wait here. Somebody be here directly. Don't move. They'll find you."*
>
> *"Thank you," she said. "I wish I knew your name so I could remember you right."*
>
> *"Name's Stamp," he said. "Stamp Paid. Watch out for that there baby, you hear?"*
>
> *"I hear, I hear," she said, but she didn't.*

Nothing about the dialogue looks terribly foreign to the reader, but we get the sense of dialect through the little touches like "Somebody be here directly" and "Watch out for that there baby, you hear?" Morrison has found the proper balance.

Another alternative to dialect is simply to state that a character has an accent or a dialect, or have another character comment on this fact, then write dialogue as you normally would. This method gets your point across without confusing the reader.

A semirelated matter: make sure that you're not making the reader experience the same speech difficulties as your characters. If you have a character who stutters, avoid showing it in this distracting fashion:

> *"I—I—I'm not sh-sure," Joe said.*

Go for the simpler:

> *"I'm not sure," Joe stammered.*

You also want to be fairly sparing with such circumlocutions as "uhm," "uh," "well," and "you know."

And, uh, well, I guess that's what I've got to say on dialogue.

CHAPTER 7
SETTING AND PACING:
I'M HERE THEREFORE I AM
BY CAREN GUSSOFF

I've lived in seven different states in fifteen years. I grew up in the shadow of the Yonkers Raceway in Yonkers, New York, my neighborhood hemmed in by squat WPA houses and freeway overpasses. I became accustomed to waking up to the smell of rotten apples and wet sheep in the fairylike mists of early-morning Marlboro, Vermont. In Boulder, Colorado, I wore layers—from shorts to earmuffs—as the whole world could seem to change in an instant as the strange weather patterns bounced off the walls of the valley, walled in by granite flatirons on two sides. I've settled, for now, in Seattle, Washington, where the meteorologists have a hundred words for rain, understandably so. I've begun to appreciate the various forms it can take, from an imperceptible mist that nonetheless soaks you through to your skivvies to a vigorous outpouring that makes you swear someone is dumping a bottomless pitcher right overhead. Yet with all the rain, there is almost never any thunder or lightning, very few true storms. Living here in the constant sop affects every aspect of my life—where I go, what I wear, how I get there.

Strangely enough, though, my earliest works of fiction blithely ignored setting, concentrating instead almost solely on character. I thought I was doing okay. All of my favorite books had memorable characters—Holden Caulfield, Leopold Bloom, Jay Gatsby—so memorable, in fact, that most of them are irrevocably etched into our cultural consciousness. I intuitively understood the importance of characters, and what they do in a piece of fiction. They not only give a reader a focal point, but they also act, interact, react, have relationships, offer judgments, tell us about other characters, speak with other characters, describe, ruminate, think . . . and, most importantly, they change.

In a way, I was right to concentrate on character. After all, without strong characters, a story will fall flat on its face. But my stories fell flat on their face anyway. My characters paced aimlessly through my stories like caged tigers, and, worse, I often couldn't even write beyond a few pages. Things just stalled. I noticed that people who read my work labeled my pieces *vignettes, anecdotes*. How frustrating. That was not what I wanted. I wanted to write great stories, full stories, stories like *The Catcher in the Rye, Ulysses, The Great Gatsby*.

Here's what I failed to realize: Jay Gatsby is who he is *because* of the Jazz Age. Leopold Bloom is who he is *because* of Dublin. Holden Caulfield is who he is *because* of Pencey Prep School and New York City. I was missing the world surrounding my characters and the enormous impact it had on them, not to mention the impact on the overall story.

When readers read a piece of fiction, they expect it to feel real, even if it's a life they don't and will never know. They want to enter into it, to live there, with the characters. Setting—which refers simply to time and place—grounds the reader in the story in the most physical sense.

Traveling to various fictional places and times can also be one of the most entertaining aspects of reading, be it a journey of escapism or straight into the familiar. Think about some of your favorite works of fiction. They've all taken you to some kind of setting—haven't they? Charles Dickens moved his characters through the sooty streets of nineteenth-century England; J.R.R. Tolkien's Hobbits in the *Lord of the Rings* trilogy are from comfortable holes in Middle-Earth; Jeffrey Eugenides's *The Virgin Suicides* uses the façade of a calm Vietnam-era American suburb to show the driving desperation hidden just beneath the surface.

It's easy to dismiss setting because, frankly, it can be easy to miss. Look carefully at effective stories and you'll find the setting is so deeply combined with the characters and the action that it's almost unnoticeable. Like a master woodworker whose joinery is invisible, the writer has embedded the setting into the story. But if you really attune your eyes, you'll see that this implanted setting has an immeasurable impact on the characters and plot and, well, everything else.

YOUR TURN:
Pick up one of your favorite works of fiction
and read the first few pages. Pay attention
to how quickly you get some indication of the
setting. Notice how much or how little
the setting is layered into the action and
description. If you want to have some fun,
try revising the opening of the story using
a drastically different place or time. For
example, put Scarlett O'Hara in contemporary
Los Angeles and see how she does. (Probably
very well.)

PLACE

When writers talk about place, they mean the specific and definite location
of a story, on a large and small level. What planet, continent, country, state,
city, neighborhood, street are the characters in? What does the office or
building or river or cabana or castle or room look like?

The idea is to ground the reader in the place, whether it is the
middle-of-nowhere Wyoming, as in Richard Ford's "Rock Springs":

> *Where the car went bad there wasn't a town in sight or even a house,*
> *just some low mountains maybe fifty miles away, or maybe a hundred,*
> *a barbed wire fence in both directions, hardpan prairie, and some hawks*
> *sailing through the evening air seizing insects.*

Or the toughest section of the Bronx from Tom Wolfe's *Bonfire of the
Vanities:*

> *It was as if he had fallen into a junkyard. He seemed to be underneath*
> *the expressway. In the blackness, he could make out a cyclone fence*
> *over on the left ... something caught in it ... A woman's head! ...*
> *No, it was a chair with three legs and a burnt seat with the charred*
> *stuffing hanging out in great wads, rammed halfway through a cyclone*
> *fence ...*

Or looking out at Dublin Bay in James Joyce's *Ulysses:*

> *Woodshadows floated silently by through the morning peace from the*
> *stairhead seaward where he gazed. Inshore and farther out the mirror*

of water whitened, spurned by lightshod hurrying feet. White breast of the dim sea.

Or a room as bleak as this one from William Faulkner's *The Sound and the Fury:*

We entered a bare room smelling of stale tobacco. There was a sheet iron stove in the center of a wooden frame filled with sand, and a faded map on the wall and the dingy plat of a township. Behind a scarred littered table a man with a fierce roach of iron gray hair peered at us over steel spectacles.

Or a room as luxurious as this one from F. Scott Fitzgerald's *The Great Gatsby:*

The windows were ajar and gleaming white against the fresh grass outside that seemed to grow a little way into the house. A breeze blew through the room, blew curtains in at one end and out the other like pale flags, twisting them up toward the frosted wedding cake of the ceiling—and then rippled over the wine-colored rug, making a shadow on it as wind does on sea.

When dealing with place, don't neglect the possibility of including weather. As I mentioned earlier, my whole existence is directly and fundamentally affected by Seattle's weather. I know my corner of the world wouldn't be the same without the continual precipitation. Chances are there's something about the weather where you live that affects you dramatically, even though you may have ceased to think about it.

It may be like this sensual sunniness from Joyce Carol Oates's "Where Are You Going, Where Have You Been?":

Connie sat with her eyes closed in the sun, dreaming and dazed with the warmth about her as if this were a kind of love, the caresses of love . . .

Or this snowstorm from Leo Tolstoy's *Anna Karenina:*

The terrible storm tore and shrieked between the wheels of the train and round the scaffolding at the corner of the station. The railway carriages, the pillars, the people, and everything that could be seen were covered on one side with snow getting thicker and thicker. Now and then the storm would abate for an instant, and then blow with such gusts that it seemed impossible to stand up against it.

Weather immediately deepens the visceral sensation of "being" in a fictional place.

When writing your fiction, you should always be asking yourself where the characters are. And you need to give the readers some indication of where the characters are, be it one setting or numerous settings. Some places you may paint in great detail, others not, but you and the reader need this awareness of location at all times.

Place also affects the action of a piece. What would be possible in midwinter Siberia differs tremendously from what is possible in Miami in May. Likewise, what's considered normal activity in the Wild West might be downright scandalous in Victorian England. (You'll notice that time and place are irrevocably intertwined.)

Consider the impact of place on the plot of Cormac McCarthy's *All the Pretty Horses*. The main character, sixteen-year-old John Grady Cole, is the last in a long line of west Texas ranchers. The conflict at the center of the story is about the disappearance of the cowboy and rancher way of life, which eventually forces Grady's mother to sell off the family ranch. Grady then travels to Mexico, hoping to find a land free of the progress and population that have started to choke the Texas cowboys. This novel depends heavily upon the arid and desolate Southwest borderlands. In fact, it just wouldn't make any sense if it were set anywhere else.

Setting is also a driving force in Flannery O'Connor's "A Good Man Is Hard to Find." While on a car trip with her family, a grandmother believes she recognizes the area they are passing through and urges the family to take a side trip:

> They turned onto the dirt road and the car raced roughly along in a swirl of pink dust. The grandmother recalled the times when there were no paved roads and thirty miles was a day's journey. The dirt road was hilly and there were sudden washes in it and sharp curves on dangerous embankments. All at once they would be on a hill, looking down over the blue tops of trees for miles around, then the next minute, they would be in a red depression with the dust-coated trees looking down on them.
>
> "This place had better turn up in a minute," Bailey said, "or I'm going to turn around."
>
> The road looked as if no one had traveled on it in months.

Chaos ensues from taking the road less traveled. When the grandmother gets upset, the cat she has smuggled along gets loose, causing a car accident that places the family face-to-face with a murderer. Could the story have taken place during a jaunt down a suburban cul-de-sac? Perhaps not. And we wouldn't want it to.

How does the place, or places, in which your story is set affect the action? If the answer is *not at all,* then you should probably look for ways to make the place play some kind of a role in what happens. Otherwise your characters just might be drifting through a vacuum.

> YOUR TURN:
> Return to something you have written,
> perhaps using one of the previous exercises.
> If you haven't dealt with the place of the piece
> fully enough, revise with an eye toward doing
> this. Don't choke the passage with too much
> setting, but ground the reader in the place
> and let place have some impact on the action.
> If you have already dealt with place fully, then
> revise the piece drastically *altering* the place.
> Whichever route you choose, you should end
> up with a visibly different piece.

TIME

The notion of time is as integral to setting as place. Time can give us a sense of the backdrop of the story in the big sense—the era, century, year—and in the small sense—the season, day of the week, and time of day.

If we're in the nineteenth century, people may be traveling as they do in Charles Dickens's *Great Expectations:*

> *The journey from our town to the metropolis was a journey of about five hours. It was a little past midday when the four-horse stage-coach by which I was a passenger got into the ravel of traffic frayed out about the Cross Keys, Wood Street, Cheapside, London.*

And a century later they may be traveling as they do in Thom Jones's "A White Horse":

> *A faded, light-green Mercedes with a broken rear spring came bouncing*

too fast across the beach and skidded, sliding sideways as it stopped near the carousel.

We may be in springtime, as in D. H. Lawrence's *Lady Chatterley's Lover:*

An English spring! Why not an Irish one? Or Jewish? The chair moved slowly ahead, past tufts of sturdy bluebells that stood up like wheat and over grey burdock leaves. When they came to the open place where the trees had been felled, the light flooded in rather stark. And the bluebells made sheets of bright blue colour, here and there, sheering off into lilac and purple.

Or autumn, as in Ernest Hemingway's "In Another Country":

In the fall the war was always there, but we did not go to it any more. It was cold in the fall in Milan and the dark came very early. Then the electric lights came on, and it was pleasant along the streets looking in the windows. There was much game hanging outside the shops, and the snow powdered in the fur of the foxes and the wind blew their tails.

Or in a busy city during the day, as in J. D. Salinger's *The Catcher in the Rye:*

Broadway was mobbed and messy. It was Sunday and only about twelve o'clock, but it was mobbed anyway. Everybody was on their way to the movies—the Paramount or the Astor or the Strand or the Capitol or one of those crazy places. Everybody was all dressed up, because it was Sunday, and that made it worse.

Which is different from the same city in the same book late at night:

I didn't see hardly anybody on the street. Now and then you just saw a man and a girl crossing a street, with their arms around each other's waists and all, or a bunch of hoodlumy-looking guys and their dates, all of them laughing like hyenas at something you could bet wasn't funny. New York's terrible when somebody laughs on the street very late at night. You can hear it for miles. It makes you feel so lonely and depressed.

As with place, you always want to locate your characters in time, whether or not you spend much space describing it. Be aware of the time, in both the big and the small sense, and give the reader whatever clues they may need to stay oriented. You may have heard the newscaster expression: "*It's ten P.M.*

Do you know where your children are?" At any given time, you should know where your characters are and what they are doing.

> YOUR TURN:
> Return to something you have written. Just
> don't use the piece you used for the previous
> exercise on place. But do the same thing as
> in that exercise, this time either dealing with
> the time more fully or drastically altering the
> time. See if your tampering with time affects
> this piece as deeply as the tampering of place
> did with the previous exercise.

SETTING THE MOOD

In addition to grounding the reader in a physical place and time, setting can actually enhance the emotional landscape of a piece, affecting the atmosphere and mood.

Edgar Allan Poe was a master of using setting to maximize the mood of his stories, as seen in the opening of "The Fall of the House of Usher":

> *During the whole of a dull, dark, and soundless day in the autumn of the year, when the clouds hung oppressively low in the heavens, I had been passing alone, on horseback, through a singularly dreary tract of country, and at length found myself, as the shades of the evening drew on, within view of the melancholy House of Usher.*

As much as painting the time and place, perhaps more, Poe is evoking a mood, an emotional state—one of bleakness and danger and melancholy. Of course it's autumn, of course night is falling, of course the clouds hang oppressively. Practically every word in this passage tolls like a solemn bell. Poe underscores the tension before you even know what the tension is . . . or could be. Descriptively, Poe may be a little over the top, but dramatically, he's right where he should be, setting the stage for the dark tale about to unfold.

In a far more contemporary example, Lorrie Moore uses the setting of a hospital to convey the emotional state of her protagonist in "People Like That Are the Only People Here":

> *The Mother studies the trees and fish along the ceiling's edge in the Save*

the Planet wallpaper border. Save the Planet. Yes! But the windows in this very building don't open and diesel fumes are leaking into the ventilating system, near which, outside, a delivery truck is parked. The air is nauseous and stale.

The setting seems even more nightmarish later with:

Red cellophane garlands festoon the doorways. She has totally forgotten it is as close to Christmas as this. A pianist in the corner is playing "Carol of the Bells," and it sounds not only unfestive but scary, like the theme from The Exorcist.

Notice that in the above examples, the setting is being conveyed through the consciousness of the POV character. Perhaps some people would have found the "Carol of the Bells" charming, but this character found it harrowing.

> YOUR TURN:
> Imagine a character who is contemplating a major change in his or her life—dropping out of school, having a child, entering a risky business venture . . . Once you have fleshed out the character a bit, write a passage where this character is dealing with the change. You may or may not choose to have other characters involved. Here's the interesting part: let weather underscore the drama of the passage, be it the first gusts of autumn or a torrential downpour or any other act of the elements.

SETTING AND CHARACTER

While we're on the subject of characters, let me point out that setting plays a great role in who your characters are—how they dress, talk, socialize, work, travel, eat, and so forth. Much like animals, people behave a certain way in their natural habitat, and you want to pay attention to how your characters are shaped by their setting.

At this pool party in a ritzy suburb from John Cheever's "The Swimmer," the characters act in a way that is quite native to their environment:

As soon as Enid Bunker saw him she began to scream; "Oh, look who's here! What a marvelous surprise! When Lucinda said that you couldn't come I thought I'd die.*" She made her way to him through the crowd, and when they had finished kissing she led him to the bar, a progress that was slowed by the fact that he stopped to kiss eight or ten other women and shake the hands of as many men. A smiling bartender he had seen at a hundred parties gave him a gin and tonic and he stood by the bar for a moment, anxious not to get stuck in any conversation that would delay his voyage.*

How are the characters in your fiction shaped by their setting? If you can easily take your characters out of their current setting and plop them elsewhere with no notable difference in who they are, then perhaps your characters are not affected deeply enough by the time and place in which they live. Don't pound setting into your characters, like forcing your Texas businessman to wear cowboy boots and exclaim *y'all* every time he speaks, but look for the subtle ways that Texas may have seeped into his being.

Stories often contain characters who are forced to go outside their natural environment, which creates interesting dynamics and situations. In such cases, you'll need to be aware of how a character acts and reacts in a setting that is somewhat foreign. Imagine a young punk girl getting fitted for an evening dress at Neiman Marcus, or a socialite in a tattoo parlor. Literature is filled with examples of this, such as middle-class midwestern Nick entering Jay Gatsby's lavish world in *The Great Gatsby,* or Earl, the car thief, being stranded for a few days in Wyoming in "Rock Springs."

At its most extreme, this becomes a "fish out of water" story, where the main conflict is between a character and a wildly unfamiliar surrounding. You may recognize the fish-out-of-water scenario from such TV shows as *Green Acres* or *Northern Exposure,* but it's also proven popular in fiction. An obvious example is Lewis Carroll's *Alice in Wonderland,* where a well-bred Victorian girl falls through a rabbit hole, landing in a topsy-turvy world where turtles sing and cats disappear into nothing but a smile. Examples abound, such as *Great Expectations,* where a boy from the English marsh country mingles with the dandies of London, or Thom Jones's "A White Horse," where an American advertising man with amnesia finds himself wandering through the squalor of Bombay without a clue as to how he got there. A fish-out-of-water story can be enormously fun, but if you tackle one by ready to deal with your setting extensively.

The Metamorphosis, by Franz Kafka, puts an interesting twist on the fish-out-of-water story, as Gregor Samsa, a young traveling salesman, wakes up one morning to discover that during the night he has been transformed into an insect. The world that was once so familiar and comfortable to Gregor has become an unnavigable and strange landscape. Here he is trying to manage a once simple task:

> *He thought that he might get out of bed with the lower part of his body first, but this lower part, which he had not yet seen and of which he could form no clear conception, proved too difficult to move: it shifted so slowly; and when finally, almost wild with annoyance, he gathered his forces together and struck out recklessly, he had miscalculated the direction and bumped heavily against the lower end of the bed.*

Throughout the story, Gregor is forced to see his familiar world from a whole new perspective. Offering a new perspective is one of the advantages of placing characters in an alien environment, because it forces the characters and the reader to see things with fresh, and often wary, eyes.

> YOUR TURN:
> Think up a character who is very much the opposite of yourself. Choose some of the following differences: sex, age, occupation, background, temperament . . . Now write a passage where this character must live for a while in an environment very similar to your own. Let the setting cause as much conflict as possible for the character. For example, if the character is a freewheeling bachelor, perhaps let him struggle tending to your houseful of kids. If the character is a spoiled rich kid, perhaps let her hold down your job for a day. Have fun letting someone else struggle with your setting!

In some cases, a setting becomes so overwhelmingly important that it actually performs as a character in its own right—it can act and change, and even become one of the most dominant features in your story. This is certainly true of most fish-out-of-water stories, where the setting is the major conflict, but it also applies to such diverse examples as the moors of *Wuthering Heights,* the Jazz Age of *The Great Gatsby,* the Depression of *The Grapes of Wrath,* the Vietnam War of "The Things They Carried," the hospital of "People Like That Are the Only People Here," and the affluent suburbia of "The Swimmer."

Virginia Woolf used this technique in her novel *The Waves,* where she traces the lives of a group of six friends from childhood to middle age. They each speak in a series of soliloquies, with the sea and roaring waves as the backdrop. *The Waves* is punctuated by descriptive interludes that show a changing view of the sea as day evolves from dawn to nightfall. The waves themselves recur and change, creating a sense of unity in the novel and adding a level of meaning. The characters' speeches seem to be fluid stream-of-consciousness pieces about what it is to be, as the waves are. When the novel opens, we see the early waves of the morning:

> *The wave paused, and then drew out again, sighing like a sleeper whose breath comes and goes unconsciously.*

As the book progresses, and the characters age, so the day progresses and the waves become bolder:

> *The waves massed themselves, curved their backs and crashed. Up spurted stones and shingle.*

And at the end of the book, in which the characters face impending age and death, the waves do as well. The novel ends with the simple line:

> *The waves broke on the shore.*

SETTING THE DETAILS

If the purpose of setting is to ground the characters, and the readers, in the physical world of the story, and perhaps reflect the appropriate dramatic mood, then you, the writer, are going to need to create that physical world. With what? With the only thing you've got—words. If you've read chapter 5 in this book, you should already have a pretty good idea of how to bring your settings to life. Largely you'll be painting your fictional settings through the artful use of sensory and specific description.

Here's a section from Henry James's *The Portrait of a Lady.* Pay attention to the sensory and specific details in this depiction of a house:

> *It stood upon a low hill, above the river—the river being the Thames, at some forty miles from London. A long gabled front of red brick, with*

*the complexion of which time and the weather had played all sorts of
picturesque tricks, only, however, to improve and refine it, presented itself
to the lawn, with its patches of ivy, its clustered chimneys, its windows
smothered in creepers.*

This is a setting you can see unmistakably, can't you? Not only does James
give you a highly detailed visual picture of the house itself but he also gives
you a sense of the house's history and he pinpoints its exact location. There
is a lot of fuel for your imagination in such a small amount of space.

Such conciseness is actually important. You don't want your setting
description to hit the pause button on the action too often or readers will
go out to have a drink or do some shopping while you're there working
carefully at the easel with your brush and paint. Readers depend on the
forward movement in a story, so your story is best served by scattering
your setting description throughout a piece rather than dropping it in giant
globs here and there. You would also do well to mix a little action into your
descriptions of setting.

Take a look at this selection from Marguerite Duras's novella *The
Lover:*

*I get off the bus. I go over to the rails. I look at the river. My mother
sometimes tells me that never in my life shall I ever again see rivers as
beautiful and big and wild as these, the Mekong and its tributaries going
down to the sea, the great regions of water soon to disappear into the caves
of ocean. In the surrounding flatness stretching as far as the eye can see,
the rivers flow as fast as if the earth sloped downward.*

*I always get off the bus when we reach the ferry, even at night, because
I'm always afraid, afraid the cables might break and we might be swept
out to sea. In the terrible current I watch my last moments. The current
is so strong it could carry everything away—rocks, a cathedral, a city.
There's a storm blowing inside the water. A wind raging.*

Duras's details are sensuous, but she weaves the setting into the story by
relating an anecdote about what the character's mother tells her to notice,
thereby providing valuable character insight alongside the description. The
flow of the story is not lost at all.

Remember the importance of telling details, those tidbits of information
that carry so much power in their little shells? Skillful use of telling details
will allow you to convey your settings quickly, yet effectively. In Richard
Russo's *Empire Falls*, Miles, the protagonist, runs a somewhat rundown

diner. Instead of giving us every shabby detail of the diner's kitchen, Russo focuses on the antiquated dishwasher:

> *Only one tub of dirty dishes remained, but it was a big one, so Miles lugged it into the kitchen and set it on the drainboard, stopping there to listen to the Hobart chug and whir, steam leaking from inside its stainless steel frame. They'd had this dishwasher for, what, twenty years? Twenty-five? He was pretty sure it was there when Roger Sperry first hired him back in high school.*

With this one detail, the reader feels as if he is standing there in the kitchen beside Miles, and the story is ready to move onward.

As a rule of thumb, ask yourself how important a particular time or place is to your story and this will help you determine how much "space" to spend describing any given setting. "The Fall of the House of Usher" takes place entirely in the House of Usher, and so a good amount of description on the house is warranted. But you don't need to spend page after beautiful page describing a drugstore if your main character simply stops in to buy a bottle of aspirin.

Do all works of fiction deal with setting in at least some detail? Well, no, actually. Raymond Carver, for example, noted for the minimalism of his prose, often doesn't put in much setting. In "Cathedral," the entire story takes place in a house, and though Carver refers to the kitchen and the sofa and the window and the TV, he doesn't give any specifics about anything there, except that his wife bought a new sofa and the narrator liked the old one. But the lack of setting detail makes sense here because this story is told in the first person and the narrator isn't really taking note of his house or especially interested in it. We can also assume from the lack of detail that this is a fairly ordinary home, neither squalid nor lavish. If it were either, then the writer should have told us so. If you have a compelling reason *not* to describe your setting, then you have permission to do so.

THE REALITY OF SETTING

Most fictional stories deal with authentic settings, portraying real places and times or at least seemingly real ones. Though, say, Thomas Hardy's Wessex County, home to several of his novels, cannot be found on any map, it's very similar to the genuine article in that particular part of the English countryside. When writing about these real or seemingly real settings, do your best to paint them accurately and vividly.

If you're writing about a setting that you know well, you shouldn't have a problem verifying the details. If you're writing about a setting you don't know well, you should do your best to gather as much information as you can, by visiting or just doing some old-fashioned research, made all the easier by the un-old-fashioned Internet. However, if you're writing about a setting with which you are not intimately familiar, you may want to give it a fictional name so as not to do something like anger the residents of Cleveland by mixing up the names of the cross-streets downtown. If you call your city, say, Leveland, you're off the hook.

Fictionalizing your location also gives you some dramatic license. In Beth Nugent's novel *Live Girls,* the main character, Catherine, in her early twenties, drops out of college to live in a seedy motel and work as a ticket taker in a rundown adult theater. The city is unnamed, and is probably an amalgamation of several places:

> *It is just another grim Eastern seaport collapsed in on itself with its own inertia, caving slowly into the dark heart at its center. It is a city full of rooms that rent by the week or the day or even the hour, and it is populated by the kind of people who would rent them; there are no families here, and no houses, and every day what respectable people there are move farther and farther away, where there are houses and families and respectable jobs and hobbies; they live in little developments built just for them, spreading outward from the city, like spores cast away from a plant.*

Though this place feels authentic, Nugent could choose her details, calibrating them to the feel of the story, without limiting herself to a literal place.

Perhaps you're using a place and time that doesn't exist, or hasn't . . . yet. Look at this passage from George Orwell's speculative novel *1984:*

> *The black moustachio'd face gazed down from every commanding corner. There was one on the house-front immediately opposite. BIG BROTHER IS WATCHING YOU, the caption said, while the dark eyes looked deep into Winston's own. Down at street level another poster, torn at one corner, flapped fitfully in the wind, alternately covering and uncovering the single word INGSOC. In the far distance a helicopter skimmed down between the roofs, hovered for an instant like a bluebottle, and darted away again with a curving flight. It was the police patrol, snooping into people's windows.*

The novel centers around Winston Smith, an average man who lives in Oceania, a totalitarian empire led by Big Brother. The setting isn't real, but the details certainly feel real. Here we have familiar sights—the flapping posters, the hovering helicopters—placed in an unfamiliar framework, helping to maintain an internal accuracy that rings true. If you find yourself creating settings that are only semirealistic, look for ways to blend the familiar with the fabricated to give your setting a sense of verisimilitude.

Even if you're creating a world that is wholly fantastical, as found in many works of science fiction and fantasy, you will still want the setting to *seem* real. Believe it or not, these kinds of settings usually demand more homework than any other kind of setting, if you really want your time and place to be convincing. While working on the great trilogy *The Lord of the Rings,* J.R.R Tolkien spent many years developing a complicated system of mythology and history, a detailed geography and a full set of maps, and the entirety of several languages (including Elvish) in order to build his imaginary world. The Hobbits didn't just live off in the ether of a fantasyland. They dwelled in a very specific place and time:

> *Forty leagues it stretched from the Far Downs to the Brandywine Bridge, and fifty from the northern moors to the marshes in the south. The Hobbits named it the Shire, as the region of the authority of their Thain and a district of well-ordered business; and there in that pleasant corner of the world they plied their well-ordered business of living, and they heeded less and less the world outside where dark things moved, until they came to think that peace and plenty were the rule in Middle-Earth and the right of all sensible folk.*

No wonder so many millions of readers seem to think this world really exists.

THE PACE OF TIME

The term *pacing* is often used to mean a number of different things in fiction, but here we're going to refer to it as the manipulation of time. The fiction writer becomes a sort of Tolkienesque wizard, able to manipulate time with the wave of a staff (or tap of the keyboard), and pacing is one of the great tools in the fiction writer's bag of tricks.

The most prevalent way you manipulate time is by compressing and expanding it to fit the needs of your story. Time passes for our characters, but the writer controls how quickly or slowly it flows. Writers do not show every moment of a plot, every instance in a character's life from birth until death, but instead speed through or skip over sections of time that are irrelevant to the story, while slowing down and expanding the sections that are most important.

If you move too quickly through an important section, the reader can feel disappointed or even confused. Likewise, if you move too slowly or dwell on irrelevant events, you can bore your reader. I bet you can remember skimming or even skipping over entire pages of a book, to "get to the good part." That was most likely because the writer slowed down the pace in a section where nothing of particular interest was happening. So pay attention to how important your scene is to the overall story, and pace it accordingly.

Do you want to see how time can be magically slowed down? Take a look at this section from Toni Morrison's *Sula,* in which Nell has just walked into her bedroom to find her husband, Jude, naked on the floor with her best friend:

> *I am just standing here. They are not doing that. I am just standing here and seeing it, but they are not really doing it. But then they did look up. Or you did. You did, Jude. And if only you had not looked at me the way the soldiers did on the train, the way you look at the children when they come in while you are listening to Gabriel Heatter and break your train of thought—not focusing exactly but giving them an instant, a piece of time, to remember what they are doing, what they are interrupting, and to go on back to wherever they were and let you listen to Gabriel Heatter. And I did not know how to move my feet or fix my eyes or what. I just stood there . . .*

This passage (which continues a while longer) covers only a few seconds of real time, but Morrison has slowed time to an excruciatingly slow pace to adequately reflect the horror of the moment in the narrator's mind. If you think about it, times of crisis do indeed seem to pass very slowly, each second exploding into an eternity. And as you can see, this is far more effective than telling readers about a character's emotions. *She felt shocked, betrayed, angry, and embarrassed* just doesn't give the reader the same kick to the heart. But by giving us every awful thought, Morrison makes us understand just how shocked and torn her protagonist is. Obviously not every moment in the story is handled with such depth and breadth, but this one deserved the attention it got.

> YOUR TURN:
> Recall the most frightening moment of your life. If it's too scary or recent, go for the second most frightening moment. Using yourself as a first-person narrator, write a passage about this moment. Chances are time slowed down for you as you were living that moment, so slow time way down as you describe this experience. Include minute details and the panoply of your thoughts. You may end up writing several pages about several seconds. Feel free to embellish, though you probably won't need to.

Let's look at how Raymond Carver handles pacing in "Cathedral."

After some initial exposition and a scene in the kitchen where the narrator and his wife argue, Carver jumps ahead to the blind man's arrival with:

So when the time rolled around, my wife went to the depot to pick him up. With nothing to do but wait—sure, I blamed him for that—I was having a drink and watching the TV when I heard the car pull into the drive. I got up from the sofa with my drink and went to the window to have a look.

Very quickly, we've cut to the important moment of Robert's arrival. Then we get a scene that covers the narrator meeting Robert and everyone sitting around having a drink (clearly not the narrator's first of the day). In the scene we fully observe the first part of the conversation, but Carver skillfully moves us through the cocktail hour (which probably included several rounds) with:

This blind man filled his ashtray and my wife emptied it.

It takes a while for even a chain smoker to fill an ashtray, so we get the sense that some time has passed, and then we cut to:

When we sat down at the table for dinner, we had another drink.

Then we get a longish summary of the dinner and corresponding conversation. Note that one of the chief ways pacing is achieved is by alternating scene and summary. Here the author has chosen summary over scene to move us more quickly through the expanse of the dinner, with things like this:

> *From time to time, he'd turn his blind face toward me, put his hand under his beard, ask me something. How long had I been in my present position? (Three years.) Did I like my work? (I didn't.) Was I going to stay with it? (What were my options?) Finally, when I thought he was beginning to run down, I got up and turned on the TV.*

And with that final line, we move on to the next stage of the evening, watching TV and drinking. In only seven pages, Carver has moved us through several hours and we don't feel we've missed anything important. We're also probably starting to feel a little drunk. Then we get a scene in which the narrator and Robert start watching television. After a little dialogue, we skip ahead further with:

> *After she'd left the room, he and I listened to the weather report and then to the sports roundup. By that time, she'd been gone so long I didn't know if she was going to come back.*

We sense they've watched some prime-time TV and are now into the news. The passing of time is now being reflected in the changing of the TV programs. Soon the news ends, the wife returns but promptly falls asleep on the couch, the narrator and Robert smoke some pot (while still drinking), and they end up watching some kind of documentary on "the church and the Middle Ages." It's beginning to feel like a long night—an aimless, drunken, stoned, claustrophobic night that is probably quite similar to most nights in this house. Then we make one more jump in time:

> *We didn't say anything for a time. He was leaning forward with his head turned at me, his right ear aimed in the direction of the set. Very disconcerting.*

The story is now approaching its apex—the narrator's transformation—and here Carver really slows down time and gives us a long scene that takes us through practically every moment of what happens, even following the details of the TV program:

> *The TV showed this one cathedral. Then there was a long, slow look at another one. Finally, the picture switched to the famous one in Paris, with its flying buttresses and its spires reaching up to the clouds.*

With agonizing slowness, we watch as the narrator vainly attempts to describe a cathedral, and, failing this, he attempts to draw one while the blind man places his hands on those of the narrator, and we hear pretty much everything that is spoken between these two men in this most dramatic of moments.

In fourteen pages, Carver has expertly taken us through a very long-seeming night in which a man's life is believably altered and every single sentence is both necessary and interesting. This is what pacing is all about.

Your pacing choices will be greatly affected by the length of your fictional work. In a short story, where there is a minimum of page "real estate," you'll need to be very choosy about what you show and don't show. With a novella or novel, you have more wiggle room, but even with a longer work you should ultimately be reluctant to include anything that doesn't have a significant impact on the tale being told. Think about your work as a whole, and plan how much time (and space) you'd like to spend on each part.

FLASHBACKS

And, yes, the fiction-writing wizard has another great trick in that he can move back and forth through time at will.

Flashbacks come in handy when there is a need to relate something that took place before the chosen time frame of the story. Instead of just having the narrator briefly allude to the event, you may want to show the event with some depth of detail, which will mean actually drifting back to the event.

"The Things They Carried" by Tim O'Brien follows the journey of a lieutenant in the Vietnam War. Though the story takes place entirely in Vietnam, the protagonist is continually wandering in his mind to memories of his tentative relationship with a young woman in New Jersey. While studying a picture of the woman:

Lieutenant Cross remembered touching that left knee. A dark theater, he remembered, and the movie was Bonnie and Clyde, *and Martha wore a red tweed skirt, and during the final scene, when he touched her knee, she turned and looked at him in a sad, sober way that made him pull his hand back, but he would always remember the feel of the tweed skirt and the knee beneath it and the sound of the gunfire that killed Bonnie and Clyde, how embarrassing it was, how slow and oppressive.*

Though the story is about Cross's experiences while in Vietnam, the periodic flashbacks give the reader a much fuller sense of all the "things" this man is carrying with him, mentally, as he wages war.

Flashbacks are usually better off not running too long, though they may include actual scenes of dialogue. But don't rely on them too much. If you find yourself needing pages and pages of flashbacks, you may have begun your story at the wrong point in time, in which case your story may take on a disjointed quality. Flashbacks can also be quite confusing to a reader unless you clearly delineate them, remembering to anchor them to the story's present. As with setting, you always want the readers to have a sense of where they *are*. And, as with anything, there are exceptions—stories, such as Toni Morrison's *Beloved,* that move fluidly through different time frames throughout the entire work. But such a feat requires a wizard of the highest order.

CHAPTER 8
VOICE: THE SOUND OF A STORY
BY HARDY GRIFFIN

When I started writing, I couldn't figure out what "voice" was, so I skipped it and spent my time learning how to create characters and plots out of nothing. I figured I'd just go ahead and write and use whatever "voice" showed up naturally.

That is, until my friend showed up instead and asked me to read some fiction in a reading series he was coordinating at the corner restaurant. Suddenly my little apartment was full of *my* nervous, frustrated, bewildered voice while I spent the better part of a week pacing from the sink to the couch and back, reading and editing a simple three-page story about a young man (half me and half fiction) at his grandparents' house for Thanksgiving. Nothing sounded right, from the Southern accents to the lemon meringue pie to the fireflies in the deep blue dusk.

I stepped into the exposed-brick basement of the restaurant where the reading was and got a gin and tonic right away (for the Southern accents, you understand). It was packed and I was freaked out. But when my turn came and I stood in front of everyone and started reading, something happened. The thing in my hands didn't feel like my story so much as my narrator's story, as if the words on the page had come together and formed a new person who was speaking and who the audience in the café wanted to listen to.

Three things popped out at me about voice after that night. First of all, the voice of a piece is what makes it special, what sets it apart and makes it feel lived. On the other hand, voice isn't half as ephemeral as critics and academics make it sound. But most important, it's essential that your narrative voice sounds natural. Your storyteller should be relaxed and absorbed in the fiction so your readers can be too. That's what worked in my piece for the reading—even while *I* was in a sweat, my narrator's voice was completely involved in telling the story.

But what *is* this mysterious thing, voice?

One of my favorite oxymorons is the often-repeated phrase "a writer's voice." Just how much sound can a bunch of black marks on a piece of paper make, anyway? I don't know about you, but the only sounds I make as I'm writing are the tap of the keys and various inarticulate groans. Obviously these aren't the voices that readers, academics, and critics are always talking about.

Simply put, voice is what readers "hear" in their heads when they're reading. Voice is the "sound" of the story.

In every strong work of fiction, one voice rises above the din to unify the piece and lead the reader through the thicket of characters' voices. This voice is the most important for the simple reason that, after finishing a good story or novel, it's this overarching voice which continues to ring in the reader's mind. And yes, you guessed it—the voice of a story is the voice of the narrator.

My fiction students often get confused between the voice of a piece and the writer's voice, and with good reason. If a number of works by the same author have a similar tone, then people often lump them together as that writer's voice or style. However, the best thing you, as a writer, can do is to concentrate on the narrator's voice of each individual piece of your fiction. Someday, a critic may see what your varied works have in common and write an admiring article that defines what your voice as a writer is like. Until then, your job is to focus on the voice in each individual story.

TYPES OF VOICE

The amazing truth is that your chosen voice can take an infinite variety of "sounds." So how do you pick what kind of voice to give your narrator?

More than anything else, your choice of voice is related to your point-of-view choice. If you're using a first-person narrator, then your voice will need to match the personality of that particular character. If you're using a second- or third-person narrator, then the narrator will be a storyteller, who may or may not sound like you. Also, the sound of the second- or third-person narrator will be affected by the emotional distance with which this narrator is telling the story. A first-person narrator will naturally tell a story in a way that is close to the action because he or she is inside the story. But this isn't the case with a second- or third-person narrator. Such narrators may be emotionally close to the characters, as in a first-person POV, or they may be telling the story from a more remote distance, as if they are standing outside the story's events, like those broadcasters on TV commenting on the golf match in whispered, reverant tones.

To help you get a sense of your voice options, let's break voice into several general types. Although these titles aren't as official as those for POV, placing voices into general types can help you make choices about your voice and also help you tell if a story has drifted from its originally intended route.

CONVERSATIONAL VOICE

Everybody knows somebody whom they don't have to dress up for, whether this person is a close friend or family member. Just like it sounds, the conversational voice feels a lot like the narrator is having a casual conversation with the reader.

Mark Twain's *The Adventures of Huckleberry Finn* is a prime example:

> *You don't know about me without you have read a book by the name of* The Adventures of Tom Sawyer; *but that ain't no matter. That book was made by Mr. Mark Twain, and he told the truth mainly. There was things which he stretched but mainly he told the truth. That is nothing. I never seen anybody but lied one time or another, without it was Aunt Polly, or the widow, or maybe Mary.*

Here Twain believably captures the voice of a hillbilly kid, namely Huckleberry Finn. Before *Huck* appeared on the shelves in 1885, most fiction had an elevated voice, but Twain threw all that away and truly let Huck speak for himself. The result is one of the most nonpretentious and entertaining voices in all literature.

J. D. Salinger's *The Catcher in the Rye* also belongs in this category:

> *If you really want to hear about it, the first thing you'll probably want to know is where I was born, and what my lousy childhood was like, and*

how my parents were occupied and all before they had me, and all that David Copperfield kind of crap, but I don't feel like going into it, if you want to know the truth.

You can probably guess from these first couple of lines that the voice is that of a personable and often sarcastic teenager. As we find out at the end of the novel, Holden Caulfield has been telling his story to a psychiatrist the whole time, which is exactly how the narrative sounds, as if a real person is speaking his mind.

Another example is Dorothy Parker's "The Waltz." Here a woman agrees to dance with a man when she doesn't want to, and then she starts to think about what she could have said instead of agreeing:

I most certainly will not dance with you, I'll see you in hell first. Why, thank you, I'd like to awfully, but I'm having labor pains. Oh, yes, do let's dance together—it's so nice to meet a man who isn't a scaredy-cat about catching my beri-beri. No. There was nothing for me to do, but say I'd adore to. Well, we might as well get it over with. All right, Cannonball, let's run out on the field. You won the toss; you can lead.

Most of the story is made up of this woman's sarcastic thoughts as she struggles with her dance partner, tearing him to pieces in her mind but every now and then exchanging pleasantries with him out loud.

> YOUR TURN:
> Take the above passage from Dorothy Parker's "The Waltz." Rewrite and expand it using the third-person objective point of view. Remember, in the objective POV you don't enter the minds of characters. You simply show the action, as it's been recorded by a journalist. In fact, keep the writing very dry and factual, distant from the actual emotions of the woman. But strive to convey the woman's thoughts solely through her actions and, if you desire, dialogue. Then compare your version with Parker's, noting how the same event can be told with very diverse voices.

The conversational voice is almost always in the first person and it usually employs colloquial speech patterns and slang. So a conversational voice would opt for *See, this woman's following me, like she has for the past two whole weeks* rather than *Two weeks ago, a woman started following me, and I saw her again behind me today.*

The great thing about this voice is that you can let your first-person narrators go full throttle with their personalities. And they can pretty much tell the reader anything. Which can also be the downside. If you're not careful, it may sound like your narrator is blabbing out all her intimate details for no good reason.

INFORMAL VOICE

You can dress down, but at least tuck in that shirt. Informal voice is a fairly broad category that's not as casual as the conversational voice, but it also doesn't quite have the dressed-up feel of the more formal voices.

Take Raymond Carver's "Cathedral" for example:

> *I remembered having read somewhere that the blind didn't smoke because, as speculation had it, they couldn't see the smoke they exhaled. I thought I knew that much and that much only about blind people. But this blind man smoked his cigarette down to the nubbin and then lit another one.*

See how this first-person narrator isn't as chatty or colloquial as the conversational narrators, but at the same time, he's an average sort of guy who drinks, smokes pot, and thinks he knows only one thing about blind people before a blind friend of his wife's comes to visit.

Another example in the first person is John Cheever's "Goodbye, My Brother":

> *I don't think about the family much, but when I remember its members and the coast where they lived and the sea salt that I think is in our blood, I am happy to recall that I am a Pommeroy—that I have the nose, the coloring, and the promise of longevity—and that while we are not a distinguished family, we enjoy the illusion, when we are together, that the Pommeroys are unique.*

The secondary-school teacher who narrates this piece strikes a balance between the "blue-blooded" roots of his family and the openness of revealing the family's problems. The informal voice allows this line to be walked.

In the informal voice, the narrator uses casual, everyday language but isn't as personality-heavy as the conversational. But, as you can see in the difference between the Carver and Cheever examples, there's a lot of leeway in what can make up casual language for different narrators.

This informality can also come through with a third-person narrator. Check out how Amy Bloom's "Song of Solomon" has a similar voice to the Carver story:

> *Sarah had stopped sucking a little sooner than usual, and Kate was so grateful she sang to her all the way through burping. Everything went smoothly; little Sarah, stoned from nursing, was completely content to lie in her crib and murmur to the world. Kate dressed like a surgeon prepping, precise and careful in every movement. She checked her watch again. Twenty-five minutes to get to the temple.*

Though the narrator isn't a character, the voice sounds rather like that of a real person, someone we might know relating a story to us in their living room. And Bloom's relatively close third-person narrator conveys Kate's slightly nervous actions and thoughts, but isn't so close to Kate as not to convey a sense of the child's serenity. A first-person narrator would not have maintained quite as much balance between the emotions of Kate and the baby.

Let's return to an example that appeared in chapter 4, from "Earth to Molly" by Elizabeth Tallent. Here you'll see an informal third-person narrator who inches very close, emotionally, to the POV character:

> *Molly was sorry for having needed her to climb the stairs, but of course the old woman complained her stiff-legged way up them all the time, showing lodgers to their rooms. Why, oh why, would anyone spend the night here? A prickly gray carpet ran tightly from wall to wall. It was the color of static, and seemed as hateful.*

Here the voice of the third-person narrator sounds pretty similar to the voice Molly might use if she were telling this story herself in the first person. If you use a third-person informal narrator, you'll usually want to make this narrator somewhat close, or very close, to the emotions of the POV characters. Otherwise your readers will feel like someone's just told them to make themselves at home in a living room packed with priceless antiques.

The main advantage of the informal voice is that it's middle of the road. If you're working in the first person but don't want the narrator's voice to dominate the story, this is a good pick. It's also a good pick if you're working in the third or second person but don't want to sound too much like a "writer."

Actually, it's hard to go wrong with the informal voice, and for this reason it's probably the most commonly used voice in contemporary fiction.

FORMAL VOICE

Even the word *formal* makes me think of some boarding-school prom night with a row of girls in strapless heels and boys in navy suits, but in practice, the formal voice doesn't have to be awkward at all.

In the old days most all fiction leaned toward the formal, as in this example from Leo Tolstoy's "Master and Man":

> *Suddenly a weird, startling cry sounded in his very ears, and everything beneath him seemed to heave and tremble. He clutched the horse's mane, yet found that that too was quivering, while the cry grew ever more and more piercing.*

As you can see, the formal voice doesn't have the same chattiness or spoken-story qualities of the conversational or informal, often conveying, instead, a certain detachment from the characters. In this passage, even though the man is panicked and on the edge of death from freezing, the third-person narrator stays fairly observational. You'll see what I mean if you compare how close you feel to this narrator's emotions with those of Huck Finn or Holden Caulfield.

This kind of dressed-up style can work in contemporary fiction too. If you're working on an epic story that, say, covers multiple generations, a number of locations, and a large cast of characters, the formal voice is a good bet because it lends itself to the story's "big screen" sweep.

Look at the opening to Gabriel García Márquez's *One Hundred Years of Solitude:*

> *Many years later, as he faced the firing squad, Colonel Aureliano Buendía was to remember that distant afternoon when his father took him to discover ice. At that time Macondo was a village of twenty adobe houses, built on the bank of a river of clear water that ran along a bed of polished stones, which were white and enormous, like prehistoric eggs. The world was so recent that many things lacked names, and in order to indicate them it was necessary to point.*

As the novel moves back and forth over a century of one family's development, strange, detailed, and beautiful descriptions of Macondo village put the reader in the setting, rather than sticking us with a single character. Which is a good thing because Márquez ends up using more than twenty major characters. And the formal voice gives the book the depth and importance of a historical (albeit fanciful) chronicle.

The formal voice is perhaps most commonly found in the third-person POV, but it's not restricted to this. It can work with the first person as long as the first-person narrator has a formal enough personality.

For example, Humbert Humbert, the narrator of Vladimir Nabokov's *Lolita,* is the son of the owner of a luxury hotel on the French Riviera. Early in the novel, we discover that Humbert attended a good English school and later became a literature scholar. So it's certainly fitting that he speaks in a formal tone, to the point of pretentiousness:

> *And less than six inches from me and my burning life, was nebulous Lolita! After a long stirless vigil, my tentacles moved towards her again, and this time the creak of the mattress did not awake her. I managed to bring my ravenous bulk so close to her that I felt the aura of her bare shoulder like a warm breath upon my cheek.*

Very few people actually sound like this, but Humbert Humbert happens to be one of the people who does.

Another example is the voice of Nick Carraway in F. Scott Fitzgerald's *The Great Gatsby.* Nick is also well educated enough to pull off the formal voice. Here he is describing his first glimpse of Jay Gatsby:

> *The silhouette of a moving cat wavered across the moonlight, and turning my head to watch it, I saw that I was not alone—fifty feet away a figure had emerged from the shadow of my neighbor's mansion and was standing with his hands in his pockets regarding the silver pepper of the stars. Something in his leisurely movements and the secure position of his feet upon the lawn suggested that it was Mr. Gatsby himself, come out to determine what share was his of our local heavens.*

It's worth noting that Nick's observations are distant enough that he sounds more like the writer than a distinctive character, and this could almost be switched into the third person. But then we would lose the sense of Nick as a witness to the story's events.

Go for the formal voice if you want a certain high style in your prose, but make sure you're not just trying to sound like a writer and, if you're using this voice for a first-person narrator, make sure it's someone more likely to write with a Montblanc pen than a chewed-up pencil.

> YOUR TURN:
> Two cars collide at an intersection. Write a brief passage describing this event from the POV of a teenager, then again from the POV of a socialite, then again from the POV of a cowboy type. You decide how these characters were involved in the collision. In all cases, let the character be a first-person narrator. So pick the voice type—conversational, informal, or formal—that seems most appropriate for your narrator. Conversational may work well for the teenager, but then that depends on your teenager, doesn't it? Whatever you come up with, each passage should sound different from the others because these are three very different characters.

CEREMONIAL VOICE

You'll have to get your tux out of storage if you want to be the master of ceremonial. A good way to get into the mind-set of this voice is to imagine you're old Abe Lincoln about to give "The Gettysburg Address": "Four score and seven years ago, our forefathers . . ."

You wouldn't think that ceremonial voice would come into play very much in fiction, but many writers have used it to great effect. Take this passage from Charles Dickens's *Oliver Twist:*

> *Oliver Twist's ninth birthday found him a pale thin child, somewhat diminutive in stature, and decidedly small in circumference. But nature or inheritance had implanted a good sturdy spirit in Oliver's breast: it had had plenty of room to expand, thanks to the spare diet of the establishment; and perhaps to this circumstance may be attributed his having any ninth birthday at all.*

Look at how detached this narrator is. Basically, Oliver's starving and abused, and the only thing that's kept him alive up to his ninth birthday is his spirit, but the narrator's far enough from the boy's suffering to be half-joking about how empty his stomach is. But perhaps this kind of mocking ceremonial is what allows the reader to absorb Oliver's painful, bleak story over the course of the novel's four-hundred-plus pages.

At the same time, the following passage from Gertrude Stein's *Melanctha,* a novella about a black woman's life in Bridgeport, Connecticut, around the turn of the twentieth century, shows a different side of ceremonial:

> *Melanctha Herbert was always losing what she had in wanting all the things she saw. Melanctha was always being left when she was not leaving others.*
>
> *Melanctha Herbert always loved too hard and much too often. She was always full with mystery and subtle movements and denials and vague distrusts and complicated disillusions. Then Melanctha would be sudden and impulsive and unbounded in some faith, and then she would suffer and be strong in her repression.*
>
> *Melanctha Herbert was always seeking rest and quiet, and always she could only find new ways to be in trouble.*

Stein creates an almost biblical rhythm through the repetitious language and the odd sentence phrasing. By using a ceremonial voice, the narrator elevates Melanctha Herbert's life nearly to the level of a prophet, and her struggles suddenly don't appear to the reader as worthless or squalid in this light.

Just as conversational is hardly ever in the third person, it's also quite rare to find a first-person ceremonial narrator. The advantage of the ceremonial voice is that it slows the reader down, giving a great sense of occasion and importance to the story. The disadvantage is that it can seem stilted and suppress the story's energy.

OTHER VOICES

Once again, let me say that these voice types are just arbitrary terms to help you get a sense of the options and to help you stay on track. Really, the voice of a story can take on any conceivable "sound" as long as you have a reason for it. Literature is filled with unusual voices that don't fit anywhere on my clothesline of types.

Take, for instance, Helen Fielding's *Bridget Jones's Diary:*

> *TUESDAY 3 JANUARY*
> *130 lbs. (terrifying slide into obesity—why? why?), alcohol units 6 (excellent), cigarettes 23 (v.g.), calories 2472.*

9 A.M. Ugh. Cannot face thought of going to work. Only thing which makes it tolerable is thought of seeing Daniel again, but even that is inadvisable since am fat, have spot on chin, and desire only to sit on cushion eating chocolate and watching Xmas specials.

The unique voice here comes from the fact that the whole book is written as a diary, the diary of a contemporary, smart, and somewhat neurotic thirty-something woman. It's very casual and often quite embarrassing, as you would expect from a diary.

A voice can become lyrical to the point of sounding a lot like pure poetry. Listen to the narrator of Jack Kerouac's *On the Road*:

The only people for me are the mad ones, the ones who are mad to live, mad to talk, mad to be saved, desirous of everything at the same time, the ones who never yawn or say a commonplace thing but burn, burn, burn like fabulous yellow roman candles exploding like spiders across the stars and in the middle you see the blue centerlight pop and everybody goes "Awww!"

Here the narrator is a soul-searching, usually inebriated beatnik (with a beatnik's bent for the poetic). You can almost see this guy stumbling and rambling drunkenly down the street.

Such poetry can stretch even further into stream of consciousness, where the writer attempts to portray a character's thoughts in the random manner in which they play through the human mind. The final chapter of James Joyce's *Ulysses* consists of a forty-five-page sentence that careens through the mind of Molly Bloom. To save paper, I'll just show the end of it:

. . .he kissed me under the Moorish wall and I thought well as well him as another and then I asked him with my eyes to ask again yes and then he asked me would I yes to say yes my mountain flower and first I put my arms around him yes and drew him down to me so he could feel my breasts all perfume yes and his heart was going like mad and yes I said yes I will Yes.

No, those aren't typos in there. Remember, there is no editor in the deeper recesses of the psyche.

Is this getting weird enough? We can perhaps get even weirder. Take a gander at this from Anthony Burgess's *A Clockwork Orange*:

The chelloveck sitting next to me, there being this long big plushy seat that ran round three walls, was well away with his glazzies glazed and sort of burbling slovos like "Aristotle wishy washy works outoing cyclamen get forficulate smartish."

Huh? What? Relax, you're not going crazy. This novel is set in the future and the writer has created a whole new vocabulary (a mix of hallucinogenic and Slavic) to suit the time and the personality of the narrator.

> YOUR TURN:
> Return to something you have written, perhaps from a previous exercise. Rewrite a portion of it using a different voice. You may do something simple, like shifting from formal to informal. Or you might want to try something fun, like using a voice reminiscent of, say, a film noir detective story or a fairy tale. Or you may go for stream of consciousness. To accommodate the new voice, you might end up using a different POV. Look for a voice that will shed an interesting light on your story.

STYLE

You've seen a number of authors parading before you and you've checked out their checks, plaids, and stripes. Now it's time to hit the sweatshop floor and see just how these voice-suits are put together.

People often use the terms *voice* and *style* interchangeably, but there's an enormous difference from the writer's perspective. Style consists of various technical choices made by a writer, and the voice is the sum result of those choices. If voice is the velvet dress, style is the fabrics, threads, buttons, and such that create the garment.

The dirty truth is that a piece's voice is created by the most elemental tools in writing—namely, what words you pick, how you string them together in a sentence, and how you mix and match your sentences to form paragraphs. Hemingway used short sentences. Short sentences and repetition. Dorothy Parker liked to throw around the slang, know what I mean. Nabokov favored amplitudinous words. Though these things may seem very technical, you'll see just how closely stylistic choices relate to the personality of the narrator and the story's content. So let's take a look at how to use these very handy tools of style.

WORDS

To see how deeply word choice, often known as diction, affects voice, consider the following two examples that both deal with a first-person narrator musing on sleep. First up is Haruki Murakami's "Sleep":

> *All I wanted was to throw myself down and sleep. But I couldn't. The wakefulness was always there beside me. I could feel its chilling shadow. It was the shadow of myself. Weird, I would think as the drowsiness overtook me, I'm in my own shadow. I would walk and eat and talk to people inside my drowsiness . . .*

Here, Murakami has used an informal voice for this man who's remembering his casual life at university. Murakami opts for everyday one- or two-syllable words, except for *wakefulness* and *drowsiness,* for which there aren't any options with fewer syllables. And I'll take these two words as random examples of how nearly everything in this quote is informal: imagine if he had switched *wakefulness* and *drowsiness* for *insomnia* and *lassitude*—these new choices would have shoved the narration right out of the informal voice and into something more formal for no apparent reason.

Look at the passage again, and watch how every word is short, to the point, and fits with a certain kind of jerky insomnia. You can feel how the narrator's movements are quick and even stunted from his lack of sleep through his simple words. *Weird* pops out as an almost conversational word, and the slight jump in voice adds to the jittery quality of the prose.

Now compare this with the opening to John Updike's "Falling Asleep Up North":

> *Falling asleep has never struck me as a very natural thing to do. There is a surreal trickiness to traversing that inbetween area, when the grip of consciousness is slipping but has not quite let go and curious mutated thoughts pass as normal cogitation unless snapped into clear light by a creaking door, one's bed partner twitching, or the prematurely jubilant realization, I'm falling asleep. The little fumbling larvae of nonsense that precede dreams' uninhibited butterflies are disastrously exposed to a light*

they cannot survive, and one must begin again, relaxing the mind into unravelling.

Throw a dart into that paragraph and chances are you'll hit a three-syllable word. This narrator uses the formal voice, marking him as a different type of person from the one in the previous example. Such words as *traversing, cogitation,* and *larvae* would feel out of place in the Murakami piece, but they feel quite natural here.

The words also help to show how the insomnia of Murakami's narrator is different from that of the Updike narrator; the former is much more zombie-esque in the way he stumbles about, having no energy to sound impressive, while the narrator in the Updike story is concentrating wholly on the act of falling asleep, and all the fancy words and modifiers help to show his obsessive personality.

Choosing the right words basically boils down to this: know your narrator and what sorts of words this person is inclined to use and make sure your word choices are working with the general type of voice that you have chosen. But don't worry about it too much as you're writing away. You can always go back and take out any incongruous fellas that sneak in.

SENTENCES

Words alone don't create the voice; how they're thrown together into a sentence is what really gives writing its flow. I'll tell you something surprising: how you place words in a sentence is the most important stylistic choice you'll make.

A sentence is just a new thought, although that can mean anything from a one-word fragment sentence to a twisting, Route 66 of a sentence. And then within any given sentence there are a thousand things that can happen. But your choices with sentences come down to two basic things: sentence length, and the structure of the sentence, which is often called syntax.

Let's check out the difference between how Hemingway and Fitzgerald handled sentences. These two contemporary writers are both credited as being voices for the Lost Generation of Americans in the years shortly after World War I. Both Hemingway's novel-in-stories, *In Our Time,* and Fitzgerald's short story "May Day" focus on the end of the war and how it affected individuals and society as a whole.

Here's the opening of Fitzgerald's "May Day":

*There had been a war fought and won and the great city of the conquering
people was crossed with triumphal arches and vivid with thrown flowers
of white, red, and rose. All through the long spring days the returning
soldiers marched up the chief highway behind the strump of drums and
the joyous, resonant wind of the brasses, while merchants and clerks left
their bickerings and figurings and, crowding to the windows, turned their
white-bunched faces gravely upon the passing battalions.*

These long, grandiose sentences almost give the writing a mythic quality.
Fitzgerald's third-person narrator picks up right after the war's end on the
night of May 1, in the midst of the victory festivities. He uses an expansive
writing style as his narrator hops among the celebrations and sufferings
of multiple main characters—an expansive voice precisely because "May
Day" is a mini-epic, a collage encompassing half a dozen of the thousands
of stories packed into ten blocks in New York City on a given night. The
long sentences reflect the mythic quality of the occasion and the busyness
of the festivities.

The sentences are also long because Fitzgerald loads them with plenty
of adjectives. (Clearly, Fitzgerald did not agree with Henry David Thoreau's
famous advice to writers: "As to adjective: when in doubt, strike it out." Either
that or Fitzgerald didn't have any doubts.) For his narrator he has chosen
a florid language to match all the flowers and parades, and you can feel the
mood of this *great city* through the modifiers he's chosen, such as *conquering,
triumphal,* and *joyous, resonant wind of the brasses.* And he has used a
somewhat complex sentence structure to accommodate all the pomp.

Now contrast this with Hemingway's description of soldiers marching
under the spell of a different kind of happiness:

*Everybody was drunk. The whole battery was drunk going along the road
in the dark . . . We went along the road all night in the dark and the
adjutant kept riding up alongside my kitchen and saying, "You must put
it out. It is dangerous. It will be observed." We were fifty kilometers from
the front but the adjutant worried about the fire in my kitchen. It was
funny going along that road. That was when I was a kitchen corporal.*

First, you'll notice shorter sentences. In roughly the same amount of space,
Fitzgerald uses two sentences and Hemingway uses eight. Admittedly, this
is partially just a stylistic difference between the two writers, but it's also

shaped by the differences in these two pieces. Hemingway's first-person narrator, Nick, fights in World War I and then travels around aimlessly after the war—shell-shocked and withdrawn from the company of other human beings, finding solace only in the natural world. No wonder his sentences are short and spare.

There also isn't a single adverb, and you can count the adjectives on one hand. Hemingway's narrator keeps all of his sentences simple—simple structure and simple words, from the adjectives—*drunk, whole, funny*—to the verbs—*was, went, kept, put.*

Whether you lean toward short or long sentences as a rule, you always want to make sure that you vary your sentence lengths once in a while. If all your sentences are exactly the same length, your reader will get bored pretty quickly, just as you would if you were talking to someone who said:

> *I went to the store and bought some milk. I saw a man I knew in aisle 4. We spoke about the price of figs and fish.*

Even if the next sentence is a real eye-opener, like *I wondered about his two-headed child,* the reader may skim right over it because the unchanging length has lulled her into a kind of reading trance.

Which brings us to the question of rhythm. Working together, sentence length and syntax often create a rhythm, and you can manipulate this rhythm to great effect. Look at this passage from Hemingway's *The Old Man and the Sea:*

> *The shark's head was out of the water and his back was coming out and the old man could hear the noise of skin and flesh ripping on the big fish when he rammed the harpoon down onto the shark's head at a spot where the line between his eyes intersected with the line that ran straight back from his nose. There were no such lines. There was only the heavy sharp blue head and the big eyes and the clicking, thrusting all-swallowing jaws.*

Here Ernest went for an especially long sentence, and a bucket-load of adjectives. Both the length of that long sentence and the structure of it, piling one thing on top of another, give a rhythm that reflects the confusion and action of this struggle between man and fish. Also notice how well Hemingway mixes up his sentence lengths, following the long sentence with a short and then a medium sentence.

Let's look at a passage from James Baldwin's "Sonny's Blues." This story is narrated by a schoolteacher whose brother, Sonny, is a jazz musician who struggles with heroin addiction and goes to prison for a short time. At the end of the story, the narrator goes to watch Sonny play his first jazz gig after he's been released from prison, and for five beautiful pages, Baldwin ushers the reader into the jazz bar and Sonny's blues:

> *Sonny's fingers filled the air with life, his life. But that life contained so many others. And Sonny went all the way back, he really began with the spare, flat statement of the opening phrase of the song. Then he began to make it his. It was very beautiful because it wasn't hurried and it was no longer a lament. I seemed to hear with what burning he had made it his, with what burning we had yet to make it ours, how we could cease lamenting. Freedom lurked around us and I understood, at last, that he could help us to be free if we would listen, that he would never be free until we did.*

Baldwin plays with rhythm throughout this passage, using longer and shorter sentences with a lot of strategic word repetitions. Not only that, but the narrator enhances the sentence rhythms by manipulating the sound of the words.

See how alliteration affects this sentence, letting the reader practically hear Sonny's breath coming faster as he works the music:

> *Sonny's Fingers Filled the air with liFe, his liFe.*

And check out this sentence that comes later:

> *I seemed to hear with what burning he had made it his . . .*

Notice how the words sound like a pair of brushes sweeping the snare drum. At first, the words begin with soft letters—*s, t, h, w*—until we get to the harder *b* in *burning* and the *d*s in *had* and *made*. Then comes the second half of the sentence:

> *. . . with what burning we had yet to make it ours, how we could cease lamenting.*

Here it seems the drum is being tapped. The *b* and *d* sounds repeat in the next phrase, except that the *b* and *d* come sooner, and then we get the drawn-out sound of *yet* followed by the hard *k* sound in *make* and *could*.

Okay, all right, maybe this is a bit much, but you can see how there's a rhythmic quality to Baldwin's sentences that matches the jazz club and, more importantly, the narrator's respect for Sonny's struggle and his music.

PARAGRAPHS

The length of your paragraphs also has a big influence on voice. As with sentences, you want to vary the length of your paragraphs to prevent a sense of stagnation or predictability. But beyond that, you can manipulate the feel of your voice by leaning toward long, winding paragraphs or short, snappy ones or somewhere in between.

Generally a new paragraph signals a shift in thought, either major or minor, or a jump in time or space. But there is a lot of room for interpretation on when you want to make these paragraph shifts. Some writers may cram a bunch of thought shifts into a single paragraph while other writers may separate each thought in a new paragraph. Similarly, you could move freely through time and space in a single paragraph or use a new one for each shift.

You can see what I mean in the first paragraph of Joyce Carol Oates's "The Fine Mist of Winter." Right off the bat, the author has made clear decisions about the paragraph (and sentence) lengths that set up the voice for the whole piece:

> *Some time ago in Eden County the sheriff's best deputy, Rafe Murray, entered what he declared to the sheriff, and to his own wife and man-grown sons, and to every person he encountered for a month, white or black, to be his second period—his new period, he would say queerly, sucking at his upper lip with a series of short, damp, deliberate noises. He was thirty-eight when he had the trouble with Bethl'em Aire, he would say, thirty-eight and with three man-grown sons behind him; but he had had his eyes opened only on that day; he was born on that day; he meant to keep it fresh in his mind. When the long winter finally ended and the roads were thick and shapeless with mud, shot with sunlight, the Negro Bethl'em and his memory had both disappeared from Eden County, and—to everyone's relief, especially his wife's—from Murray's mind too. But up until then, in those thick, gray, mist-choked days, he did keep what had happened fresh in his mind; memories of the fine driving snow that fell on that particular day, and of his great experience, seemed to recur again and again in his thoughts.*

This paragraph containing several thought shifts and one time shift could easily have been broken into two or more paragraphs. Throughout the story, the twisting, rambling voice (shown often with long paragraphs) contrasts with the simple life that the people of Eden County enjoy (shown with dialogue and humdrum actions). Oates has also made a decision regarding time throughout the piece in the first paragraph by not splitting the previous winter and the current springtime into two separate paragraphs. You can sense that time's a bit fluid in this piece because even as Murray has forgotten the day that began *his second period*, the narrator hasn't—and the narrator makes sure to circle back to it.

At the other extreme, you shouldn't be afraid of using short or even one-line paragraphs.

For example, the main characters in Arundhati Roy's *The God of Small Things* are a twin sister and brother who are so close that one can recall the other's dreams. But as children, they become separated. Have a look at how the short paragraphs (and sentences) work soon after brother and sister are reunited as adults:

> *But what was there to say?*
>
> *From where he sat, at the end of the bed, Estha, without turning his head, could see her. Faintly outlined. The sharp line of her jaw. Her collarbones like wings that spread from the base of her throat to the ends of her shoulders. A bird held down by skin.*
> *She turned her head and looked at him. He sat very straight. Waiting for the inspection. He had finished the ironing.*
>
> *She was lovely to him. Her hair. Her cheeks. Her small, clever-looking hands.*
>
> *His sister.*

You can feel the push and pull of the siblings' intimacy and awkwardness simply through the spaces between the paragraphs. Then the last paragraph—containing only two words—stands out dramatically, as if it were a tear on his cheek and yet not so melodramatic.

These short paragraphs have a dramatic feel to them. Contrast the punch each one carries with the descriptive winding of the earlier Oates example. In each piece, the general paragraph lengths are largely determining the quality of the voice's energy. Oates gives a circuitous discussion, while Roy is blunt to the point of being brutal.

Another use of paragraph breaks is to separate narration from dialogue.

This shifting between narration and dialogue also offers an interesting energy to a story's voice because the narration and dialogue often have different levels of language from each other. Either the language of the narration is more formal than the dialogue or vice versa.

Take Virginia Woolf's story "Kew Gardens." In the following passage, you can see how a simple, nearly laughable conversation between a young woman and man in love can be turned into an interchange of great (and almost lewd) importance:

> *"Lucky it isn't Friday," he observed.*
> *"Why? D'you believe in luck?"*
> *"They make you pay sixpence on Friday."*
> *"What's sixpence anyway? Isn't it worth sixpence?"*
> *"What's 'it'—what do you mean by 'it'?"*
> *"O, anything—I mean—you know what I mean."*
> *Long pauses came between each of these remarks; they were uttered in toneless and monotonous voices. The couple stood still on the edge of the flower-bed, and together pressed the end of her parasol deep down into the soft earth. The action and the fact that his hand rested on the top of hers expressed their feelings in a strange way, as these short insignificant words also expressed something, words with short wings for their heavy body of meaning, inadequate to carry them far and thus alighting awkwardly upon the very common objects that surrounded them, and were to their inexperienced touch so massive; but who knows (so they thought as they pressed the parasol into the earth) what precipices aren't concealed in them, or what slopes of ice don't shine in the sun on the other side?*

Who knew you could get so much out of pushing an umbrella into the earth and a simple conversation about a park entrance fee? And the beauty of the story is that it's all like this—spare conversations are reinvented by the narrator as deep connections are made between different pairs of people. The dynamic tension between what's actually said and the narrator's elegant interpretation continuously gives off interesting sparks.

YOUR TURN:
Find an annoyingly dry and difficult piece of writing, preferably a legal document or a manual for some kind of appliance or equipment. Then rewrite the piece, turning the writing around 180 degrees, making it

ecstatically poetic or down-home friendly or anything else you like. Use the third person. But employ drastically different words and sentences and paragraphs than found in the original document. You'll begin to see the profound effect of stylistic choices. And you will certainly provide a more entertaining document than the original.

CONSISTENCY

In addition to being determined from words, sentences, and paragraphs, voice is a result of every type of choice made in a work of fiction, sticking its dexterous fingers in every slice of the larger craft-element pie. Is there a lot of description or are there just a few telling details? Is the language filled with imagery and poetic devices or is it straightforward? Are the characters described from their hair to their shoes, or is a lot left to the reader's imagination? How many characters are there, a multitude or a few? Does the story have a plot with tight curves, or does the plot seem to be almost meandering? What's the balance of dialogue and narrative?

It's important that all of these elements coalesce into a unified voice. The key is consistency. As with POV, you make an unwritten agreement with the reader about how the general voice of the piece is going to sound. Readers like the sense that someone is telling them a story and they want the same storyteller to be there at all times, unless you are using a multiple-vision POV. If the narrator seems to change unwittingly from Uncle Remus to Ishmael in the middle of the tale, the reader will become confused, and, worse, the reader will stop believing any of it.

Unless . . . you purposely take a leap away from the original voice to achieve a certain effect. The narrator won't necessarily change to another narrator, but he may change his voice to suit the moment. A great example of this is found in J. D. Salinger's "A Perfect Day for Bananafish." The story begins with the following satirical voice:

> *There were ninety-seven New York advertising men in the hotel, and, the way they were monopolizing the long-distance lines, the girl in 507 had to wait from noon till almost two-thirty to get her call through. She used the time, though. She read an article in a women's pocket-size magazine, called "Sex Is Fun—or Hell."*

This woman, you discover, is the fiancée of the main character, Seymour

Glass. Most of the story focuses on Seymour as he jokes around with a little girl that he runs into on the beach. The voice continues in the same witty vein as the beginning until the narrator starts to walk back to the hotel. At that point, Seymour changes, moving into a much less humorous frame of mind, and the third-person narrator makes the shift with him. Check out how different the voice has become once Seymour comes into the hotel room:

> *He glanced at the girl lying asleep on one of the twin beds. Then he went over to one of the pieces of luggage, opened it, and from under a pile of shorts and undershirts he took out an Ortgies calibre 7.65 automatic. He released the magazine, looked at it, then reinserted it. He cocked the piece. Then he went over and sat down on the unoccupied twin bed, looked at the girl, aimed the pistol, and fired a bullet through his right temple.*

The quick turn in the voice shocks the reader, and works with the action.

FINDING YOUR VOICE

Salinger, ceremonial, Parker, Hemingway, Murakami, chellovecks—all these voice choices are probably about to melt your brain. But don't get all discombobulated. The biggest key to voice is not worrying about it.

Bad style often comes when a writer is trying too hard to imitate the style of other writers. You can and should admire and study the works of other writers, but if you find yourself writing in the voice of Charles Dickens or John Cheever or Toni Morrison, you're in danger of sounding like one of those phonies that Holden Caulfield fears so much. Those folks aren't you and their narrators aren't your narrators. If you have to go through a Hemingway phase for a while, fine, do it, but don't stay there too long.

Your own natural voice will come from regular writing practice, whether it's in writing stories or writing in your journal or doing the exercises in this book. The more you write, the more your own voice will emerge because you'll grow more confident and you won't continuously pause to edit every word.

YOUR TURN:
Write a letter to someone you know well.
Not a short e-mail note but a longish letter
where you really talk about something. Don't

worry about voice or style or anything else. Just
write the letter. Then . . . when you're done,
analyze the voice and style of the letter. Chances
are it will be a good reflection of your natural
voice, which may be similar to a storytelling
voice you choose to use in your fiction. If you're
so inclined, go ahead and send the letter.
If you get a response, you can analyze *that*
person's voice.

You can also find the voice of a story by listening to the story's narrator. If you're using a first-person narrator, look at all the choices you have made about that character and get a sense for how this person would tell his or her story, whether the character's illiterate, like Huck, or pretentious, like Humbert. If you're working with a third-person narrator, figure out what this narrator should sound like by tailoring the voice to the characters, story, POV choice, setting, and how intimate your narrator is with both the reader and what's happening in the story. Of course, if you've chosen a multiple-vision POV, you may have to juggle more than one narrative voice.

But again, don't let the details hold you back. If you have a plot or character burning in your mind but you're agonizing about the voice for the piece, stop worrying and just write the story.

When you've finished a first draft, then you can think about the voice a bit more. Go back and check to see if the voice wavers in its general level of personality and formality. Pay attention to the way your words, sentences, and paragraphs are contributing to, or detracting from, the voice. If the voice sounds terribly unnatural or ill-suited to the story, try changing it to something that's more familiar to you or something in which your story fits more comfortably. Just as you should experiment with different POVs for a story, it's not a bad idea to do the same with voice.

At some point, you may get bolder about modifying the style to fit the story—you might, say, adopt longer sentences for a story about an obsessive person, or shorter, curt sentences for a story about an unemotional parent. You might pay closer attention to when a switch in style matches the specifics of a particular moment. For example, you might change the style of a piece to accentuate a moment of tension, as in the earlier passage from *The Old Man and the Sea*.

On the other hand, you can allow voice to guide you at the outset. If you're starting a piece but no plot or subject comes to mind, start writing from the perspective of someone who has a very distinctive way of speaking and thinking, and see where that voice will take you.

Last of all, you should always test your voice with a real voice. After a draft or two, you should read the whole piece from start to finish aloud, letting your actual speaking voice merge with the voice of the writing. See if the sound of the piece fits with the voice you wanted. Perhaps you could persuade someone to read the story aloud to you so you can simply listen to the voice. Either way, you should mark down places where the voice feels particularly natural and where it feels strained. Soon enough, you'll be able to spot the voice hiccups right away and wash them away with a glass of water.

CHAPTER 9
THEME: SO WHAT'S YOUR STORY REALLY ABOUT?

BY TERRY BAIN

Some years ago, I had a lot of stories that I thought were finished and on their way to publication. I thought I was ready to become a famous writer, making appearances before jealous young writing students worldwide, answering questions from the audience, and going out for cocktails afterward. But magazines weren't accepting my stories, and when people read them, they often said things about them that I didn't understand, such as "I don't get it."

What is there to get? I thought. *It's a short story.*

So I set out for a writer's conference, to get some advice from a real writer, from someone who knew what he was talking about, someone who would "get it" and praise me beyond compare and introduce me to his agent, who would also "get it," and who would send my manuscript to publishers who were just dying to jump on the bandwagon, whether they "got it" or not.

Instead I met the leader of my workshop, the fiction writer Mark Richard (a last-minute replacement author who I'd never heard of). He reviewed my story, and we talked about it, and in his final analysis he ended up asking me this: "What's your story about?"

I looked at Mark Richard, my head spinning a little, wondering if he'd said what I thought he'd just said.

I didn't know what to say. I reacted as you might imagine I would react in such a situation.

"I . . ." I said, "I guess I don't know."

"Find out," he said. Though I know he said more than just "find out," it was these words only that I remembered. Did he really mean to say that I had to know what my story was about before I could finish writing it? He seemed to be saying this as if it were the most obvious advice in the world. This was a world with which I was not yet familiar.

Of course, I think I was confusing plot with what my story was "about." He wasn't asking, *What happens,* but rather, *What's the big picture? Why should I care?* He wasn't just asking what the story was about plotwise but what was the story *really about*? He wanted me to take a closer look at this story and arrive at some conclusion about it. He wanted me to distill my story and arrive at its thematic center.

I decided to reread my story. It wasn't about anything. It was all over the place. It was about everything. It didn't hang together. It simply moved forward willy-nilly like a movie spliced out of sequence.

When I got home from the conference, I set out searching for the theme in another story I'd begun well before the conference. I had nearly abandoned this story, thinking it pretty boring. To make a long story short (though I fear it's already too late), the revised version of my story was accepted and published in *The Gettysburg Review*. And several months later the story was republished in the *O. Henry Awards*. I don't believe it would have been published in the first place had I not revised it with theme in mind, and this is why I'm here to harp on the topic of theme.

WHAT IS THEME?

The theme is the container for your story. Theme will attempt to hold all the elements of your story in place. It is like a cup. A vessel. A goblet. The plot and characters and dialogue and setting and voice and everything else are all shaped by the vessel. In many cases the vessel will go unnoticed by readers, but it would be very difficult to drink a glass of wine without the glass itself. The glass itself is, of course, part of the experience, but it is not one we always pay much attention to.

Okay, okay, so I used a nice metaphor. But now you want to know: what the heck is a theme? First, the word *theme* is confusing and may do you as much harm as good. You shouldn't think of theme as the ponderous sort of explanations given by critics and academics. That doesn't have much to do with writing a story. And you'll get into an equal amount of trouble if you think of theme as synonymous with *message* or *moral*. That kind of thing is best left to pundits and philosophers.

The novelist John Gardner wisely said: "By theme here we mean not a message—a word no good writer likes applied to his work—but the general subject, as the theme of an evening of debates may be World Wide Inflation." You see, the theme may be simply *world wide inflation* without there being any elegant solution for inflation or even a single point of view on the subject. The great Anton Chekhov also said something smart. He said that the fiction writer does not need to solve a problem so much as state the problem correctly.

So, you see, you're off the hook. You don't have to create themes that will solve the problems of the world. You just have to shine your flashlight on some aspect of life and let the reader see what's there. Not *every* aspect. *Some* aspect. And that's a key point because a theme should give a story some kind of focus, in a manner similar to how plot gives a story focus.

We're probably best off by just saying that theme is some kind of unifying idea in a story. Any kind of unifying idea will do, truth be told.

Ever read the children's picture book *Goodnight Moon* by Margaret Wise Brown? The story is simple. A bunny is going to bed, and all the things in his room are introduced to the reader. The story, or perhaps the bunny, then proceeds to say good night to all the things in his room: socks, clocks, kittens, mittens, brush, and mush. But there is a point in the book at which the page is blank, and the caption reads, "Goodnight nobody." I am always surprised and delighted when I come to this page, and it has only recently occurred to me why this is.

When I read the caption "Goodnight nobody," I see the author's hand. I see the background to the story. I begin to look for a deeper meaning there. I think to myself, *What does Margaret Wise Brown want me to be looking for when I read the line "Goodnight nobody"?* And what I understand, eventually, is that I am moved to create meaning from this very simple book. The meaning I take from it is this—that at the precise moment we arrive at the blank page, the bunny has fallen asleep. The room is filled with the quiet breathing of sleep. The theme of *Goodnight Moon*? Simple, silent sleep.

A well-defined theme gives a story a kind of focus, a center. A well-defined theme allows a writer to distill the ideas, to present them in a simple fashion, to tell the story that will last longer than half an hour. *Goodnight Moon* is a classic children's book not because it has fancy pictures or a high-concept plot, but because it's a story, with a deeper, more meaningful theme than can be found on the surface.

Have you ever read a story and said to yourself, *Well, that was nice, but what does it matter?* Don't you want someone who reads your story to instead think, *Wow, I can't stop thinking about that story!* Of course you do. And one of the ways to achieve that effect is by cultivating a theme and making an appropriate vessel from which your reader may drink.

By working with theme, you will take what may be an okay, nice, lovely, charming story, and help it become myth—turning it into a part of the consciousness of the reader, something that lasts longer than half an hour.

You may not think it's possible to crystallize the themes of great and profound works as neatly as I did for *Goodnight Moon,* but I maintain that you can. At the risk of sounding like a fusty old professor, let me give you a sampling of themes from some great works of fiction, and all of these are, of course, open to interpretation.

> *War and Peace* by Leo Tolstoy—*the myriad ramifications of war and peace*
> *The Great Gatsby* by F. Scott Fitzgerald—*the corruption of the American dream*
> "The Lady with the Dog" by Anton Chekhov—*the contrast between romantic love and the constraints of marriage*
> *1984* by George Orwell—*a police state like this could happen*
> "A Good Man Is Hard to Find" by Flannery O'Connor—*the possibility of finding grace through facing evil*
> *Lolita* by Vladimir Nabokov—*the power of desire*
> "Where Are You Going, Where Have You Been?" by Joyce Carol Oates—*the forming of identity*

And sometimes a theme *is,* more or less, a message. *A Christmas Carol* by Charles Dickens probably falls into this category. You remember it. There's a mean old greedy geezer named Ebenezer Scrooge and he really doesn't give a damn for anything in the world but his hordes of money. Then one Christmas Eve the Ghosts of Christmas Past, Present, and Future visit Scrooge and show him that he's a lonely soul who has squandered his life and may soon lie unloved and unremembered in a cold grave. Lo and behold,

Scrooge sees the error of his ways and instantly transforms into a new man. Though the story certainly deals with greed, the real theme is something like: *Learn to correct the errors of your life before it's too late.* Yes, that's a message, but Dickens gets away with it (as he gets away with so many things) because he knows how to tell an absolutely wonderful story.

> YOUR TURN:
> Think of one of your favorite works of fiction, perhaps one of the stories you referred to in a previous exercise. Do your best to state the dominant theme of the story in a single word, phrase, or sentence. More than anything else, what is that story *really* about? Some hints: look for recurring images; ponder the title; examine the climax. But please don't cheat by calling up your college literature professor.

KNOW THY THEME

Most great stories have themes and your story probably needs one too. And you should know what it is. Yeah, I know you're shaking your head, hoping I'm not saying what you think I'm saying. You think that you don't have to know what your story is about any more than you have to know what the moon is made of. You think writing is too mysterious and magical to ever figure out your story's theme.

But, no, I'm telling you that you can write your story better—craft a more appealing vessel—if you actually know your story's theme. You don't have to tell anyone, even if they ask you in interviews for fancy publications, but you need to know.

For another thing, should you neglect to supply your readers with a theme, they are likely to grab one that is handy, quite possibly the incorrect one, the one that does not contain the warning *"Caution: contents may be hot."* Provide them with a theme so that they do not mistake your story about natural consequences for a story about the cuteness of puppies.

Can a story have more than one theme? Probably. But it is best for the short story writer to have a dominant theme in mind. The novel writer will probably have a greater opportunity to allow several themes to creep into the novel, just as the novelist may use subplots. When the contents are vast, it's possible that a more complex vessel is necessary. But even the novelist might be best off working with a single, dominant theme in which everything is contained.

In her collection of essays, *Mystery and Manners,* Flannery O'Connor gives the reader a clue as to what she has found in her own story "A Good Man Is Hard to Find." She shows us that she does, indeed, know what her stories are about, and has set out to make her readers aware of exactly what it is that's going on in the story:

> *A good story is literal in the same sense that a child's drawing is literal. When a child draws, he doesn't intend to distort but to set down exactly what he sees, and as his gaze is direct, he sees the lines that create motion. Now the lines of motion that interest the writer are usually invisible. They are the lines of spiritual motion. And in this story you should be on the lookout for such things as the action of grace in the Grandmother's soul, and not for the dead bodies.*

O'Connor worked with theme. You can sense that she knows what she's writing about, that she has a complete handle on what is at the center of her stories, and she's able to keep a grip on it from beginning to end. As a result, her stories expand. They are able to slip off the side of the page somehow, to work their way into your life.

Interestingly, though, in the above passage, O'Connor makes the mistake of believing that it is important for her readers to know exactly what it was she was writing about, when the truth is far more interesting, and almost magical. A reader will perhaps get something entirely different out of reading a good story than what the writer intended. Maybe the readers will be paying too much attention to the dead bodies to notice the grace. Or they may see the grandmother's actions as something entirely different from *grace*. But, if the writer was confident enough in her thematic resonance, the theme will still be absorbed, in some way, by the reader.

So while you should be aware of your theme, you should also beware forcing it down the reader's throat (which O'Connor never did). Forcing readers into understanding what we want them to understand is what will get us into trouble. We'll end up writing didactic, forgettable stories. If we overadorn our theme vessel with bright colors and too many words and signposts, the reader is likely to care less about the wine inside the vessel.

Though you are looking for theme, and you will be revising with a theme in mind, don't spend any time making sure your readers are going to "get it." Don't overclarify your theme. If you're writing about the destruction of the rain forest, it's probably enough that you've included lush scenes from just such a forest, and described how the place has changed your main character. Your protagonist does not need to stand on a soapbox and promote the welfare of the forest. In fact, your protagonist can be the enemy. He could be a forester who devotes his life to destroying the damn forests. The point will eventually come across.

After all, little children don't ponder, discuss, and write dissertations on *Goodnight Moon*. But, on some subconscious level, they most certainly "get it." Theme does not have to instruct; it merely has to connect on some kind of deep level.

> YOUR TURN:
> Imagine a soldier has just returned from a war and is having a strange time readjusting to his previous life. You can pick the war, even using an imaginary one. Flesh out the character and the setting. Then write a brief passage where this character is going about some everyday activity, but having difficulty with it. Whatever you do, *do not think about the theme of this piece*. Just focus on the character and what he or she is trying to do. Once you have written the passage, write down three to seven possible themes for this piece. Pick the theme that seems the most interesting. Ponder what direction the story may take using this theme in a *subtle* way.

SLEUTHING OUT YOUR THEME

One way to avoid overemphasizing your theme is by not beginning there. The writer who begins to write with a theme in mind almost invariably ends up with a didactic and forgettable tract. If you begin thinking, *I'm going to write about the politics of academia,* then you will probably end up with something. You'll have a lot of words and sentences and commas and periods, but it most likely won't be good fiction, something that lasts longer than a few moments. Begin writing elsewhere.

Just start by telling a story.

Telling a story will take you into the heart of the story, and at the heart of the story there will be a theme that you can dig out and crystallize, and I'm willing to place a pretty big bet on that.

Take *A Christmas Carol*. Did Dickens begin by thinking something like, *I wish to write a story that will instruct my numerous readers that they should correct the grave errors of their ways before it is, indeed, too late*? Or did he simply begin by telling a story? I like to think the latter answer is correct. He began by writing about Scrooge, and arrived at the rest based on the characters in the necessary actions that take place to tell the story that is told. You have to create the world from scratch no matter what you do. So that's what you do. You start with story, and later you go back and try to retrofit the story to the theme.

> YOUR TURN:
> Just to see how difficult it is, write a short piece starting with a theme. Here is your theme: *faith*. Spend some time contemplating characters, situations, settings, and so forth that may illustrate this theme in an interesting, noncliché manner. Once you have some ideas in place, start writing a story with *faith* as the theme. You can write just a passage or you can write a whole story. Who knows? Starting with a theme may just give you a focus that allows you to write a wonderful piece, in which case you're free to write a story, every now and then, that *does* begin with theme.

Once you've written the first draft of your story, this really isn't a bad time to start thinking about theme. If something occurs to you during the first draft, don't be afraid to jot it down. Also, don't be afraid of changing your mind later. If it turns out your first impressions were wrong, no problem. The worst that could happen is that you would have to revise your story, and you have to do that anyway.

The key thing in this process is to let the theme emerge naturally from the story you are telling, not impose the theme from above. This means that you'll have to look at what you've written and sleuth out the theme.

Yes, it's possible that as you're working on a story, a theme simply comes to you. *Oh,* you might think, *this is really about the search for truth.* If that happens, great. Go ahead and let yourself be aware of this theme, and allow it to shape your story. But it's not always quite that simple. So let me give you some tips for finding the crucial clues that will lead you to the theme of your story.

A great technique is to start asking yourself questions. Do the characters' actions imply any universal truths? Does the superhero's triumph over the green-faced man represent a broader theme of good triumphing over evil? Does the postman's role in saving your character's life imply the presence of everyday angels? Does your protagonist's hunt for her keys represent a more universal search for the keys of meaning in life?

You can also see if there is a social context to your story. Does your protagonist's relative poverty tell you that your story is about poverty in general? Does the ruthlessness with which your forester destroys tell you that your story is about destruction?

Another way to search for theme is by doing a kind of reduction or condensation. Think, as you try to discover what your story is about, *How do I reduce my story thematically?* Try to simplify your ideas into a few words: my story is about the inevitability of love; it's about abuse of all kinds; it's about addiction; the beauty of fruit; fear; longing; loathing. Death! It's about death!

It may seem like cheating to reduce your profound work of art to a single word or phrase, but Flannery O'Connor wasn't afraid to say her story was about "the action of grace," and I assure you Ms O'Connor was no cheat.

Here's a good one. What made you start writing this story in the first place? Is the theme of your story buried in your impetus to write it? Why did you decide to write a fictional tale of your grandparents' move from North Dakota to California? Is your story about alienation? Travel? Seniors trying to break into the movie business?

Or just start looking very closely at what is already there. Remember that story I told you about? The one I revised with theme in mind and eventually published? Here's what I did in my revision process:

The story was partially set in the game room of a house—a pool table, a strobe light, a bar—and concerned the head games of teenagers. Specifically, the more dominant of two friends was trying to force his friend to kiss the neighbor girl by kissing her himself. It was a kind of game for him, to manipulate his friend. So I figured my theme must be *the games people play with one another.* Then I zeroed in a bit closer and decided that my story was about *the games of adolescence,* which was more specific than *the games people play with one another* and sounded less like a Top 40 hit. I titled my story "Games." I added a new ending. I removed some of the details and scenes that weren't necessary, that weren't fitting into my thematic vessel. I added a few new details and scenes that seemed appropriate, always with an eye toward *the games of adolescence.* And, as I mentioned earlier, the story got published and won some recognition. Also let me point out that the editor who accepted the story had already rejected it once, liking it but not quite enough.

Perhaps certain things keep recurring in your story, almost functioning as symbols and metaphors, as did my games. Perhaps the story occurs in a restaurant, and the symbols are mostly food items. Your theme might be related to consuming, eating, satiating, or desire, among other things.

You can also watch for repeated words or images. Or words and passages that strike you as particularly poignant. When you were writing these things, you had something in mind. Chances are good the theme is buried in there. For instance, the word *ring* can mean more than *ring.* It can also mean marriage, boxing, entrapment, even communication. Where you go with this word depends on what theme you choose for the story.

You can also look at individual sentences and glean something from them. The kernel of your story might be in there. For instance, if you look at your first sentence and it reads, "She walked between the Dumpsters, watching for rats," there are several thematic elements to the line that you can take note of. Someone walking between the Dumpsters might be homeless. Rats and Dumpsters imply a kind of filth. Watching for rats implies a kind of fear, or perhaps hunger. Some of the thematic elements in this sentence will depend on where the rest of the story goes, whether your protagonist is homeless or not, whether this is a familiar setting or not, whether there are actually any rats or not.

Write in the margins of your story what the possible themes or clues to themes might be. When a character seems to be playing with another character in the story, you might write *games* in the margin. When the protagonist tries to beat the sales record for the quarter, you might write *competition* in the margin. Hopefully some kind of commonality will begin to form. Or one of your notations will strike you as particularly relevant to the story. Circle words or phrases that seem especially poignant, that seem to point to a larger theme, or that seem to be the most essential pieces to the story. Don't do anything with these notations just yet. Just circle them. You can come back to your notations later, maybe making further notations, maybe just rereading it, slapping yourself on the head and saying, *Of course, it's about the importance of everyday heroes.*

Let's use *Goodnight Moon* as an example again. If you were writing the story to *Goodnight Moon,* you might read your text one line at a time and make the following notes:

> Text: *"In the great green room"*
> Notation: *Life. Depth. Solitude. Peace. Quiet.*
>
> Text: *"There was a telephone"*
> Notation: *Busyness. Life.*
>
> Text: *"And a red balloon"*
> Notation: *Play. Fun.*
>
> Text: *"And a picture of—the cow jumping over the moon*
> *And there were three little bears sitting on chairs"*
> Notation: *Childhood. Nursery rhyme.*

Later in the story you might have notations as follows:

> Text: *"Goodnight comb*
> *And goodnight brush"*
> Notation: *Night / sleep for everything.*
>
> Text: *"Goodnight nobody*
> *Goodnight mush"*
> Notation: *Simplicity. Sleep. The bunny has fallen asleep.*

Hopefully, as you accumulate these details, a theme will appear. (In this case: sleep.) This theme may not be the exact theme that you will end up with, but it will certainly be better than the vague notion you had before. *And I thought the story was about rabbits!*

However you go about finding your theme, you will find it. Then what? Well, you might write your theme in big block letters on the first page of your story or on a sign posted over your workplace. Or, if you're still zeroing in, you might keep a list of possible themes on a piece of paper or on a document in your computer. Or you might have a fabulous memory for this sort of thing.

By whatever method, you'll want to be keeping your theme in mind as you return to work on your story.

You might ask, *What if I don't get the theme right?* And I would answer, *You will.*

Why? Because it's critical that you are confident in your skills. So you will get it right. You are the single most knowledgeable person regarding the theme of your story. The theme of your story is whatever you discover. You can shout down your friends and relations by telling them emphatically that your story is about *death* because you absolutely get to decide. They can decide too, of course, and they can disagree with you, and that's part of the fiction game.

> YOUR TURN:
> Take one of the pieces you wrote for an exercise in a previous chapter. Sleuth out the theme that may be lurking behind the words. Does a character's situation say anything about human nature? Is there a particular phrase or sentence that resonates for you? There's no telling where the clues lie, but they are probably there. Once you've identified a possible theme, write it down. Then revise the piece, keeping your theme in mind. If you have to alter or even throw out most of the original piece, so be it. A theme demands attention.

THEME TOUCHES EVERYTHING

As you may recall, I said you probably won't be working much with theme on the first draft of your story. What I'm implying, of course, is that you won't be writing just one draft of your story but many. And on the second and third and fourth (and so on) drafts, yes, sir, that's when you'll be thinking about theme a great deal.

The choices you make about theme will strongly influence how you revise your story. For one thing, the theme will help you make sense of what is there. If the protagonist's hunt for her keys does indeed represent a more universal search for truth, then perhaps her visit to the palm reader makes more sense. And maybe, while she's at her mother's house, she could be looking *for something* in the photo album rather than just at the pictures. What is she looking for? Perhaps her flipping channels on the car radio means more than just hating the music playing on the airwaves. She's looking for something. She can't find it. Not only does this give us an excellent way to revise our story, it allows us to expand or enliven the plot in a more natural and thematic way. Continue to cultivate these thematic threads. Choose them. Allow them to shape your story.

You see, knowing your theme actually helps you make key decisions about what to keep and what not to keep. If my story was about, say, *immortality,* then anything in it that didn't somehow relate to immortality could be cut. And I could add things to my story without fear of becoming confused or confounded. So long as what I wrote had something to do with immortality, then I was safe.

I may end up looking at a sentence for an hour, thinking, *Is this sentence about immortality?* In the end, maybe that particular sentence doesn't matter so much. Maybe it's just the sentence you need to get a character from the door to the kitchen. Maybe whatever's in the kitchen has to do with immortality. Or maybe she just wants a cucumber sandwich and you cannot deny her a cucumber sandwich because she's hungry.

But once you find a theme and begin working with it in the revision process, you should focus the story with that theme in mind, letting most, if not all, of what's there relate, in some way, to your theme. Thus, the story will attain depth, since the repetition of thematic elements will naturally pile up, one upon another, creating a kind of resonance within the story. Yes, thematic repetition is good. If you are able to provide enough elements relating to your theme, eventually the reader will begin to have a clearer picture of a story with a center, rather than a story that proceeds as life proceeds, without much structure or resonance.

At this point, you may be wondering two things: 1) Does most everything in a story *really* relate to its theme? 2) How do I go about revising a story so most everything relates to the theme? Good questions, both. I think the best way to answer these questions is by looking at a particular story from the viewpoint of its theme. Since we've been discussing Raymond Carver's "Cathedral" in this book, let us use that one. While we're doing this, you may be able to see how Carver made decisions joining his theme to all the major craft elements of fiction as he took this story through the revision process.

For starters, we should ponder what the theme of "Cathedral" actually is. If I had to crystallize it, and I do, I'd probably say the theme of "Cathedral" is *True vision is much deeper than the physical ability to see.*

Carver gets working on the theme right from the get-go. The story begins:

This blind man, an old friend of my wife's, he was on his way to spend the night.

And a few lines later the narrator says:

I wasn't enthusiastic about his visit. He was no one I knew.

Already we're getting the sense that the narrator, a man who can physically see, is emotionally blind because of his lack of interest in meeting a good friend of his wife's. The wife's friend is named Robert, but the narrator is so disinterested in this fellow that he refers to him simply as "the blind man." The narrator, in fact, isn't interested in much of anything. He stumbles through life blindly oblivious to just about everything. He's blind to Robert and his life, because everything he learns about Robert is limited by his intense focus on Robert's blindness. He's shocked to see a blind man with a beard, and without dark glasses, and smoking, and having a diverse work history. The narrator is also oblivious to his wife and her interests. He doesn't get into her poetry, or poetry in general, and doesn't want to look closely at her past or, for that matter, her present. Perhaps most importantly he seems to want to be oblivious to his own life—his job, his bad habits, and so forth. We sense his ideal evening is getting drunk, getting stoned, and watching TV. Perhaps this personal obliviousness is why he never even reveals his *own* name.

The protagonist, the narrator, fits perfectly into the story's theme. But so do the other two characters. If the man who can physically see is emotionally "blind," then it helps to have the physically blind character someone who can "see" in the emotional sense. Such is the case with Robert. He grabs life with gusto, seemingly interested in anything that comes across his path. We sense he loved his recently deceased wife deeply and has cultivated many friendships, and even his vigorous drinking and smoking seem to be social tools rather than crutches. Hey, he even has two television sets and he prefers the one with color!

The narrator's wife, the only other character in the story, seems to be an absolutely lovely person, cherishing her friendship with Robert and doing all she can to treat him graciously. If the wife were a shrew, we might understand why the narrator takes her for granted, but her loveliness reinforces the narrator's emotional "blindness."

These important character traits are revealed clearly with just about every line of dialogue in the story. For example:

> I said, "Let me get you a drink. What's your pleasure? We have a little of everything. It's one of our pastimes."
>
> "Bub, I'm a Scotch man myself," he said fast enough in this big voice.
>
> "Right," I said. Bub! "Sure you are. I knew it."
>
> He let his fingers touch his suitcase, which was sitting alongside the sofa. He was taking his bearings. I didn't blame him for that.
>
> "I'll move that up to your room," my wife said.

It's all there—the narrator's disinterest, Robert's gregariousness, and the wife's sweetness. What the characters say supports the theme, though, of course, they don't know it.

Carver chose the first-person point of view for this story and, in relation to the theme, it seems an inspired choice. We're not just watching the narrator's lack of "vision," we're experiencing it with him as we live inside his mind. Interestingly, the narrator's blindness makes him a somewhat unreliable narrator. We don't trust his opinions, and we're right not to. He tells us close-minded things that we, the reader, know to be silly, like:

> This blind man, feature this, he was wearing a full beard! A beard on a blind man! Too much, I say.

Also notice how the voice of the narrator reinforces his lack of "vision," the voice being tinged with cynicism and ignorance. Throughout the story, the POV and voice are working hand in hand, perfectly, to convey the narrator's limited scope.

Perhaps you're wondering about the setting. The entire story takes place in the narrator's house. But we never get a real good sense of that house. As a rule, Carver is sparing with detail, but it seems especially appropriate in this case. Even in his own home, the narrator seems unable to "see" things. This lack of giving detail, or "seeing," extends really to most of the description in this story. Nothing—the house, the food, the liquor, the wife—is described with any relish or specificity. Notice the apathy in such a description as this:

> *The news program ended. I got up and changed the channel. I sat back down on the sofa.*

If we didn't know better we might be tempted to think that Raymond Carver wasn't a very good writer. Oh, but he is, though, because he is merging his POV, voice, and description choices to fully reveal the narrator's "blindness," and, thus, his story's theme. And, tellingly, the descriptions become more specific and vivid when the narrator finally does begin to "see" toward the story's end, as when he is watching a documentary about cathedrals on TV:

> *The camera moved to a cathedral outside of Lisbon. The differences in the Portuguese cathedral compared with the French and Italian were not that great. But they were there.*

Now this incredibly oblivious narrator is even starting to notice the difference between Portuguese and French and Italian cathedrals. That's quite a leap.

The theme is certainly apparent in every progression of the plot. Plot is usually a living illustration of theme—theme in motion, you might say. If you show the theme through the actions of the characters, then you never really need to state the theme, and, in this story, Carver never does.

As we saw in chapter 3, the major dramatic question of this story is whether our narrator will ever come to truly "see," which certainly works together with the theme of *True vision is much deeper than the physical ability to see.* All the events of the story, from beginning to end, push the narrator closer and closer to the moment when he finally does come to "see." The narrator tries with all his might to remain detached, and Robert never lets up on the narrator, being charming and inquisitive and caring until finally the narrator is quite simply unable to resist Robert's life-affirming "vision." At the story's climax—where the narrator draws a cathedral—the plot and theme come together in one blindingly bright moment of glory.

At the climax, you have these two guys watching television, and they see this cathedral. Well, no. The narrator, who has physical sight, sees the cathedral. Of course Robert, the blind man, has never seen a cathedral. So, what happens? The sighted man describes the cathedral to the blind man, at the blind man's request. Only the sighted man is emotionally "blind," so he doesn't know *how* to describe it adequately. He confesses to Robert:

"It just isn't in me to do it."

He's been the way he is for a very long time. He doesn't know how to be any different. Will he ever "see"? Maybe, maybe not.

But the blind man, Robert, will insist on it because, of course, he does possess true "vision." He knows that the narrator can't "see." He knows this is important, to help this man, or maybe to help his friend who has married this emotionally "blind" man. So Robert encourages the narrator to get paper and a pencil, and the two of them get down on the floor, and the narrator attempts to draw the cathedral with the blind man's hand resting on top of his own hand, the hand doing the drawing. Robert claims this will help him get a sense of the cathedral, but maybe Robert really just wants to offer the narrator the courage it will take to accomplish this task. And the narrator does accomplish the task. He ultimately manages to draw a cathedral. When he's done, he closes his eyes. And finally, miraculously, he can "see."

And perhaps by now you are seeing how every major craft element of this short story converges on its theme. But there is one more thing worth mentioning—the symbol of the cathedral. Something becomes a symbol in a story when it takes on a meaning larger than what it really is. Symbols are nothing a writer should worry about too much; rather, they should emerge naturally, as probably happened with this story. But at some point, Carver must have become aware of cathedrals as something symbolic because he chose to call the story "Cathedral."

Why a cathedral? Think about it. Cathedrals are perhaps the most magnificent and awe-inspiring man-made structures on earth, and they were built to bring humans closer to God, to elevate the human soul as high as it could possibly travel. When the narrator learns to "see" a cathedral, he has elevated himself about as far as he can go. By story's end, not only does the narrator have the physical ability to see, but he has gone deeper to achieve *true vision*. In a big way.

YOUR TURN:
Return to the favorite work of fiction for which you figured out the theme. Get your hands on a copy of it. Focus on several pages of the text. Write down everything you see there that seems to relate to

your chosen theme for the work. Anything is
fair game—the characters, setting, voice, title,
opening line . . . If not much seems to relate to
your theme, what does that tell you? That the
theme is illustrated with great subtlety? Or not
illustrated well enough? Or do you have the wrong
theme?

Can you do what Carver did with this story on your own works of fiction? Can you, as they say, try this at home? Of course you can. Simply discover the theme of your story, after a draft or two, then revise and revise. And with each revision look for ways to make all your choices fluidly and delicately flow inside the vessel of your theme. If you find this difficult, do as the narrator of "Cathedral" did—simply close your eyes and "see."

CHAPTER 10
REVISION: REAL WRITERS REVISE
BY PETER SELGIN

I write fiction for the same reason people believe in God, to give meaning and order to life, or at least to give it some shape here and there. Like many people, I'm uncomfortable with chaos and disorder. The studio where I write contains a medley of tidily arranged shelves, bookcases, and surfaces, jars neatly bristling with writing implements, and notebooks arranged by size, category, and date, all within arm's reach. I'm pathologically tidy. But I'm far from alone. For damning evidence of man's fixation with order look no farther than heaven; what are the constellations, but tidy boxes in which we've shelved the stars? The Big Dipper is cosmic fiction.

When I teach fiction, I alarm my students right up front by announcing that I'm not going to teach them how to write, that, as a matter of fact, I *can't*. I can only teach them how to rewrite, to reconsider what they've written, and then revise it. The writing, the getting something down on paper, that's really all up to them. Once they've got something written down—when they're ready to make order from chaos—then I may just have something to offer.

FIRST DRAFTS

Before we decide how to revise, it helps to have something *to* revise, namely, a first draft. "All that matters," said Hemingway of first drafts, "is that you finish it." Elsewhere I've heard it said that a first draft should be written with the heart, whereas subsequent drafts must bring to bear that more critical organ, the brain.

Papa Hemingway, not one to mince words, also called first drafts "excrement." That's harsh, but also liberating. It's okay if a first draft sucks; it should suck; it's supposed to suck. The only thing a first draft *needs* to do is get finished. Get something down on paper. Be reckless, be shameless, be grossly irresponsible and self-indulgent, even, but get something down.

And remember: when writing first drafts, you should not be editing. A writer friend of mine who owns a collection of hats wears one—a red baseball cap with KEROUAC stitched in gold over the visor—while writing her first drafts, and another—Chinese, tutti-frutti, shaped like a funnel—when revising them. This, I'll admit, is pushing things, and I also think it odd that the funnel should be for the editor, but it illustrates a point: that though they share the goal of creating a work of literary art, editing and writing are different disciplines requiring different temperaments, different skills. While the woman in the red baseball cap may be driven by pure instinct and emotion, half-poet, half-ape, whosoever dons the tutti-frutti Chinese cap must be an emotionless diagnostician, probing each word, sentence, and paragraph with a screwdriver in one hand and a scalpel or a hatchet in the other.

However inspired, first drafts can always stand improvement. "No sentimentality about this job," wrote Daphne du Maurier of the editor's task. And while there may be nothing sentimental about revision, though by turns terrifying, cold-blooded, and brutal, editing can be enjoyable. With experience the fiction writer learns not only how to find and solve technical problems but that solving such problems in a manuscript can be as creative as writing that first draft. In fact, editing can be edifying, so beware: you may never want to take off that conical, tutti-frutti Chinese hat.

Still, you're reluctant. You've finished the first draft. It sits on your desktop, next to your computer, a stack of pages sprinkled with words—your words. Maybe you worked in a white heat, following Jack Kerouac's famous dictum "First thought, best thought," flinging sentences like Jackson Pollock flinging paint. Or else you worked cautiously, glacially, like William Styron, who, writing his extra-long novels, felt compelled to hone each sentence to perfection before proceeding to the next, his perfected prose accruing like plaque on the teeth. Either way, you think the work done. And maybe it is.

But most likely it's not. Few of us are William Styrons, who called his own working method "hell." Be honest with yourself and you'll admit that for every sentence hurled down onto your page like a lightning bolt from

Zeus, ten others must be dug up like root vegetables from the humble soil, from which they emerge covered with dirt and manure.

Some writers may feel that once their raw genius has been spilled onto the page it's up to someone else to clean it up; that's what editors are for. In the good old days of publishing this may have been slightly true. There was a time when a guy like Thomas Wolfe could plop a manuscript as bulky and disheveled as himself onto an editor's desk and hope to have it published—and would, providing the editor was Maxwell Perkins, the legendary Scribner's editor who whipped Wolfe and notable others into print.

Those days, sadly, are gone, as are men like Perkins. Today the typical editor is a harried creature, with more urgent things to do than edit your novel or story. Darken his or her desk with a manuscript in need of editing and it will be read "very quickly." So, you should revise. In fact, if there isn't one already, there ought to be a bumper sticker: REAL WRITERS REVISE!

PRELUDE TO REVISION

Before revision can begin, however, before we slice open the body of our stories or novels and muck around in search of tumors, extraneous organs, and signs of internal bleeding, our words, together with our emotions, need to have grown cold, sober, well rested. Insomnia, intoxication, frenzied passion, and/or too much caffeine are not things wanted in a surgeon.

Hence, do not revise in the throes of creative ecstasy, or when angry, upset, exhausted, depressed, or filled with self-doubt, dread, or loathing. You've printed out your first draft? Good. Let it sit. Do something else for a while, work on another project, take two weeks and tour the Greek Islands—bring your watercolors and your scuba gear. Soak your weary soul in the wine-dark sea, while letting your manuscript grow clammy-cold. Distance, we're told, makes the heart grow fonder. It also makes editing easier. A paradox: the less we recognize our own words, the better equipped we are to judge them. Just as distance makes the heart grow fonder, familiarity breeds contempt, or, worse, a false sense of inevitability, turning our sentences into ruts in an oft-traveled road.

Still, you needn't go as far as Neil Armstrong went to gain distance on your words. Some writers write in the morning, and then, in the afternoon or evening, revise what they've written. Others wait until the next day, when they can be sure they're no longer in love or hate with what they wrote the day before. But revising in too much of a hurry has its perils. Here's Virginia Woolf in her diary *The Voyage Out* on revising:

> *When I read the thing over (one very gray evening) I thought it so flat and monotonous that I did not even "feel" the atmosphere: certainly there was no character in it. Next morning I proceeded to slash and rewrite, in the hope of animating it, and (as I suspect for I have not re-read it) destroying the one virtue it had—a kind of continuity; for I wrote it originally in a dream-like state, which was at any rate, unbroken . . . I have kept all the pages I cut out, so the thing can be reconstructed precisely as it was.*

Woolf makes a good case for saving all drafts. And given the luxury of more time she might not have, as it were, thrown out the Wedgwood with the dishwater.

But what if, after a day or two, you still can't see clearly what you've written, and you can't afford a trip to Greece, or you don't have or want the luxury of more time? Or you're on deadline, with an editor's hot breath wilting the short hairs behind your neck? How, then, to cool a manuscript quickly, and make your all-too-familiar words less familiar?

Try reading your words aloud to yourself, sharpened pencil in hand. Read loud and clear—hurling each word like a stone at an imaginary audience. Imagine that somewhere in that audience is your ideal reader. Maybe he or she is your favorite writer, the ghost of Jane Austen or Bill Faulkner. See her sitting there with her own sharpened pencil, or, in Faulkner's case, a flask of bourbon. As you read, imagine her facial reactions; see her twitching, scowling, smiling, or wincing at certain words. And listen to yourself. Words sound different to our ears than to our eyes. You'll hear not only faulty rhythms and errors in logic but pretentious language, clichés, digressions, and a host of other sins. You'll be surprised how much editing pencil gets on your pages this way. If reading aloud to Faulkner's ghost is too intimidating, select a more benign imaginary listener, your grandmother or the freshman comp teacher who gave you an A+ on that essay about truffle hunting in Normandy with your crazy French uncle.

Some people don't even like going to the movies alone, and may balk at reading alone to themselves, in which case they should find someone to read to. Not an editor, or even a fellow writer, just someone who likes to be read to (believe it or not, such people exist). They needn't comment. In fact, better if they don't. They aren't there to critique, but to react, to help you hear in your own words what you need to hear.

Or have someone read your words *to* you. Having your own words thrown back to you in another's voice—with their inflections, stumbles, laughter, tears, wincing, and cringing—can greatly enhance the revision process. You can also read your own words into a tape recorder and then play it back. Me, I prefer a warm body.

> YOUR TURN:
> Return to something you have written,
> perhaps from one of the previous exercises.
> Read it aloud. As you read, make notes on
> what you think can be improved. If you
> find yourself bored as you read, odds are
> the readers will be bored too. Ask yourself
> why the piece is less than thrilling. And any
> words or sentences that make you (or your
> imaginary reader) wince or cringe should be
> treated as suspect. As a bonus round, revise
> the piece based on your notes.

Two other solutions remain. The first is so simple it's almost embarrassing, yet it works. Print out your chapter or story in an unusual, but legible, font. Your words will seem like strangers to you, and you can begin to edit them.

The ultimate solution is to get help, that is, if you're lucky enough to know a sympathetic reader who is also a skilled editor. By *sympathetic* I mean sympathetic to your intentions as well as to your overall style. Their ranks being swollen by struggling writers, professional editors are by no means hard to come by; for a price you can have your pick of them. But beware, even the costliest and most experienced editor may be, if not plain wrong, a poor fit for your writing. Professional or not, an editor's opinion is still an opinion. And many a good writer has had the guts yanked out of his or her prose by some "expert" editor. Remember that last botched haircut? Editors are like barbers. If you find a good one, consider yourself blessed and chain yourself to her. Better still, give her your manuscript, and go to Greece.

That said, no editor's advice should be followed slavishly. It's your work. You've got to know when to listen to suggestions, and when to say no, thanks. Sometimes an editor's efforts will tighten and clean up your prose when you want it ragged and filthy. Also bear in mind that editors tend to err on the side of caution. As Tennessee Williams said to Gore Vidal after Vidal finished editing one of his short stories, "You have corrected all my faults, and they are all I have!"

THE REVISION PROCESS

So, you're willing and ready to revise. But what to revise, how to revise, how much to revise?

> *"Revise till your fingers bleed."*
> —Donald Newlove

> *"Don't f— with it too much."*
> —Lawrence Durrell

Two great writers, two seemingly irreconcilable pieces of advice. How to reconcile them? Whose advice to take?

The purpose of multiple drafts is to discover what we're writing, and then to refine it into its ultimate form. Think of a painter with a canvas. She paints all day, perhaps for days, then scrapes and starts over. She may go through this process a dozen times, more, before emerging with a masterpiece. Are all those scraped efforts wasted? Of course not; they're all part of the process.

Initially, revision is often a matter of reenvisioning. From our first drafts we may take only a good character, or a scene, maybe a description, an opening sentence, possibly a theme—the rest is a shroud of disposable words. And yet, if it has served up any one of those things, all that writing wasn't in vain.

Suggestion: having finished a first draft, start over again. Put in a fresh piece of paper or open a fresh document on your computer, and start typing, this time with a sure, or surer, sense of what it is that you're writing. Refer to your draft, if and when it contains something worth referring to. Otherwise, write from scratch. D. H. Lawrence did so three times with *Lady Chatterley's Lover,* producing three novels on the same subject, never referring to the existent versions. Old words can block fresh insights.

YOUR TURN:
Return to something you have written,

perhaps from one of the previous exercises.
Reenvision the piece. Read it through several
times, asking yourself what is most original
or powerful about this piece. It may be a
character, a theme, a stray idea, even a single
line. Now be bold. Toss out everything but this
one promising thing. Start over, writing the
piece entirely from scratch.

But two drafts may be just the beginning. It's not unheard of for a writer
to go through twenty drafts, or more, on a single story. I know. I've done it.
And twenty drafts later some of those stories still molder in a file drawer,
unpublished. Does that make me a fool? No, because after twenty-*one* drafts,
they may be published. On the other hand, I've had stories published that
took only two drafts.

The fact is, some stories are easier to write than others. But the hard
ones are no less worth writing. Be prepared to see your work through many
revisions. Raymond Carver, one of this country's best short-fiction writers,
has confessed to revising his stories on average no fewer than a dozen times.
He understood as well as anyone that real writers revise.

THE BIG PICTURE

If a first draft is the place to write from the heart, free of worry, subsequent
drafts are the place to worry about *everything,* and heed all the sage advice
on craft doled out in this book. You may choose to spend whole drafts focusing
only on a single craft element. Perhaps you go through each scene finessing
only dialogue, then spend the next draft coalescing elements of theme.
Whatever your approach, before addressing little things—like whether to
use a dash or parentheses—you want to make sure the Big Things are
in order.

Some of the Big Things to consider:

CHARACTER

When you get down to it, people are interested in people. That's why they
read fiction.

Some questions to ask about the characters in your work: First, *Do I have all the characters I need to tell my tale?* If so, *Can I afford to lose a few? Can my protagonist do with two buddies, or one, instead of three?* When considering the number of characters with which to tell a story, as with so many things, less is more. It's also less work.

Once you've established that you have all the characters you need and no more, then ask yourself: *Are any of my main characters too flat? Do they fulfill their roles too neatly, too glibly?* When we assign characters narrow, predictable roles in our fiction, we are essentially condemning them to be archetypes, if not stereotypes. As F. Scott Fitzgerald wrote, "Begin with an individual, and before you know it you find that you have created a type; begin with a type, and you find that you have created—nothing."

Finally, ask yourself: *Are my main characters sufficiently motivated?* A character with no goals to struggle toward, who exists at the mercy of outside forces, we call a cipher. Voltaire's Candide is such a character; so is Mersault in Camus's novel *The Stranger*. But unless you're writing a satirical fable or an existential novel, your characters should want things.

PLOT

If I had to choose a formula for plot, I'd go with the English poet Philip Larkin, who described a story as consisting of three parts: a beginning, a muddle, and an end.

Beginnings are crucial. If the beginning of a story is weak, chances are no one will ever get to the "muddle," let alone the end. Writers are routinely advised by editors and other meddlers to grab their readers by the throat within a paragraph or a page. Sometimes this works. There's something irresistible about:

> *Hale knew they meant to murder him before he had been in Brighton three hours.*

—the opening of Graham Greene's *Brighton Rock*. But not all readers want to be grabbed by their throats. Some prefer to be gently seduced, in which case a sly wink or a wiggled finger may trump a grappling hook, as with *Moby-Dick*'s come-hither opening:

> *Call me Ishmael.*

The point is you don't have to be sensational to be amusing, entertaining, or interesting. Think of yourself as a guest who has just arrived at a party. You wish to make a strong impression. You can strangle the hostess; that should do it. Or tinkle your wineglass and tell a story in your own beguiling voice, a story filled with charm, eccentricity, and colorful details, that takes place in a provocative and/or magical setting. In other words, you can hook your reader without breaking, or even bruising, her neck.

The other good news about beginnings—one can often be obtained simply by amputating the first paragraphs, pages, or chapters of a draft, what editors refer to smugly as "throat clearing." Ask yourself, *What's the first interesting thing that happens in my story?* Begin there.

Having finished your first draft, you can be fairly sure the muddle's there, right where it ought to be, in the middle. The middle is the meat of the sandwich. It consists of an event or group of events, leading to the biggest event of all, the *climax.* As I've said, motivate characters sufficiently, and select a limited number of telling moments from their lives, and, providing you've chosen and shaped each of those scenes to something near perfection, the middle more or less takes care of itself.

The question to ask is, *Have I judiciously selected the necessary events with which to tell my story?* John Gardner speaks of the "rule of elegance and efficiency," meaning if you can tell a story in four scenes, don't tell it in five. When, in *The Great Gatsby,* Fitzgerald paints us a wonderful scene of Gatsby heaving his multicolored shirts onto his bed before Daisy's sparkling eyes, he feels no subsequent need to escort us into Gatsby's garage and have him show off his Studz Bearcat.

With endings, though we may aim straight for a point on the horizon, it's better if we don't arrive there, exactly. It's also likely that we won't, since our characters, being motivated, are apt to find their own solutions to their goals and frustrations, and these in turn will have their own dramatic repercussions. Assuming all does not go as expected, the ending of a story should be unpredictable not only for the reader but for the writer.

That said, an ending that's surprising but also unlikely, if not impossible, is by no means satisfying. The thing to aim for, in novels and stories, is the ending that's both surprising and inevitable. Ideally, the reader's first response should be *My God!* followed shortly thereafter by *But of course!*—since a good ending is always the direct result of everything that has come before.

POINT OF VIEW

Decisions about point of view are often made for the writer, dictated, so to speak, by the nature of the material. And most of the time our writer's instincts won't steer us wrong. But telling a story a certain way instinctively doesn't make it the right, let alone the only, or the ultimate, way.

Having finished your first draft, ask yourself: *Have I chosen the best possible point of view? Should I stick to this one character's viewpoint, or alternate between characters?* These are big questions, indeed. Still, to not ask them would be a mistake. True, what you've written may work just fine, in which case why change it? Then again, if a story or scene isn't working, the first culprit to round up and sit under the interrogator's lamp is point of view.

Each point-of-view option has its advantages and disadvantages. The third-person POV is the least problematic. A third-person narrative is more flexible, allowing for a wide range of diction and greater perspective. On the other hand, who would want *The Catcher in the Rye* in third person? Or *Huckleberry Finn*? Had Melville written, "His name was Ishmael," well, what a shame. A first-person narrator is all intimacy, all voice; we're getting the goods straight from the hero's mouth.

Then again, as a first-person narrator, Madame Bovary would be insufferable, if not impossible. Nor could Jay Gatsby by any means tell his own story.

And, of course, whatever POV choice you make, keep it consistent.

DESCRIPTION

"Go in fear of abstractions," said the poet Ezra Pound. And though he went nuts, Ezra was right about some things.

When writing description, you want your reader to hear, see, smell, taste, and feel what your characters hear, see, smell, taste, and feel; you want specific sensations that grip the senses, not the intellect. Though abstract words like *beautiful* and *mysterious* seem to convey qualities of universality and timelessness, they leave most readers snoring. To say *Sally had beautiful strawberry-blond hair* is to say next to nothing. But *Sally's hair streamed like turnings of steaming copper and bronze from a spinning lathe, down both sides of her face*—now, that says something.

With description, the particular always trumps the general, and concrete always trumps abstract. Here's Shakespeare writing up a storm:

> *Blow, winds, and crack your cheeks! rage! Blow!*
> *You cataracts and hurricanes spout*
> *Till you have drench'd our steeples, drown'd the cocks!*
> *You* sulphurous *and* thought-executing *fires*
> *Vaunt couriers of* oak-cleaving *thunderbolts,*
> *Singe my* white *head! And thou,* all-shaking *thunder,*
> *Strike flat the* thick rotundity *o' the world!*
> *Crack nature's moulds, all germens spill at once,*
> *That make* ingrateful *man!*
> *Rumble thy bellyful! Spit fire! Spout rain!*

A vast improvement over *It was a dark and stormy night,* don't you agree? I've highlighted the modifiers; there are a few. But what modifiers! *Thought-executing* and *oak-cleaving* are nouns and verbs pressed into service as adjectives, and so they give us the concrete jolt of solid, moving objects. Likewise *all-shaking. White,* like all words standing for colors, is a concrete abstraction. As adjectives go, *sulphurous* is also concrete; you can almost smell it. The one truly abstract word here is *ingrateful.* (Even the Bard nods, occasionally.)

Still, when choosing concrete details, it pays to be selective. D. H. Lawrence, talking about details, draws a distinction between what he calls "the quick and the dead," the quick being "lifeblood," and the dead being . . . well, dead. The first things you notice about a person or a place are most likely the "quick" things; the rest are likely dead.

DIALOGUE

A few words on dialogue. Concise: the fewer words to make a point, the better. Subtext: it's not what characters say, but what they mean, that counts. Illogical: people are illogical, especially when they speak, especially when they argue. Adversarial: and they *should* argue. We learn much more when characters disagree, or have different philosophies. Dialogue should never be tape-recorder real; a few hours spent in the company of a courtroom transcript will drive that point home. But it should be speakable, another reason to read your words out loud.

Try not to force dialogue into your characters' mouths. If you know your characters well, and have motivated them successfully, they should know what to say and when to say it, placing you in the humble role of stenographer.

Pay attention to the ratio of scene to summary, of dialogue to description. (This matter relates to pacing as well as to dialogue, affecting your decisions on which events to compress and which to expand.) A skilled author layers scene with summary, weaving and blending the two, aware that the best narratives are like roller-coaster rides, with slow climbs of exposition leading to swift falls of dramatic conflict. But there's no one way to build a roller coaster. And while one author favors dialogue over summary (Elmore Leonard springs to mind), another, say, Jens Christian Grondahl, author of the novel *Silence in October* (about a man whose wife has left him and who spends the novel's 280 pages reflecting on this and other matters) eschews dialogue entirely. When we call a work of fiction fast-paced, that's a quantitative, not a qualitative, judgment. Writing fiction isn't the Indy 500. Sometimes slow and steady wins the race, else we'd all have to agree that Thomas Mann, Virginia Woolf, and Malcolm Lowry, to name but a few, are snail-paced, and hence lousy, writers.

SETTING

Context is everything, and our fates are determined as much by landscape as by geography. Set *Madame Bovary* in Beverly Hills in the 1990s, and you have no story. Our readers should be grounded in the time and place of our stories. This can be as easy as popping in a date here and there, or as subtle as a poster promoting the Works Progress Administration. A story set in Los Angeles hangs in a buttery layer of smog, while one set in New Orleans drips wrought iron and Spanish moss; a romance pitched against a "dark and stormy night" is bound to play out differently than one set on a bright, sunny day. Setting is character, after all, and imposes its own demands on plot.

Also look for ways to use setting metaphorically. The ubiquitous fog through which we view the London of Dickens's *Bleak House* evokes perfectly the dreary murkiness of the British court system that is the book's subject. In Marilynne Robinson's *Housekeeping,* the novel's setting is also its primal image: a lake that literally and figuratively drowns both the past and the present.

FLASHBACKS

In his early novel *The Centaur,* John Updike spends three tightly packed pages taking his reader on a side trip to New York City that has little, if anything, to do with the scene at hand, which takes place in a car on its way to a school on a snowy morning in Brewer, Pennsylvania. Strictly speaking, this sort of thing is what writers call a digression, except it isn't. Updike gets away with it, so we call it a flashback. Essentially, a flashback is a digression that works. How does Updike get away with a three-page flashback? First of all, by writing like John Updike, which never hurts. Second, by knowing just how far a reader's attention can be diverted from a scene before she either forgets the scene entirely or, worse, bails out.

Beginning authors often lose sight of their own scenes, letting them drift into flashbacks like Arctic explorers into snowstorms, never to be seen or heard from again. A master like Updike always knows what scene he's writing within, and how much tension it can hold. He knows he's got three pages in which to reminisce and sightsee, then the train leaves without him. Updike is also smart enough not to break into full-blown dialogue, knowing this might confuse the reader into thinking he's abandoned one scene to enter a new one, and to the same end limits his flashback to a single paragraph, however long.

Thus a general (and, to be sure, breakable) rule for flashbacks: keep them very brief. If a flashback insists on turning into a full-blown scene, consider putting it elsewhere, or giving it its own section or chapter.

VOICE

With the first few paragraphs of a story or novel, you make a contract with your reader. You agree to tell a particular kind of story in a particular voice. Whatever you contract to do, as with POV, you contract to do it *consistently*. And though it may be the hobgoblin of little minds, half of what we do as editors is done in the name of consistency.

It can even be argued that what we call *style* is little more than a writer's tics and mannerisms rendered consistent through editing to produce a narrator's voice. Do something weird once in a while and it's a mistake; do it consistently, and it's a style. A stylist, then, is a writer who pays particular attention to what I'll call the details: to language, punctuation, the use of figurative devices, sentence rhythms, and the overall music of words. I can't teach you to be poets, I tell my students, but I can teach you to be stylists. For the fiction writer, that's close enough.

But the very thought of a style throws many good writers, and their writing, into disarray. That's because many beginning writers worship an ideal of style that has nothing to do with its practice. Think of an actor wanting to look and sound like Marlon Brando, who assuredly had no such intention himself. Just as actors are born with certain equipment, each writer has particular strengths and gifts and must learn to work with, and not against, them.

The term *journalese* was, I think, coined by Hemingway to describe prose that, like most newspaper stories, is made to be read once, if that. If a story or book gets read twice or more, it's not for the story or even for the plot, but for the language, for the unique pleasures offered by a specific arrangement of words. Hence, if you want your stuff read only once, skip this part.

With journalese the reader gets all of the necessary information in the proper order. But the sentences just sit there; there's concision, but little if any music; there are characters, but there's no voice. As for poetry, or music, or something approximating those things, there's none to speak of. You've told your story, you've done an adequate, journeymanlike job. Which is to say your prose is dull, if not dead.

Try pitching your voice higher. Remember *His name was Ishmael*? The third person makes it weak. But suppose Melville had stuck to his first-person guns and written, *My name is Ishmael*. Or: *They call me Ishmael*. Or even: *You can call me Ishmael*. Compared to *Call me Ishmael,* all three versions frankly suck. This doesn't mean that by casting all of your sentences in the imperative you too can write a masterpiece. It means that writing powerfully means taking risks, daring to have a strong character like Ishmael pound out his first spoken words like a sledgehammer pounding red-hot steel. Or, at the other extreme, having the guts to let a spineless character like John Barth's protagonist in *The End of the Road* introduce himself like so: "In a sense, I am Jacob Horner . . ." One way or another, the author must take a stand with his material, must assume a position of authority, even the authority of weakness, and hold it, and not let go, ever.

THEME

As I've said, we read fiction to learn about people. And though we may start with some notion of a theme, we needn't know exactly what we're writing about until we've written it. As the historian Daniel J. Boorstin famously said, "I write to discover what I think." By writing we stumble upon our themes. They are the result, not the cause.

Still, when themes emerge, as writers we're responsible for recognizing and highlighting them. For instance, in *The Great Gatsby,* as the theme of financial greed grew out of his material, Fitzgerald chose to color the light at the end of Daisy's dock green, and to mention it not once but several times, including the most conspicuous place, at the novel's conclusion.

Writers don't plant themes, they find and nurture them, make them resonate for the reader, dress them up and display them. And, if they're as good as Fitzgerald, they do so with a subtlety bordering on the invisible.

> YOUR TURN:
> Return to something you have written, perhaps from one of the previous exercises. Revise the piece, making some kind of major adjustment—changing the point of view, overhauling the dialogue, altering the setting . . . As you revise, force yourself to focus solely on this single craft element. If so desired, you may take another round of revision, focusing on another major craft element. With so many craft elements to juggle, often it's nice to focus on just *one* thing at a time.

SWEATING THE SMALL STUFF

Now, with the Big Things in place, comes the time for microrevision. You've heard the saying *"Don't sweat the small stuff."* Now's the time to sweat it. But fear not: this part can be as much fun as that fevered first draft. This is where you get to sharpen your editing pencil and line-edit yourself into the next best thing to a poet: a literary stylist.

Once again, this is a good time to read your stuff aloud. Any little thing that trips you up as you read is worth marking and reconsidering.

It's also a good time to hand your work over to a trusted colleague for some feedback, with the understanding that you are the final judge of what stays and goes.

Some Little Things to consider:

GRAMMAR AND PUNCTUATION

Grammar is a convention, something that civilized people can agree upon, and, like all conventions, creative souls are free to depart from it, with good reason. In writing this sentence, I spell the words according to Webster's dictionary, pause with a comma after the word *sentence,* capitalize the first word, and end with a period. but what if i chooz not to dew so what if i chooz to dispenss with speling an punkchewayshun an yooz ownlee lowurkaze ledderz My guess is you'll be confused, if not flabbergasted.

Grammar is one of the few things, maybe the only thing, that keeps writers civilized. Use it. Not slavishly or mindlessly, but with due respect for the powerful minds that have brought it to bear over the ages. An indented paragraph is a lovely thing; why so many choose to dispense with indents is beyond me. Punctuation marks are dramatic personae: the ebullient exclamation mark, the impulsive dash, the coy ellipse, the intellectual semicolon. A simple comma, improperly placed, can make all the difference. *Pardon, impossible to be hanged,* wrote the king's page, when what he meant to write was, *Pardon impossible, to be hanged.* In both cases he should have used a semicolon, but let's not quibble.

But this is no place for a grammar lesson; a good book on English usage can give you that. Also, if you haven't done so already, buy a copy of *The Elements of Style*, by William Strunk and E. B. White. This modestly slim volume takes up no more space than T. S. Eliot's poem *The Waste Land,* and it's as good. Whatever you need to know about the uses and abuses of English is in there, and more, including such disarming advice as "Be clear."

Not that you should sell your artistic soul to Messrs. Strunk and White, or to anyone else. But before breaking conventions, know them, at least. Only once mastered can they be broken with flair. Otherwise, people may just think you're dumb.

THE LESS-THAN-PERFECT IMPERFECT TENSE

When it comes to good prose, the imperfect tense—i.e., *he was talking; she was going; they were screaming*—could not be more aptly named. The words *is, was,* and *were* are all variants of the verb *to be*, which, among dead verbs, wears the heavyweight crown. While most verbs are chosen for their evocative powers, *to be* paints no picture in the mind, conveys no action, makes not the slightest dent in the reader's psyche. It says practically nothing. To find a deader word, one must reach for an article or a conjunction, such as *the* or *and* or *but*.

Which begs the question: why do writers use, let alone overuse, the imperfect tense? Why write, *Sam was wearing a pink rugby shirt*, when you could say just as easily that he *wore* one? Why *Susan was running*, when if she *ran* she'd get there faster?

True, in conversation people tend to use the imperfect tense. It sounds friendlier, softer. Which explains why, in the merry, merry month of May, I didn't *walk* down the street one day; I *was* walk*ing*. For sure, the past imperfect has its place, and not just in corny old songs. But used too frequently, out of sheer lazy habit, like a carnivorous wasp it sucks the meat out of otherwise healthy writing. That space taken up by *was* might have held a stronger, more active verb. *My cousin Gilberto was at the dinner table*. Okay. *My cousin Gilberto slumped at the dinner table*. Better.

MIND YOUR METAPHORS

A metaphor is a poetic device whereby one thing is described in terms of another. *Lester's mouth is an open sewer* is, we hope, a metaphor. Add the word *like,* and you get the watered-down version, *Lester's mouth is like an open sewer*—a simile. My rule, if there is one, being this: if you can change a simile into a metaphor without confusing people, do so. Why say what something is *like,* when you can say what it *is*? Your reader isn't stupid. The reader knows you're being figurative; to be told so is an insult. And you must never insult, or underestimate, your reader.

About mixing metaphors: don't. If the art deco hotel in your novel starts off looking like an ocean liner, don't turn it into a wedding cake. If a metaphor starts out watery, keep it watery. If the stage floor under the spotlights looks like *a strip of sandy beach,* the shifting, murmuring audience may be likened to *surf,* but not *a field of Kansas corn.* Steinbeck wrote, "Words pick up flavors and odors like butter in a refrigerator." Metaphors are onions. Be careful, or they'll stink up everything in the icebox.

MIND YOUR MODIFIERS

A modifier is a word—adjective or adverb—that modifies another word. One hopes that in modifying, the modifier adds meaning that isn't already there. The trouble with most adjectives and adverbs is that they're dead wood. *Desperately lonely* is such a case. The desperation of loneliness is implied by the word *lonely;* it doesn't need help; it can manage fine on its own. Choose the right nouns and verbs, and you won't need adverbs and adjectives. Go through and strike out any adjective or adverb that is either not doing much work or can be replaced by a noun or verb that will work much harder.

Of course, adjectives and adverbs needn't be shunned entirely. The reason why modifiers have earned a bad reputation is because writers use them perfunctorily, and not as they ought to be used, to boldly send a noun or adjective somewhere it's never been before. When, in his novel *Catch-22,* Joseph Heller, who loves his modifiers, describes General Dreedle's *ruddy, monolithic face,* he adds something to that face that wasn't there. When he modifies a silence with *austere,* the reader hears the silence differently. And when he endows obsequious military doctors and colonels with *efficient mouths* and *inefficient eyes,* the reader suspects she knows precisely what he means, even if she has no idea. "Go in fear of modifiers" doesn't mean don't use them; that's the coward's way out. It means use them boldly, bravely, but sparingly, as a chef uses spices.

KILL THOSE CLICHÉS

The novelist Martin Amis calls all writing a "campaign against cliché." "Not just clichés of the pen," he writes, "but clichés of the mind and clichés of the heart."

A cliché is a figure of speech that once had its moment in the sun. Once upon a time, the phrase *It's raining cats and dogs* was poetry worthy of Shakespeare. Now it's just a poor little tired old cliché. Were you the first to coin that expression, you'd be rightly proud. But you're not, and neither am I, and should either of us commit that particular string of words to paper, except as dialogue in the mouth of a bland character, we should be ashamed. We're supposed to be writers; we're supposed to come up with our own strings of words to describe the rain.

And that's really all there is to cliché. When, reading over your draft, your eyes come upon a familiar grouping of words, odds are you've authored a cliché. It needn't be as obvious or extravagant as *It's raining cats and dogs*. *A heart of stone* is a cliché; so are *baby-blue eyes;* so is whatever gets handed to someone *on a silver platter*. Most cliché s, in fact, are fairly prosaic: *desperately lonely* qualifies; so does *wreaked havoc;* so do *abject poverty* (what other kind is there?) and *sweating profusely* and *every name in the book*. Said too often, even "the heaventree of stars hung with humid nightblue fruit," Joyce's most gorgeous line in *Ulysses,* risks turning into a cliché.

WATCH YOUR ATTRIBUTIONS

Said—that most watery of words—is the perfect host to dialogue: smooth, discreet, all but invisible, like the butler in Kazuo Ishiguro's *Remains of the Day*. Therefore stop killing yourself to come up with new, improved ways of saying *said*. No need for she *chuckled, barked, sighed, groaned*. No need to have your characters *intone, utter,* or, worse, *opine* things, or *spit* or *blurt* them out. Nor is there good cause to have them *affirm* something *with* or without *conviction,* when they could just as easily say *yes*. Or, better still, nod.

I don't mean to imply that *said* is the only allowable attribution. In its 340 pages, no character in Nelson Algren's delectably odd-ball *The Man with the Golden Arm* ever *says* anything. Instead they: *agreed* / *wanted to know* / *pointed out* / *assured* / *replied* / *demanded* / *told* / *warned* / *called* / *mourned* / *decided* / *put in cunningly*. Algren is a master at avoiding *said*. On the other hand, Robert Stone, no less an author, never uses any other attribution. Both are brave, honorable men.

EXCOMMUNICATE THOSE LATINISMS

By my definition, a Latinism is an unnecessarily bulky word, typically derived from the Latin, when a simple, plain one would do. Hence, don't have people *converse* when they can *talk*. If Hank goes to the package store, he can *buy* a bottle of rock and rye; he needn't *purchase* it. As for words like *variegated, ascertain, beneficial, extrapolate, resumption, extemporaneous,* and *preliminary* (to give just a few *exemplary* examples), they belong in jargony annual reports, not in good fiction.

Why is so much academic writing bad? Because it's pretentious; because it imitates clear, concise writing while being neither clear nor concise. People say lawyers write badly. But legal writing, done well, can be gorgeous (see Judge Woolsey's opinion on *Ulysses*). Bad legal writing isn't bad because it's legal, but because it's *bad*. To paraphrase Tolstoy, all bad writing is bad in pretty much the same handful of ways, pretentiousness being the worst.

The easiest way to be pretentious is to use pretentious words, words like *ascertain* and *perpetrate*. *At this point in time we have ascertained that the perpetrator was apprehended* . . . At this point in time I want you to forget forever the phrase *at this point in time*. Likewise forget *the fact that* and *the question whether*. Be on the lookout for words ending in *tion*. Ditto *ism, acy, ance, ness,* and *ment*. Such words are for politicians, not poets, and maybe for a few pretentious narrators like Nabokov's Humbert, who'd be lost without his lexicon.

When in doubt, cross out or replace the overripe words. Simplify. Your readers will ~~extend gratitude to~~ thank you.

YOUR TURN:
Return to the piece from the previous exercise, upon which you tampered with something major. Even if you're sick of it by now, stick with it. Revise the piece doing the following: 1) check the grammar; 2) weed out the *be* verbs, modifiers, cliches, and pretentious words, reserving the right to keep any of them you find absolutely necessary; 3) unmix any mixed metaphors; 4) adjust any attributions that call attention to themselves. You may look for all of these things at once or do them one at a time. When done,

congratulate yourself for graduating to the role of an editor.

CUTTING AND TWEAKING

Readers are rude. They'll put your story or novel down in the middle of that sublime passage you spent ten hours on and never pick it up again, without apology. The reader holds all the cards; he has no obligation to the writer, while the writer has every obligation to him. That's why writers cut and tweak, mercilessly, throughout the revision process, down to its final stages.

There comes a time when you must cast a stern, judgmental eye on each and every one of your sentences, like a hanging judge whose noose is a sharpened pencil. No mercy here. As Don Newlove, the man with the bleeding fingers, says, "It's best to cut, not just scrape." And so your lead scalpel hovers over every line, every word.

"Omit needless words," say Strunk and White. I couldn't have said it better. For sure I couldn't have said it more concisely.

So much cutting may seem masochistic, but the fact is a piece of writing that can work well in five thousand words shouldn't run to ten thousand. And you'll be surprised what you can cut. So much of what we state is implied; so much that we've spelled out can be deduced or imagined. Remember, the reader wants to participate in the story. Do all their imagining for them, and they feel left out. Furthermore, the reader's imagination is a better writer than you or I will ever be, so why not let it do some of the work? And what we cut none but ourselves will ever miss. Unlike oil paints, words cost nothing; use as many as you like, scrape them all away, use some more—no charge. There's no excuse, in other words, for saving your words.

By tweaking I mean crafting sentences and paragraphs, reorchestrating them, shifting and changing the words around until they're as clear and pungent and crisp as possible. Like nipping and tucking, cutting and tweaking go hand in hand.

Tweaking may be less painful than cutting, but it's trickier. It calls for experience. For every paragraph I've improved through tweaking, I've mutilated dozens. Literary surgeons, we practice on our own bodies, without anesthesia, and learn from our mistakes. But we learn.

Let me share with you, if I may, the evolution of a troublesome paragraph from my own novel, *Life Goes to the Movies*. The scene: a restaurant floating on the East River. In the book's earliest draft the scene is merely sketched, with no attempt to evoke mood or atmosphere. It's hardly written:

> *The wedding took place in August of 1985 on a barge on the East River, Brooklyn side. As if to celebrate the occasion the stars were out. A twelve-piece jazz orchestra played.*

Journalese. Now strap yourselves into a time machine and skip ahead several drafts:

> *The wedding reception took place on a barge on the East River, with the Brooklyn Bridge humming its harpsong in the warm damp air high above us. Across the water, Manhattan's rhinestone tiara glittered. Carved ice statues cradled sterling caviar buckets, while a twelve-piece swing orchestra in vanilla jackets and gold derbies bounced brass noodles and spun ribbons of silver into the breezy dark night.*

My God, look at all those modifiers! Here the author reaches for a Fitzgeraldian lushness, and falls on his face. The *rhinestone tiara* is a cliché unfit for a pulp novelist. And then comes the adjectival parade—*carved, sterling, vanilla, gold, brass, silver, breezy, dark*—that leaves this reader lurching for a private barge from which to throw up. The *brass noodles* and *silver ribbons* were a valiant but misguided attempt at synesthesia, to turn notes for the ear into images for the eye. But the metaphor strays too far from its subject.

Glide your time machine forward eight months, through two more drafts, and read:

> *Montage. Night. A canvas-tented barge docked on the Brooklyn side of the East River. Summer drizzle softens the mucky air as the fabled bridge rasps with car traffic overhead. Ice mermaids cradle silver buckets of caviar, oysters on cracked ice squirm in ragged shells; shrimp cling for dear life above flaming seas of cocktail sauce. A swing orchestra in vanilla jackets and paper derbies weaves and thumps rhythms into the drizzling dark. Across the river, meanwhile, the Manhattan skyline wastes as much electricity as possible.*

Better, but still too many modifiers. Here cutting will become part of the improvement process, as it usually does. How 'bout this:

Montage. Night. A tented barge docked on the Brooklyn side of the East River. Summer drizzle softens the air as the bridge rasps with traffic overhead. Ice mermaids cradle buckets of caviar, oysters on cracked ice squirm in shells; shrimp cling for dear life above flaming seas of cocktail sauce. A swing orchestra weaves and thumps rhythms into the dark. Across the river, the Manhattan skyline wastes as much electricity as possible.

Now the *brass noodles* and *silver ribbons* have been swept off the dance floor, replaced instead by *clinging shrimp* and *thumping rhythms*. In keeping with the novel's theme of life blending with movies, the screenplay language has been added. Here the emphasis is on verbs: *tented, softens, rasps, cradle, cracked, squirm, cling, flaming* (used adjectivally here, but keeping its verbal punch), *weaves, thumps*. *Wastes as much electricity as possible* strikes me now as passive, weak, but I could think of no active way of expressing that thought. Maybe you can.

For better or worse, that's how the passage stands in the novel. You may disagree with my choices. But I think you will agree that overall the passage has been improved.

> YOUR TURN:
> Return to something you have written and, yes, you may use a previous exercise. Cut it by a third. It may seem impossible, but it probably isn't. Be ruthless. Then take a break from the piece—a half hour or several days. See if the piece isn't actually better, improved simply by the act of reduction. If you're so inclined, get back in there and start tweaking, elevating what remains to a higher level of quality.

How do we know when we're done? How do we know when our fiction has been improved to the point where it can be improved no more? Some writers claim they never really finish their stories or books; they abandon them. When the law of diminishing returns sets in, that's as good a time as any to declare victory, or throw in the towel. For some writers, no story is finished until it's between the covers of a published book. And even then they can't stop tweaking.

And then there are those who say they simply know when the work is done; when all the planets seem to have aligned themselves, when form and meaning are so of a piece they seem indistinguishable, and every word feels inevitable, if not carved in stone. For me, it's like raising children; at a certain age, ready or not, out they go. They must complete themselves out in the cruel, cold world. Perhaps some stories will never please certain people; perhaps they will never be universally loved and admired. But like their author they will have done their best.

CHAPTER 11
THE BUSINESS OF WRITING: DRIVING YOURSELF NUTS FOR FUN AND PROFIT

BY CORENE LEMAITRE

My first memory of meeting with an editor is of being soaking wet. I was sitting in the office of the director for fiction at HarperCollins UK, in damp shoes, clutching a cup of coffee and wondering what to say.

My newly acquired agent was there. She, of course, knew exactly what to say. "Eleven people for dinner tonight," she confided to the director, with the savoir faire of the literary insider. *I don't even know eleven people,* I thought.

But there I was. I'd gotten lost en route, in the rain, and I'd lacked the foresight to bring an umbrella. Pitifully early, I'd stopped at a café to tidy myself up in their makeshift restroom while suspicious staff reeking of bacon hovered outside.

"This isn't really happening," I told myself. "There's no meeting. Hell, there's no building."

For the large yet discreet edifice that is HarperCollins UK had eluded me to the point where I'd ceased to believe it existed—or that, as soon as I stepped up to it, it would disappear into the mist.

But it didn't. I approached and babbled into the intercom. The gates opened. I walked by a chauffeured Jaguar that I later learned belonged to the CEO and then past the security guards—more garbled explanations—all the while feeling as though I were committing a terrible crime.

The lobby was cold. I felt very small. But I walked out of there with an offer and, yes, it changed my life.

The writing life. Why do so many crave it? Few professions hold the degree of uncertainty that writers endure. The emotional and financial ups and downs are extreme. Nevertheless, I've yet to go to a party where nine out of ten people—successful, rational people—don't want to be writers.

If you're reading this, then I assume you crave it too.

Part of me wants to say, "Go for it." The other part is shouting, "Stop! Don't do it. You'll drive yourself nuts. You'll endure crippling poverty. And however much you assert your normalcy, people will regard you as either an object of envy or a freak."

But if you're sure . . .

THE HOLY GRAIL OF PUBLICATION

"Okay," you say, "I've written some stories and I've got a novel in the works. I'm ready to launch my literary career. So, tell me how to get published."

Enthusiasm. I like it. The desire to get published can be powerfully motivating. But though the benefits are myriad, publication should not be your only goal. In an industry as competitive as writing, it's essential that you commit to the journey, the grail-quest of becoming the best writer you can be. Indeed, there are those who write solely for the love of it.

"Is it possible to make a lot of money as a writer?" is one of the questions I'm asked most often. My reply, consisting of various statistics and an explanation of royalty structures, invariably disappoints. What they want to hear is a simple *yes*.

As writing is hard work, your desire to profit from your efforts is understandable. But if you want to make serious money, fiction is probably not the best way to go about it. This is a feast-or-famine industry, where famine is much more common, and even well-established authors gnaw on the carrion bone. So, if you equate writing with winning the lottery, you are bound to be disappointed.

Without the incentive of wealth, you need to be very clear about your reasons for pursuing publication—and potentially, there are many. Getting published opens doors. You'll meet lots of great people and get invited to nice parties. The prestige alone will improve your life. Opportunities to travel, give talks, and be thoroughly nosy will come your way. Writing credits will provide you with personal and professional validation. Your confidence will grow. And it will really piss off your enemies.

But you'll pay the price. Getting published takes time. Editors and agents rarely respond quickly, and when they do, chances are that they'll reject your work. Identifying markets and preparing manuscripts will consume your leisure hours and take their toll on your personal life.

"But I don't want a life," you say. "I want to write and write and then send my material out until my knuckles swell and my brain turns to petroleum jelly."

Good. I can work with that. So let's proceed.

THE PRODUCT

"Typescripts arrive daily in the last stages of filth and decay. Breadcrumbs, bootlaces, long hairs, tobacco ash, and all sorts of other refuse appear between the pages . . . The first impression, therefore, is bad."
—Frank Swinnerton, *Authors and the Book Trade*

So, what exactly does it take to get published? Think of the process as a two-part equation. First, you create the product—in other words, the novel, novella, or short story. Then, you sell it. Very simple. Write, then sell. Neither is easy, and in order to get published, you will need to be good at both.

Note the business terminology. Product. Sell. Inappropriate? Not at all. As a writer, this is what you're going to be doing—running a small business.

Let's take a look at the first part of the equation, writing. You've just read ten chapters on craft (unless you've been naughty and skipped ahead), so you should have some understanding of how to create the product. Yes, that's what a novel or short story is. *Pride and Prejudice* is a product. "Cathedral" is a product. What makes them products? The price tag.

And as with any business proposition, you need to make that product appealing. So what does it take to make agents and publishers want what you've got?

First, you will need a completed piece of writing. Not an idea, not a few pages, but a fully finished work. This is essential, though many aspiring writers would like to believe otherwise. I was once treated to a "pitch" by an acquaintance convinced he had a great idea for a novel. He detailed every twist and turn. When finished, he turned to me.

"So, what do I do now?" he asked.

"Well, you have to write the book."

He stared at me, aghast. "The whole thing?"

Yes, the whole thing. Beginning, middle, and end. From the first agonizing word to the final draft that you cast, clammy-fingered, into the mailbox. No one is going to do it for you.

> YOUR TURN:
> It's time to finish something. If you have an unfinished short story lying around, finish it. If you don't have a short story under way, start and finish one. You should complete a short story even if you're mostly a novel person because you'll be able to finish it in a relatively short amount of time. If you're not sure what to work on, simply take your work from one of the exercises in this book and use that as a springboard for your project. If you want to be a fiction writer, the most important thing is to start a project and the second most important thing is to finish the first draft. Of course, if you're really serious, you'll need to take your project through numerous drafts. So do that too.

"But what about those authors who get huge advances on the basis of partial manuscripts?" you ask.

Well, those writers probably have previous best-sellers under their belts, with a sales record so good that their very name functions as a brand (there's that business terminology again). Best-selling authors achieve their status by writing books—genre or literary fiction—that for any number of reasons, including quality, sell well.

Which brings us to the next point, quality control. Editors and agents are busy people with little time to commit to development, so don't expect them to discern the hidden merit in your work. You must ensure that your product is outstandingly good.

"So, how do I do that?" you ask.

Well, it's tough, especially if you're new to the game and don't know exactly what editors and agents want. Given this difficulty, you might want to consider consulting a manuscript analyst.

Manuscript analysts, also known as freelance editors, professional readers, and book doctors, are expert in figuring out what's wrong with your writing and how to put it right. If requested, they will also evaluate the novel or short story's market potential. The advantage of working with an analyst prior to submitting to an agent or editor is that you benefit from industry-level criticism before approaching the industry. By identifying weaknesses and showing you how to fix them, an analyst may greatly increase your chances of acceptance.

There are many analysts out there—the good, the bad, and the ugly. Reputable analysts work freelance or through writing schools, and often advertise their services over the Internet or through writing magazines. Check their credentials. Published authors and individuals with a background in the industry are generally a safe bet. Don't hesitate to ask for references and sample reports.

So, let's assume that you've ensured that your work of fiction is first-rate. What next? Let's shift for a moment from content to format—in other words, how your manuscript should look.

If you want to make a good impression on an agent or editor, you must follow certain formatting guidelines. Your adherence to these rules of presentation will set you apart as a professional. Indeed, if you fail to follow standard format, you'll be dismissed as amateur and your work will not be seriously considered.

The standard format for all types of fiction is this:

- Use black type on white 8 1/2-by-11-inch paper.
- Choose a 12-point font, preferably Times New Roman, Courier, Courier New, or Arial.
- Double-space.
- Indent paragraphs.
- Place at least a one-inch margin all around.
- Number the pages in the upper right-hand corner.
- Spell-check and proofread—and I do mean old-fashioned proofreading, which is done by a human, not a computer.
- Include a title page with the title, word count, your name, address, phone number, and e-mail address. (Also include this information on the first page of the manuscript.)
- Keep your pages loose-leaf.

Some absolute no-no's:

- Fancy graphics or typesetting.
- Stapling or binding pages.
- Anything gimmicky, unless it is so apt and witty that it won't be viewed as an attention-getting device.
- Your head shot, photos of your kids or pets, pencil drawings . . . you'd be surprised at the things people will send to catch an agent's eye.

Having correctly formatted your manuscript, all that remains is to place it in an envelope (along with a cover letter). Although electronic submissions are becoming more popular, your initial approach will probably be by postal mail.

One more important point. Whenever you send anything to an agent or editor, *always include a stamped self-addressed envelope.* Use a large one if you'd like the manuscript back, a small one if you'd prefer a reply only, in which case specify in your accompanying letter that the manuscript need not be returned. No SASE, no response.

"But wait, how do I protect my work?" you say. "I've worked hard on this story. How do I keep some talentless schmuck from stealing my stuff?"

Not to worry. Copyright is automatic. In other words, you acquire federal copyright protection by the very act of putting words to paper. There are, however, advantages to registering your manuscript with the United States Copyright Office (www.loc.gov/copyright). While you cannot copyright an idea—for instance, the premise of a novel—it is possible to protect the execution. And for writers, this registration will allow you to file a copyright infringement action if someone plagiarizes your work.

That said, don't get too paranoid. Publishers are unlikely to steal a novel or story they can buy at minimal cost. There is no need to refer to copyright in your query letter or on the manuscript itself—indeed, as with incorrect formatting, this screams *amateur.* Send out your work with confidence. Remember, no one can steal your individual voice.

Corene Lemaitre
111 Little Street
Smalltown, PA 19876
Tel (987) 654-3210
writer@publishme.com

90,000 words

April Rising

by Corene Lemaitre

Chapter One

It doesn't take me long to figure out that something is wrong. To begin with, my key doesn't turn in the lock. I try all the old tricks – rattling the doorknob, lifting the door half an inch off the ground – but same verdict. No entry. Access denied.

I'm being observed. Our next-door neighbor is giving me the evil eye. She doesn't look as though she recognizes me. I wonder how long it will be before she calls the police.

The lock has been changed. It's a good one, state of the art, the kind that could probably perform a citizen's arrest – more than could be said of the old lock, which had been more of a formality. Anyone could have broken in. No one ever had, of course. There is no crime in Philmont, or pain, or unhappiness, or anything resembling the usual range of human emotions. The streets are safe, divorce is rare and everyone has health insurance. The only thing likely to kill you is boredom.

Dragonlady is definitely on to me. She's exacting, believes in "love thy neighbor" provided it's on her own terms. Keeps her lawn trimmed down to the

Sample manuscript page from April Rising *by Corene Lemaitre*

THE QUERY LETTER

"My manuscript is shipshape," you say, "so can I please, please put the damned thing in the mail?"

Be patient. We're almost there. You need one more item, a query letter.

A query letter is a cover letter, specifically one designed to pique an agent's or editor's interest in your work. With short fiction, this letter will be simple and will accompany the story. The query for a novel, which will probably accompany a portion of the work, is a bit more involved. Part of the query letter's function is to "hook" your target, so you must craft it in such a way that it impels the professional in question to request the entire manuscript.

Typically a query letter works something like this:

- An opening line or two introducing your short story or novel and explaining why you've contacted this particular agent or editor. Perhaps you've been referred to him by one of his authors, or maybe he handles work that resembles your own.
- A brief pitch of your story. Showcase character and situation. Pretend you're writing book-jacket copy. Intrigue, don't explain. For short stories, a line or two is sufficient, and for novels, one well-crafted paragraph.
- A bit about you. Don't sell yourself too hard; just try to convey a sense of who you are. Include anything relevant—writing credits, personal or professional expertise related to the subject matter, promotional experience . . . If you have none of these things, don't worry. Many don't.
- The closing. State that you've enclosed a self-addressed stamped envelope and that you look forward to the recipient's response.

The salutation must include the agent's or editor's name. *Dear Sir or Madam* won't cut it. And while it's a good idea to craft your letter along the guidelines above, feel free to make it your own. Be professional and concise but allow your style and personality to shine through. Remember, this is as much a demonstration of your writing ability as the short story or novel itself. Ensure that the end result reads well.

Mr. Frank Miller
Four Winds Quarterly
321 Main Street
Yellow Plains, WI 19123

Dear Mr. Miller,

Please consider my short story "Hard Cider Seesaw" (2,300 words) for your magazine.
As *Four Winds Quarterly* publishes fiction with a strong narrative line, I thought this tale
of a young man's confrontation with his childhood adversary (a most unlikely bully)
might be of interest to you.

My prose has been short-listed for the Mid-States New Writer Award and the *Lexicon*
First Fiction Prize. My poetry has been published in several literary magazines, and I'd
love to add *Four Winds Quarterly* to my list of credits.

An SASE is enclosed for a reply, but I don't need the manuscript back. I wish you
continued success with your magazine.

Best,

Matthew Piper

Sample query letter for a short story

YOUR TURN:
Pick a short story or novel that you have worked on,
are working on, or would like to work on. Then write
a query letter for it. Even if the project is unfinished,
it will be helpful to write the query because that
will force you to zero in on the essence of the story.
Strive to make the query both professional and
reflective of your personal voice. If your short story or
novel is ready to send out, then start doing so!

THE SLUSH PILE

So, what happens when you finally send out your work? Well, your submission is probably headed for the slush pile.

"What is that, like the Dead Zone?" you ask.

Not exactly. The slush pile is the industry's pet name for the accumulation of unsolicited (meaning unasked-for and largely unwanted) manuscripts received by editors and agents—and they receive many. Fortunately

Ms. Pam Goodwin
The Goodwin Agency
123 Fourth Avenue, Suite 567
New York, N.Y. 10000

Dear Ms. Goodwin,

Please find, enclosed, the first three chapters of *April Rising* (90,000 words). As your agency handles emerging writers, including J.J. Porter, whose work resembles my own, I wondered if this mainstream novel might be of interest to you.

Ellen Kaplan, carefree and twenty-three, returns to her affluent suburban home, only to discover that someone has taken her place. The culprit is April, former farm girl, HerbElixir saleswoman and proud owner of a porcelain Jesus collection. Rescued from destitution by Ellen's older brother, April has cast a spell of familial love on the entire Kaplan clan. Ellen sets out to topple her rival but in so doing discovers more than she bargained for, including the possibility that April may not be the enemy after all. This blackly comic tale explores friendship and family values at their most dysfunctional.

A bit about me. I have a B.F.A. from New York University, where I co-founded the Rough Draft writers' workshop, and was published in *The Minetta Review*. I've traveled extensively and currently live on a plane.

I've included a stamped self-addressed envelope for a reply only. I very much look forward to hearing from you.

Sincerely,

Corene Lemaitre

Sample query letter for a novel

for you, most of them will be poorly written, incorrectly formatted, or both. So although there is no guarantee of a response, a well-crafted and -presented manuscript may stand out. Initial screening will probably be done by an assistant. They know exactly what to look for, as agents and editors choose their staff with care. As your first point of contact, you could do worse than to catch the eye of a savvy editorial assistant or agent-in-training who is eager to discover new work.

Exercise rigorous quality control, and you have a better chance of surviving the slush pile than most.

SUBMITTING SHORT STORIES TO MAGAZINES

"I've got a few short stories ready to go," you say. "So, what do I do? Should I contact an agent?"

No. While an agent might consider a book-length collection of short stories, the effort required to market individual short stories is not worth the meager profit they command.

You're going to have to go it alone, so let's start by exploring potential markets for short stories.

At the top of the tier are the big glossies—the few large-circulation consumer magazines that (bless them) still publish fiction: *The New Yorker, Atlantic Monthly, Harper's, Esquire, Playboy, GQ, Jane, Seventeen,* among others. There's no harm in approaching them, but these high-profile markets are difficult to crack. But fear not, because you have access to the vast and glorious world of literary magazines.

What exactly is a literary magazine, or litmag? Well, it's a smaller-scale publication, often published quarterly, with a circulation of anywhere from several hundred to a few thousand. Many are associated with universities and nonprofit organizations. As they cannot attract vast sums from advertising, they often depend on foundation grants to survive. They are run by (generally unpaid) staff who do it for the love of literature or the work experience or the high cool factor. And many have an excellent reputation.

There are hundreds of litmags, from top-tier publications like *Zoetrope* and *The Paris Review,* which are almost as difficult to get into as the glossies, to small-scale efforts that exude the appealing whiff of the mimeograph and are the literary equivalent of garage pop. In addition, there is a growing body of litmags on the Web. Some correspond to print versions, others are published solely on-line. What they have in common is a willingness to work with new writers.

"But if there are so many of them, how do I choose?" you ask.

Easy. You begin by consulting the market guides.

Market guides are industry directories and periodicals that provide essential information on book and magazine publishers—who they are, what they want, and how to submit work to them. (Contact names should be confirmed by telephone or e-mail, as turnover in publishing is notoriously high.)

Among the most comprehensive market guides:

- *Writer's Market.* The largest guide. Covers both fiction and non-fiction.
- *Novel and Short Story Writer's Market.* Focuses on fiction and may be your best bet.
- *The International Directory of Little Magazines and Small Presses.* Title tells all. An exhaustive source.
- *The CLMP Directory of Literary Magazines and Presses.* Produced by the Council of Literary Magazines and Presses.
- *Poets & Writers* magazine. Plenty of market listings, plus features on writers and writing-related topics.
- *The Writer* magazine. In existence since 1887, it contains valuable tips, news, and advice.

These guides are widely available in bookstores and public libraries, and some have an on-line presence. You might also check out *The Best American Short Stories,* an annual anthology of short fiction gleaned largely from literary magazines. This will point you in the direction of a number of promising markets.

Your next step is to select which magazines to target. Based on the above guides, choose a few that look as though they might publish the kind of fiction you write. Send away for copies. Alternatively, check out your local bookstore or newsstand. If you're good at squatting, you may be able to keep the sum you shell out to a minimum.

Then study them to ensure that the type of fiction they publish corresponds to your own. Analyze the stories for both content and style—subject matter, tone, syntax, and so on. Do they focus on narrative? Or are they more "slice of life"? Is one POV favored over another? Does setting play a central role? How about the language and sentence structure? Simple? Or more complex?

"Once I've determined the right magazines," you ask, "am I ready to send?"

A resounding *yes.*

Note in your query letter that you've read their publication. It doesn't hurt to mention that you really liked it. If you can slip in that you've actually bought a copy . . . well, let's just say that these editors, overworked and underappreciated, may look upon your work that much more favorably.

With the exception of a few, litmags pay nothing or very little, but the benefits of publication are huge. Preparing a story for submission will help you to hone your work to a high standard. Seeing your work in print will provide you with a sense of accomplishment. And when you are ready to submit a novel or collection, your writing credits will increase your chances of catching a book editor's or agent's eye.

> YOUR TURN:
> If you're interested in writing short stories, go track down some literary magazines and read them. Do this with at least three different litmags, keeping an eye out for the publications that feel most right for your work. If none of the litmags you read look right for you, go find some others. You'll find a wonderfully diverse selection of literary magazines out there. Certainly one of them is perfect for your fiction.

BOOK PUBLISHERS

"Publishers are very simple, innocent people, so far as books are concerned. They often do not know one book from another. But they are optimists, sentimentalists, and experimentalists . . ."
—Frank Swinnerton, *Authors and the Book Trade*

"Speaking of books," you say, "I've got one of those too—a novel. Any chance of it finding a home?"

Certainly. To this end, let's take a closer look at the world of book publishing.

The quote above was published in 1932. As you may have guessed, things have changed a bit since then. Publishing, once widely regarded as a "gentleman's industry," has become a behemoth governed by big business. At one time, small publishing "houses" dominated the scene. But they merged, then merged again, to become the conglomerates we know today. Some of the houses survived in the form of imprints—subsidiary branches that specialize in particular types or styles of writing. Other houses survived as independents. Today, publishers can be divided into these two basic categories: conglomerates and independents.

The conglomerates are mostly located in New York City and include Random House, Simon & Schuster, HarperCollins, Penguin Putnam, Harcourt Brace, and others. They carry a lot of clout and most best-sellers display their corporate seal. The independents, among them such places as Algonquin, Soho Press, and Coffee House, range from small literary and university presses scattered throughout the country to larger New York City–based firms. In recent years, their marketing savvy has increased and distribution is often excellent.

As a writer, it's important that you acquaint yourself with this increasingly complex and profit-driven industry. Study the market guides, read books on the business, visit publishers' Web sites, peruse trade magazines. Learn as much as you can about this world you are entering. Knowing the context can help you to break in.

Some writers prefer to join forces with large publishers, finding their prestige and influence advantageous. Others swear by independents, citing the in-house attention their work receives. In the end, the size of the company has little bearing on success. You may work with a small team inside a large publishing house. You may work with virtually everyone at a small publishing house. Triumph will depend on commitment and creativity, not corporate dimensions.

If you submit a manuscript yourself to a publisher, what are your chances of acceptance? With the conglomerates, very slim. You can streak up to Simon & Schuster stark naked and hurl a manuscript over the transom, but it won't make any difference. Your manuscript will be heaved onto the slush pile or, more likely, just sent back. Independents and small presses may be more open. You will find *Literary Market Place, Writer's Market,* and Jeff Herman's *Writer's Guide to Book Editors, Publishers and Literary Agents* helpful in your search for a publisher willing to read unsolicited work.

But if you really want to increase the odds of acceptance, you are going to need an agent.

AGENTS

Agents. Those literary archangels who lift you out of the slush pile and carry you through the pearly gates of publication. They read your work, buy you hot dinners, and introduce you to influential talk-show hosts. Every waking moment (and half of their sleeping ones) they network furiously, always with you in mind. And, of course, they make you large amounts of money.

Too good to be true? I'm afraid so. Agents are, in fact, merely mortal.

But they are an extraordinary breed of hardworking industry professionals who can help you get your work into print.

What exactly is an agent? An agent is someone who will sell your work to a publisher in exchange for a commission, generally 10 to 15 percent of the sale price. Why do you need one? Primarily because no one is better equipped to match and deliver a manuscript to an editor at a publishing house. Editors are often criticized for their reluctance to read unsolicited work, but the simple fact is that they can't. Their time and resources are limited, so they depend on agents to do the initial screening.

An agent's fundamental role is to sell your work. As part of this, he or she will:

- Read your work and provide suggestions for revision.
- Submit your work to the most appropriate editor.
- Negotiate the best possible terms for you.
- Exploit additional rights—foreign, serial, film, etc.
- Examine the contract, clause by clause.
- Track payments from publishers.

Once that (hopefully juicy) contract is signed and sealed, your agent may take on further roles in the areas of promotion and grievance resolution. She may buy you a celebratory drink and, if the going gets tough, give you a shoulder to cry on.

So, what does an agent look for in a writer? Given the increasingly competitive market for fiction, what would persuade a top agent to take on a first-timer? "What I look for is originality," says Suzanne Gluck, co-director of the William Morris Agency literary department. "Be it a singular literary voice, a new perspective on the human condition, or a view of a place we've not seen before. And anyone who can make me laugh is a winner in my book."

In describing the ideal author, Gluck is unequivocal. "My dream client is someone whose work I have genuine passion for, and for whom my advocacy is a natural outgrowth of my admiration. And to tell you the truth, over the years I've learned to limit myself to these folks."

So we're back to the beginning. You've got to write a good book.

You also want to hook up with an agent who is right for you. "The two most critical elements in an agent/author relationship are trust and a shared vision," notes Gluck. "Agents serve as creative sounding boards, fiduciary advocates, and, I hope, fierce professional champions. There are a lot of decisions of all sizes to be made along the way. When the client trusts that the agent has their best interests at heart, and the agent trusts that the client will always put their heart into their work, there's a greater chance the rest will fall into place."

"Sounds good," you say. "I want an agent of my own. So, how do I choose?"

Well, there are a number of reference books that provide lists. The most high-profile are *Writer's Market, Literary Market Place, The Writer's Digest Guide to Literary Agents,* and Jeff Herman's *Writer's Guide to Book Editors, Publishers and Literary Agents.* These guides are revised regularly and some have online counterparts. If these sources prove too costly, check out your local library. Always call to confirm the contact names and addresses you find in the guides.

But the staggering amount of information these books provide about agents—who they are, what they want, and how to get in touch with them—poses a bit of a problem. How do you narrow it down?

Your best bet, in the first instance, is to identify a few writers whose work is similar to your own, and figure out who represents them. Some sleuth work may be necessary, as agency client lists are often confidential, so try these methods. Open a novel by one of these writers and check the acknowledgments—authors often thank their agents. Search the Internet—you may find the information you need in an interview or on the author's homepage. Finally, visit the publisher's Web site—you may find the agent listed under film or subrights, or mentioned in a press release. Similarly, check the publisher's catalog.

An alternative way to pick an agent is to identify a good one and then investigate the kind of writing they represent. To this end, read the "Hot Deals" column of *Publisher's Weekly,* which details who's selling what, and for how much. Good to know.

YOUR TURN:
If you're interested in writing a novel, get the names of several agents who might be right for the kind of novel you have written, are writing, or plan to write. This will take some detective work, but you'll end up with the names of some agents who might be

interested in seeing your novel when it's ready to be sent out. And maybe those names will give you the incentive you need to finish the novel.

Agencies come in three sizes—small, medium, and large. The smallest are the sole traders, whose agencies often bear their name. Medium-sized agencies will employ several people, sometimes quite a few. Others are huge, and represent screen and television writers as well, often "packaging" book-to-film deals from their own pool of clients. Throughout the entirety of this range, you will find excellent agents.

Many agencies have both established and new agents. So, which is better? Some top reps exceed their authors in notoriety, acquiring odd nicknames and granting interviews to glossy magazines. Their clients benefit from their experience and high profile. But up-and-coming agents have their own advantages. What they may lack in clout and contacts they make up for in determination and drive. Ultimately, it boils down to the individual. Look for someone who respects your work and is willing to fight on your behalf.

SUBMITTING TO AGENTS

"I've made a list of suitable agents," you say, "and now I'm ready to submit my novel. Should I send them the whole manuscript?"

No. They won't have time to read it, nor do they need to, because they can tell from just a sampling whether or not you can write well.

So, what do you send? Well, you have two options. Your first is to follow the specifications under each agent's entry in the previously listed reference books. Check these guides, and you'll find that some agents ask for a query letter only, or a query and a synopsis (a plot summary of one to several pages), while others want to see a few pages of the book itself. Very rarely do they request the whole novel.

Your second option is to ignore the agent's request and send a query letter with about fifty pages of the manuscript. The reasoning behind this approach is as follows: Many first novels have little structure, if any. They are episodic, merely a series of scenes strung together, and this is one of the primary reasons why agents reject work. Fifty pages will demonstrate that you can shape a story.

Should you include a synopsis? Perhaps, but there's a danger that they will read the synopsis and lose interest. A synopsis will not demonstrate that you can craft prose. Better to try to hook them on that first page and impel them to read on. No one can resist a good audition.

"Should I send my query to every agent on my list?" you ask. "All twenty-five?"

That's probably too many. Begin with three or four. As with every endeavor, there's a learning curve, and you don't want to use up every promising agent you've found. Select a variety and see what kind of response you get.

Some agents have a no-"multiple"- or -"simultaneous"-submission policy. This means that they would prefer an exclusive while considering your manuscript. This is understandable. Agents don't want to fall in love with your work only to discover that you've accepted another offer. But approaching agents one by one may take too long, as each will take several weeks or even months to respond. So, sending your initial query to three or four is a reasonable compromise that doesn't violate the no-multiple-submission policy.

Once an agent expresses an interest in your work, it's important to respond quickly. If she requests the entire manuscript, send it right away. Allow her eight weeks to get back to you. At this point, it's permissible to send a polite follow-up letter inquiring after the status of your manuscript, but don't pester her by e-mail or telephone.

There are several possible outcomes. You may be rejected by all of them. If this happens, try to figure out why. Your manuscript may need a bit more work, or you may have simply hit the wrong agents. Select several more, and try again. Then again, each may love your manuscript and ask to meet with you in person or at least have an extended phone conversation. Get in touch with them immediately and arrange to have this talk. Remember, a "shared vision" is desirable. Your relationship with your agent will be a crucial one, and this discussion will help you to determine whether or not he or she is right for you. After speaking with you, each may offer you representation. If this happens, try to make a decision as swiftly as possible. Remember, this is very much like a proposal of marriage (a metaphor often employed in the agent-author relationship), and you don't want to leave anyone "hanging on." Once you've selected your agent and informed him or her of your decision, send a polite thank-you note to the others. After all, your professional relationship with your agent of choice may not work out, and you don't want to burn bridges.

If only one agent expresses an interest in your work, but after meeting it doesn't feel right, then don't sign with him or her. Contact a few others. If your work is strong, you will find the right agent for you.

BEWARE NONLEGITIMATE AGENTS

"Hey, check out this classified ad," you say. "'Established literary agent now accepting manuscripts from new writers. All genres.' Hot damn. Should I send?"

No. The "invitation to submit" is a danger sign. Bona fide agents receive more work than they can handle. They don't need to place ads. This particular "agent" is a fraud and the request for manuscripts is a scam.

These so-called agents do not make money from sales to publishers but rather from "reading fees" solicited from the author. Contact them about the possibility of representation, and you will receive a request for money—at least several hundred dollars. Alternatively, they may refer you to an "editor" who will charge you quite a lot for not much (rest assured that the "agent" gets a kickback).

Legitimate agents don't charge you for reading your manuscript or for signing you as a client.

So, how can you be sure that your agent is legit? Well, most reputable agents are members of the Association of Authors' Representatives (www.aar-online.org). To qualify, an agent must meet professional standards specified in the AAR's bylaws and agree to subscribe to its canon of ethics. Members cannot charge reading fees. So, find out if your agent belongs, though not all legitimate agents do. You may also interview your potential agent, once she has expressed an interest in your work. An excellent list of questions can be found on the AAR's Web site. If in doubt, ask for a list of recent sales, and investigate her track record.

RESPONSE AND REJECTION

"Well, I've got a lot of stuff out there," you say. "I guess I'm going to get a lot of rejections, huh?"

Initially, yes. But there are different types of rejections, some of which are quite useful and constitute reason to be of good cheer. And at some point, there could be an acceptance, if you just hang in there.

The types of responses you may receive are more or less the same whether coming from agents, editors at publishing houses, or magazine editors. Let's go over some typical examples:

- *No response:* Why not, when you'd enclosed the SASE? Who knows—too busy, too disorganized, too jaded . . . Whatever the reason, let it go. Their loss.
- *Form rejection:* A standardized letter, but don't lose heart. This is the most common type of response. It does not necessarily mean that your work was poor or even inappropriate. Rather, it suggests overworked agents and editors.
- *Personalized rejection:* This could be anything from a form rejection with a handwritten note scrawled in the margin to a neatly typed missive detailing exactly why your story doesn't work for them. This is rare, and may be a sign that they regard your writing as having promise.
- *Rejection with invitation to resubmit:* Consider this encouraging. You'll receive suggestions for improvement and a request to see the revision. If possible, try to incorporate at least some of their recommendations into a rewrite. Then send the story back to them with a photocopy of their letter and a thank-you note.
- *Acceptance:* This may come as a letter or a phone call. Celebrate. You've earned it.

You may have good fortune and receive an acceptance right away, but chances are that you will face a lot of rejection. If so, you will be joining an illustrious list of writers, including Herman Melville, Margaret Mitchell, Charles Dickens, Virginia Woolf, James Joyce, Beatrix Potter, Dylan Thomas, Emily Brontë, and Marcel Proust, who have faced this setback and lived to tell the tale. Over time the sting of rejection may diminish to a pang of disappointment, but it always hurts.

The best way to deal with it is by writing. Turn over the rejection slip and throw down some words. Brainstorm. Freewrite. Draft a short story.

Don't let the setback of rejection get under your skin. If possible, have several projects on the go. Submit manuscripts regularly and keep working on more, and rejection will cease to seem like such a big obstacle.

As you send out your writing, it's a good idea to keep track of what you're sending to whom and when. You don't want to target the same individual twice. Also, you may need to chase people, especially if others are interested in the same material. If your work is rejected, recording the reasons may help, as this may reveal a pattern. Acceptances are enlightening as well—you may discover, for instance, that you're having success, or getting warm, with a particular sort of magazine. Finally, keeping a list, even of rejections, is good for morale. Remember, every *no* brings you closer to a *yes*.

You may regard keeping track as yet one more task that robs you of time for your actual writing, but remember that you're running a business, and, as with any small business, you are responsible for day-to-day operations, including administration. So, develop good record-keeping habits. Once you've established a system, you'll find that you've actually maximized your writing time, with increased job satisfaction and peace of mind.

MONEY AND CONTRACTS

"So, what if an agent or editor expresses an interest in my work?" you ask. "How much money can I expect to make?"

A reasonable question. Anything from zero to upward of several hundred thousand dollars (though the latter sum is quite rare). These days a typical sum for a novel ranges from five thousand to twenty-five thousand dollars. The sum will be based on a number of factors. One is the estimated market value of your work—in other words, the amount your publishers think your book will bring in. Another is luck. But the important thing is to secure a fair deal.

Having interested a publisher, your agent will try to negotiate an advance. An advance is essentially a loan, which you will pay back through your royalties. The term *royalty* refers not to your newfound status as a writer but to your slice of the financial pie—generally 7 to 15 percent of the cover price of the book, often stepped to reward greater sales. New writers seldom get big advances, but you will probably get something.

So, let's say that your book comes out as a paperback original, an increasingly common practice. At ten dollars a book, assuming your royalty schedule starts at 7 percent, you'll get seventy cents. Okay, it's a bit like holding out a hat, but it adds up.

Also, bear in mind that getting published has a domino effect. Having a novel or story in print can lead to paid talks, teaching engagements, and even writing commissions. If these opportunities don't come your way, create them. Think laterally and be entrepreneurial. Remember, you're running a small business.

You must also be prepared to deal with contracts. A contract is a written agreement between you and your publisher concerning the use and sale of your work. At some point, you are probably going to be given one. Not so much with short fiction, unless you are published by one of the glossies or issuing a collection, but certainly with novels.

When offered a contract, it's a good idea to have it scrutinized by an expert. A publishing contract is a complicated document, particularly with the advent of electronic rights, and needs to be examined with care, preferably by more than one person. Initially, your agent will take a look at it. This is part of her job, and she should have the necessary expertise. If you would like added reassurance, consult an entertainment or literary property lawyer. Finally, contact a professional organization such as the National Writers Union (www.nwu.org) or the Authors Guild (www.authorsguild.org). Joining fees are minimal, and members are offered free contract advice.

But though these individuals and organizations will help, you too must become an expert. Ultimately, you are responsible for protecting yourself. There are a number of guides to contract law for writers. Obtain one, and peruse the document clause by clause. Above all, don't ever feel pressured into signing a contract that you don't feel comfortable with.

AFTER THE BOOK DEAL

Celebrate. You've completed a long and difficult journey, and chances are that you'll be experiencing a variety of emotions, ranging from elation to bewilderment. But it's important to remind yourself that you've achieved a significant goal, and a good way to do that is to mark the occasion. Buy yourself a present, break out the champagne, do a private victory dance. Enjoy your accomplishment—you've earned it.

There are many further stages to come, and you will undertake a lot of hard work. So, once you've given yourself a chance to get used to this new state of affairs, roll your sleeves up and get ready to plunge into the prepublication process, beginning with the editorial department.

Once you've closed the deal, you will work with your editor to make your novel or short story collection the best it can be. You will receive notes, oral or written. These comments may be extensive and revision will probably require more than mere tinkering. Be prepared to dig in. But your editor will serve another important function, as your "in-house ally," ensuring that other departments, such as sales, marketing, and publicity, are aware of your upcoming release. Your publisher will have other books on their list and yours may not be prioritized. But however fierce the internal competition, your editor will champion your work and ensure that it gets as much attention as possible.

At some point, probably well before your book is published, you will be assigned a publicist who will endeavor to promote your book. Publicists will do mailings to various literary editors and critics, in an effort to secure reviews. They may recommend you to journalists as an interviewee. If you're very fortunate, they will arrange for you to participate in readings at bookstores and literary festivals. They may also contact radio and television producers with an eye toward getting you "on the air."

Should your publicist neglect you in favor of another, more profitable author, don't worry, because there is plenty you can do for yourself. There are several excellent guides to do-it-yourself book promotion and marketing, so invest in a few and make a plan. Prepare a media kit containing a press release, an author photo, your bio sheet, contact details, any prepublication endorsements, and a copy of the book or at least the jacket. Then send it to producers, journalists, and newspaper and magazine editors, with a personal note. Call booksellers and offer to do signings or conduct workshops, always with an eye toward making their job as easy as possible.

Whichever form your promotion takes, an "author Web site" is essential. In fact, you will benefit from being on the Web from the day you begin submitting your work. Acquire a domain name and establish your presence. If you can't design it yourself, pay a professional or recruit a technologically expert friend. As with the press kit, include your photo, bio, and so forth, but don't hesitate to give the contents a personal spin. Your

Web site should reflect not only your skills but your style and sense of humor.

SELF-PUBLISHING

A brief side note. If no publisher accepts your book *and* you have an entrepreneurial bent, you might want to try self-publishing. With the advent of digital print-on-demand, this option has become much more affordable. You can hire a publishing service that takes care of producing your book—everything from typesetting to cover design. Bear in mind, though, that these companies are not selective—they'll publish anybody's manuscript. Their job is solely to get your work into print. If you go this route, you would do well to hire a good freelance editor, to ensure quality control. Also bear in mind that self-published books seldom turn a profit for their authors.

One word of caution. Beware "vanity publishers." Both vanity publishers and publishing services are sometimes referred to as *subsidy publishers,* as they charge a fee for putting your work between two covers. So, what's the difference? Vanity publishers pretend to be something they're not—namely, real publishers. They will send you a letter telling you how wonderful your novel or collection is, suggesting that it has strong commercial potential. Having hooked you, they will gently introduce the delicate matter of payment. Don't fall for it. This is a cousin scam to the fee-charging agent. They will produce shoddy work and the charge will be exorbitant.

While self-publishing is a legitimate option, you will probably retain your dream of having work accepted by an established publisher.

COMPETITIONS, GRANTS, AND AWARDS

Getting your work published is not the only way to gain prestige and money as a writer.

Explore writing competitions. You will find details on these in the market guides and magazines. An Internet search is also a good idea. Many charge an entry fee, so make sure the competition is legitimate. Research the sponsoring organization or magazine. Awards sometimes include publication of your short story, novel, or collection. Your work may be brought to the attention of a literary agent. There is often a money prize. With high-profile competitions, even semifinalist status will enhance your query letters.

Your story may get a close reading or a cursory one. In the end, it's a lottery. Great work is often overlooked, but it's worth the risk. Someone's got to win, and it could be you.

Many writers receive some financial sustenance from literary grants, fellowships, and awards. These are administered by a variety of organizations—academic, nonprofit, and governmental. Among the best known are those administered by the National Endowment for the Arts. State arts councils often make similar provisions. An excellent guide is *Grants and Awards Available to American Writers,* published by PEN American Center, which lists more than one thousand opportunities complete with contact details. The market guides and magazines are also good sources of information.

Though many grants, fellowships, and awards require writing credits or nomination by a publisher, they are worth looking into. After all, they're designed to assist authors in financial need, including those at the beginning of their careers.

THE WRITING COMMUNITY

Published or not, give some thought to joining the writing community. Launching your literary career requires extreme patience; connecting with others may help you to sustain excitement and hope, and pick up some knowledge in the process. Communities, both actual and virtual, exist all over the globe and can be accessed from as far off as Uzbekistan. So, let's take a look at ways to hook up with kindred spirits.

Writing conferences and retreats are excellent ways to access the community. But they are very different, and each serves a particular function.

Conferences offer a chance to meet publishing professionals and learn about the industry. Locations range from Maui to Prague. Unless the conference is local, you will pay travel and housing costs in addition to an attendance fee, but the benefits are significant. Seminars, workshops, and networking opportunities abound. Agents are often invited to give talks or participate in panel discussions, and may be available afterward to speak with attendees.

Retreats, on the other hand, are just that—a chance to withdraw from the world and do some writing. Also known as writers' colonies, they provide an opportunity to work in the company of like-minded people. Some are open to all, and charge a fee for room and board. Others are selective and pay all costs save travel. Two of the better known are Yaddo and the MacDowell Colony. Everything is designed to minimize distractions and facilitate writing. Lunch is often brought to your door. But though there may be a rule of silence during the day, evenings are often social.

For lists of conferences, visit www.awpwriter.org/wcc and writing.shaw-guides.com. For retreats, check out *Artists & Writers Colonies: Retreats, Residencies, and Respites for the Creative Mind. Poets & Writers* is a great source for both.

You may also find fellow writing enthusiasts at literary readings or events in your corner of the world. These generally take place at colleges, bookstores, community centers, literary festivals, and cafés. Check your local newspaper or "what's on" guide for locations, dates, and times.

If you find your motivation flagging or yourself desperately in need of feedback on your work, consider joining a writing class or a writing group, or both. Both classes and groups are available on-line, as well as "live."

A writing class provides several advantages—specifically, expert advice, instruction, and feedback. The teacher will enlighten you on the art and the business of writing. You may be given exercises designed to strengthen your craft. You will have the opportunity to submit your work for criticism by your peers. Though classes are not a substitute for the actual writing, they can be an incredibly helpful way to keep you learning and feeling good about the process.

Writing groups, also known as "writing circles," often grow out of a class or are formed by several writers who decide to meet on a regular basis. Participants evaluate each other's work, share information on getting published, and offer all-around support. Such groups can last for years and become invaluable to their members.

Finally, consider joining a professional organization. There are many such bodies—national, regional, and local—but among the most prominent are the National Writers Union (NWU) and the Authors Guild.

The National Writers Union is the trade union for freelance writers of all genres, including fiction. Both published and unpublished writers are eligible. The benefits include networking opportunities, agent databases, market information, contract advice, grievance resolution, health insurance at competitive rates, and job banks. There are chapters all over the country. Join. Attend meetings, if time permits, and participate in forums and events. You'll be glad you did.

The Authors Guild is the oldest and largest professional society of published writers in the country. The Guild lobbies on a local and a national level on such issues as copyright, taxation, and protection of authors' rights under the First Amendment. Its considerable achievements include clearer royalty statements and improved contractual terms. While not technically a trade union, the Guild provides many of the same services as the NWU, including forums and events.

Bear in mind that there is a worldwide community of writers. If you'd like to connect with this global network, you might want to check out International PEN (www.pen.org), which campaigns on behalf of persecuted authors, much as Amnesty International crusades to free prisoners of conscience. PEN has an American branch. Learn about their activities and get involved.

For the most part, writing is a solitary journey, so consider joining forces with others who share your mania. Solidarity can help. There is strength in numbers.

> YOUR TURN:
> Find some ways in which you can join the writing community, either in your vicinity, or by traveling somewhere, or through the Internet. You can choose between conferences, retreats, literary readings/events, classes, writing groups, and writing organizations. Then join or participate in one of those for real.

BEING A WRITER

"Having read (and believed) the depressive truths I have communicated, do you still wish to become a writer?"
—Frank Swinnerton, *Authors and the Book Trade*

At some point, you will realize that you've made the transition from becoming a writer to being one. How will you know? Well, you'll find it a bit easier to sit down and work. You'll have adjusted to the daily discipline of writing. Submitting manuscripts will be accomplished swiftly. Rejection will sting a bit less. Every so often, you may receive an acceptance, and these credits will bring you personal and professional satisfaction. Most importantly, crafting fiction will have become part of the fabric of your life.

Though the rewards are abundant, adjusting to the writing life takes time. Like characters in your own stories, you will face obstacles and challenges. So, let's a take a look at how to circumnavigate some of these hazards.

You've probably heard the expression "Don't give up the day job." Your internal censor (that destructively critical voice in your head) may have told you this, or a well-meaning friend, or a colleague who just doesn't get it. Although you may have reasonable faith in your abilities as a writer, this advice rings in your ear with all the portent of a dire warning.

Relax. Though you may not be able to leave paid employment right away, it's not the end of the world. Most fiction writers, even those with impressive publication credits, supplement their income through other means, and successfully reconcile their day jobs with their writing life. Anton Chekhov, for instance, maintained a medical practice for part of his literary career, and claimed to have gathered much of his insight into human nature during this period.

You may even find that a day job gives you forced distance from your writing and helps keep feelings of isolation at bay. Also, as Chekhov found, the human comedy and tragedy of the workplace may prove a rich source of character and situation. And time away from your writing may increase your hunger and drive.

Regardless of your job, make sure to set aside a period every day, or at least several days a week, for writing. Treat that time as sacrosanct. Rise an hour earlier in the morning or go to bed a bit later. Watch less television. Try using ritual to ease the transition from the day job to your creative work. This may be as simple as preparing a cup of tea, but it will help you to drift into your fictional dream world.

"The problem is," you say, "that as soon as I enter the dream, someone I know tries to drag me out."

A common problem. The sad fact is, you will need to counteract the intrusion of family and friends. If you're lucky, your loved ones will turn cartwheels when you express your desire to write. But their initial enthusiasm may wane when they discover that you are *really going to do it* and that this activity will make you less available to them. Anticipate sabotage.

Seriously, expect the worst. They will knock at your door. Shout your name from downstairs. Walk into your study and burst into tears. You will pick up your pen, only to be interrupted by someone who needs a favor or simply desires your company.

Talk to them. Explain that this endeavor is important to you, and that shutting yourself away in a room with a pad of paper doesn't mean that you don't care about them. Then bolt the door and get on with your work. And don't use their demands as an excuse to procrastinate. Learn to say *no*. You'll find this liberating. There may be occasions when you need to put people first. To the extent that you can, however, prioritize your writing, as those who write may become enraged and dangerous if prevented from doing so for too long.

You may encounter even darker perils . . .

You're at your table scribbling. Or perhaps you're at work, writing on the sly. All is well, until you stop . . . look up . . . and the bottom drops out of your soul. You feel crushed, discouraged, and utterly alone. Suddenly, you don't know *what* to write or *how* to write or *why* you should write. In short, you are facing the Abyss.

The Abyss refers to the anguish that can strike you at any given moment. This feeling is as likely to come to you in the midst of a crowd as when you are by yourself, but it's a particular hazard in solitary occupations such as writing. This emotional chasm may shake your confidence and temporarily diminish your ability or desire to write. So try the following antidotes.

Stay in touch with the human race. However much you want or need to be alone, communication (with real people, not just fictional characters) is important. Make the most of any time you spend with family and friends. As discussed, connect with the writing community, where you will find others who know exactly what you're going through.

Also, develop a healthful lifestyle. Writing is intensive, all-consuming work, and there's a danger that you'll end up living on coffee and whatever convenience food is at hand. Mood is tied to health, as is productivity, so eat sensibly and try to get enough sleep. Step outside and breathe some fresh air. Take a walk. Writing is tiring, and physical activity will energize your body and mind.

YOUR TURN:
Make a list of ten things that you can do to make writing more of a priority in your life. This can include anything from waking up earlier to hiring a baby-sitter to exercising (to give yourself more energy) to signing up for a writing class. Post this list somewhere, say, above your desk or on the refrigerator. Then really *do* those things, at least some of them. The best way to become a writer is to get serious about being a writer. And the best time to start is right now.

Finally, write. Just lose yourself in the process and let it flow. Writing is the best stimulant in the world. Not when it's going badly, perhaps, but when it's going well . . . oh, baby. Your mood lifts, the Abyss recedes, and your confidence returns. Creative blocks vanish and words flood the page before you. By the very act of writing, you will have accessed your subconscious and tapped into something larger than yourself. You will have become a conduit for the world.

CHEAT SHEET

CHARACTER

- Do your characters have desires?
- Are your characters distinctive enough not to be types?
- Do your characters have contrasting traits that make them complex?
- Are your characters consistent despite their contrasting traits?
- Do your characters have the ability to change?
- Do you know your characters well enough?
- Are the right characters "round" and the right characters "flat"?
- Are you showing your characters more than telling about them?
- Are you utilizing all four methods of showing—action, speech, appearance, thought?
- Do your characters have the right names?

PLOT

- Do you have a major dramatic question?
- Do you have a protagonist with a strong goal and plenty of obstacles?
- Does your protagonist have both external and internal obstacles?
- Do you have a beginning, middle, and end?
- Is your beginning not clogged with too much exposition and not too long?
- Does your conflict escalate in the middle?

- Are the events of your middle linked by cause and effect?
- Do you have crisis, climax, and consequences at the end?
- Is your ending plausible, satisfying, and not too long?

POINT OF VIEW

- Does your story work best in first, second, or third person?
- Does your story work best with a single-vision or multiple-vision POV?
- Is there any reason your story might work best with the omniscient or objective POV?
- If you're using a second- or third-person narrator, how close emotionally is the narrator to the story and characters?
- Are you keeping your POV consistent?

DESCRIPTION

- Are your descriptions utilizing all five senses?
- Are your descriptions specific enough?
- Are you overusing adjectives and adverbs?
- Are you using figurative language and lyrical techniques where appropriate?
- Are your descriptions overdone, choking your story?
- Are you using telling details?
- Are you watching out for such description traps as clichés and mixed metaphors?
- Do your descriptions reflect the consciousness of your POV character or characters?

DIALOGUE

- Are you using dialogue and scenes for the more important points in your story?
- Does your dialogue sound real yet also get to the point quickly?
- Do your tags call too much attention to themselves?
- Are you using stage directions to enhance your dialogue?
- Do your characters sound distinctive from one another and appropriate to who they are?

- Is there anywhere your dialogue can be improved by using subtext?
- Does your dialogue contain clunky exposition or off-putting dialect?

SETTING/PACING

- Have you grounded your story in a specific place, or places?
- Have you grounded your story in a specific time, or times?
- Do the place and time of your story affect the action?
- Are there opportunities to let the setting enhance the atmosphere or mood?
- Do your characters act in a way that reflects either their comfort or discomfort with their setting?
- Are you describing your settings so much that they slow down the action?
- Have you chosen the right places either to expand or to compress time?

VOICE

- Have you picked a voice that works in harmony with your POV choice, the personality of your narrator, and the narrator's emotional distance to the story?
- Do your word, sentence, and paragraph choices support your voice?
- Does your voice remain consistent throughout the story?

THEME

- Have you identified a theme for your story?
- Does your theme surround your story with a light enough touch?
- Do all the elements of your story work to support the theme?

REVISION

- Have you gotten enough distance from your story to begin the revision process?
- Have you considered reenvisioning your story?

- Have you looked through a magnifying glass at all the Big Things in your story?
- Have you looked through a microscope at all the Little Things in your story?
- Have you cut and tweaked as much as you possibly can?

APPENDIX
CATHEDRAL
BY RAYMOND CARVER

This blind man, an old friend of my wife's, he was on his way to spend the night. His wife had died. So he was visiting the dead wife's relatives in Connecticut. He called my wife from his in-laws'. Arrangements were made. He would come by train, a five-hour trip, and my wife would meet him at the station. She hadn't seen him since she worked for him one summer in Seattle ten years ago. But she and the blind man had kept in touch. They made tapes and mailed them back and forth. I wasn't enthusiastic about his visit. He was no one I knew. And his being blind bothered me. My idea of blindness came from the movies. In the movies, the blind moved slowly and never laughed. Sometimes they were led by seeing-eye dogs. A blind man in my house was not something I looked forward to.

That summer in Seattle she had needed a job. She didn't have any money. The man she was going to marry at the end of the summer was in officers' training school. He didn't have any money, either. But she was in love with the guy, and he was in love with her, etc. She'd seen something in the paper: HELP WANTED—*Reading to Blind Man,* and a telephone number. She phoned and went over, was hired on the spot. She'd worked with this blind man all summer. She read stuff to him, case studies, reports, that sort of thing. She helped him organize his little office in the county social-service department. They'd become good friends, my wife and the blind man. How do I know these things? She told me. And she told me something else. On her last day in the office, the blind man asked if he could touch her face. She agreed to this. She told me he touched his fingers to every part of her face, her nose—even her neck! She never forgot it. She even tried to write a poem about it. She was always trying to write a poem. She wrote a poem or two every year, usually after something really important had happened to her.

When we first started going out together, she showed me the poem. In the poem, she recalled his fingers and the way they had moved around over her face. In the poem, she talked about what she had felt at the time, about what went through her mind when the blind man touched her nose and lips. I can remember I didn't think much of the poem. Of course, I didn't tell her that. Maybe I just don't understand poetry. I admit it's not the first thing I reach for when I pick up something to read.

Anyway, this man who'd first enjoyed her favors, the officer-to-be, he'd been her childhood sweetheart. So okay. I'm saying that at the end of the summer she let the blind man run his hands over her face, said goodbye to him, married her childhood, etc., who was now a commissioned officer, and she moved away from Seattle. But they'd kept in touch, she and the blind man. She made the first contact after a year or so. She called him up one night from an Air Force base in Alabama. She wanted to talk. They talked. He asked her to send him a tape and tell him about her life. She did this. She sent the tape. On the tape, she told the blind man about her husband and about their life together in the military. She told the blind man she loved her husband but she didn't like it where they lived and she didn't like it that he was a part of the military–industrial thing. She told the blind man she'd written a poem and he was in it. She told him that she was writing a poem about what it was like to be an Air Force officer's wife. The poem wasn't finished yet. She was still writing it. The blind man made a tape. He sent her the tape. She made a tape. This went on for years. My wife's officer was posted to one base and then another. She sent tapes from Moody AFB, McGuire, McConnell, and finally Travis, near Sacramento, where one night she got to feeling lonely and cut off from people she kept losing in that moving-around life. She got to feeling she couldn't go it another step. She went in and swallowed all the pills and capsules in the medicine chest and washed them down with a bottle of gin. Then she got into a hot bath and passed out.

But instead of dying, she got sick. She threw up. Her officer—why should he have a name? he was the childhood sweetheart, and what more does he want?—came home from somewhere, found her, and called the ambulance. In time, she put it all on a tape and sent the tape to the blind man. Over the years, she put all kinds of stuff on tapes and sent the tapes off lickety-split. Next to writing a poem every year, I think it was her chief means of recreation. On one tape, she told the blind man she'd decided to live away from her officer for a time. On another tape, she told him about her divorce. She and I began going out, and of course she told her blind man about it. She told him everything, or so it seemed to me. Once she asked me if I'd like to hear the latest tape from the blind man. This was a year ago. I was on the tape, she said. So I said okay, I'd listen to it. I got us drinks and we settled down in the living room. We made ready to listen. First she inserted the tape into the player and adjusted a couple of dials. Then she pushed a lever. The tape squeaked and someone began to talk in this loud voice. She lowered the volume. After a few minutes of harmless chitchat, I heard my own name in the mouth of this stranger, this blind man I didn't even know! And then this: "From all you've said about him, I can only conclude—" But we were interrupted, a knock at the door, something, and we didn't ever get back to the tape. Maybe it was just as well. I'd heard all I wanted to.

Now this same blind man was coming to sleep in my house.

"Maybe I could take him bowling," I said to my wife. She was at the draining board doing scalloped potatoes. She put down the knife she was using and turned around.

"If you love me," she said, "you can do this for me. If you don't love me, okay. But if you had a friend, any friend, and the friend came to visit, I'd make him feel comfortable." She wiped her hands with the dish towel.

"I don't have any blind friends," I said.

"You don't have *any* friends," she said. "Period. Besides," she said, "goddamn it, his wife's just died! Don't you understand that? The man's lost his wife!"

I didn't answer. She'd told me a little about the blind man's wife. Her name was Beulah. Beulah! That's a name for a colored woman.

"Was his wife a Negro?" I asked.

"Are you crazy?" my wife said. "Have you just flipped or something?" She picked up a potato. I saw it hit the floor, then roll under the stove. "What's wrong with you?" she said. "Are you drunk?"

"I'm just asking," I said.

Right then my wife filled me in with more detail than I cared to know. I made a drink and sat at the kitchen table to listen. Pieces of the story began to fall into place.

Beulah had gone to work for the blind man the summer after my wife had stopped working for him. Pretty soon Beulah and the blind man had themselves a church wedding. It was a little wedding—who'd want to go to such a wedding in the first place?—just the two of them, plus the minister and the minister's wife. But it was a church wedding just the same. It was what Beulah had wanted, he'd said. But even then Beulah must have been carrying the cancer in her glands. After they had been inseparable for eight years—my wife's word, *inseparable*—Beulah's health went into a rapid decline. She died in a Seattle hospital room, the blind man sitting beside the bed and holding on to her hand. They'd married, lived and worked together, slept together—had sex, sure—and then the blind man had to bury her. All this without his having ever seen what the goddamned woman looked like. It was beyond my understanding. Hearing this, I felt sorry for the blind man for a little bit. And then I found myself thinking what a pitiful life this woman must have led. Imagine a woman who could never see herself as she was seen in the eyes of her loved one. A woman who could go on day after day and never receive the smallest compliment from her beloved. A woman whose husband could never read the expression on her face, be it misery or something better. Someone who could wear make-up or not—what difference to him? She could, if she wanted, wear green eye-shadow around one eye, a straight pin in her nostril, yellow slacks and purple shoes, no matter. And then to slip off into death, the blind man's hand on her hand, his blind eyes streaming tears—I'm imagining now—her last thought maybe this: that he never even knew what she looked like, and she on an express to the grave. Robert was left with a small insurance policy and half of a 20-peso Mexican coin. The other half of the coin went into the box with her. Pathetic.

So when the time rolled around, my wife went to the depot to pick him up. With nothing to do but wait—sure, I blamed him for that—I was having a drink and watching the TV when I heard the car pull into the drive. I got up from the sofa with my drink and went to the window to have a look.

I saw my wife laughing as she parked the car. I saw her get out of the car and shut the door. She was still wearing a smile. Just amazing. She went around to the other side of the car to where the blind man was already starting to get out. This blind man, feature this, he was wearing a full beard! A beard on a blind man! Too much, I say. The blind man reached into the back seat and dragged out a suitcase. My wife took his arm, shut the car door, and, talking all the way, moved him down the drive and then up the steps to the front porch. I turned off the TV.

I finished my drink, rinsed the glass, dried my hands. Then I went to the door.

My wife said, "I want you to meet Robert. Robert, this is my husband. I've told you all about him." She was beaming. She had this blind man by his coat sleeve.

The blind man let go of his suitcase and up came his hand.

I took it. He squeezed hard, held my hand, and then he let it go.

"I feel like we've already met," he boomed.

"Likewise," I said. I didn't know what else to say. Then I said, "Welcome. I've heard a lot about you." We began to move then, a little group, from the porch into the living room, my wife guiding him by the arm. The blind man was carrying his suitcase in his other hand. My wife said things like, "To your left here, Robert. That's right. Now watch it, there's a chair. That's it. Sit down right here. This is the sofa. We just bought this sofa two weeks ago."

I started to say something about the old sofa. I'd liked that old sofa. But I didn't say anything. Then I wanted to say something else, small-talk, about the scenic ride along the Hudson. How going *to* New York, you should sit on the right-hand side of the train, and coming *from* New York, the left-hand side.

"Did you have a good train ride?" I said. "Which side of the train did you sit on, by the way?"

"What a question, which side!" my wife said. "What's it matter which side?" she said.

"I just asked," I said.

"Right side," the blind man said. "I hadn't been on a train in nearly forty years. Not since I was a kid. With my folks. That's been a long time. I'd nearly forgotten the sensation. I have winter in my beard now," he said. "So I've been told, anyway. Do I look distinguished, my dear?" the blind man said to my wife.

"You look distinguished, Robert," she said. "Robert," she said. "Robert, it's just so good to see you."

My wife finally took her eyes off the blind man and looked at me. I had the feeling she didn't like what she saw. I shrugged.

I've never met, or personally known, anyone who was blind. This blind man was late forties, a heavy-set, balding man with stooped shoulders, as if he carried a great weight there. He wore brown slacks, brown shoes, a light-brown shirt, a tie, a sports coat. Spiffy. He also had this full beard.

But he didn't use a cane and he didn't wear dark glasses. I'd always thought dark glasses were a must for the blind. Fact was, I wished he had a pair. At first glance, his eyes looked like anyone else's eyes. But if you looked close, there was something different about them. Too much white in the iris, for one thing, and the pupils seemed to move around in the sockets without his knowing it or being able to stop it. Creepy. As I stared at his face, I saw the left pupil turn in toward his nose while the other made an effort to keep in one place. But it was only an effort, for that eye was on the roam without his knowing it or wanting it to be.

I said, "Let me get you a drink. What's your pleasure? We have a little of everything. It's one of our pastimes."

"Bub, I'm a Scotch man myself," he said fast enough in this big voice.

"Right," I said. Bub! "Sure you are. I knew it."

He let his fingers touch his suitcase, which was sitting alongside the sofa. He was taking his bearings. I didn't blame him for that.

"I'll move that up to your room," my wife said.

"No, that's fine," the blind man said loudly. "It can go up when I go up."

"A little water with the Scotch?" I said.

"Very little," he said.

"I knew it," I said.

He said, "Just a tad. The Irish actor, Barry Fitzgerald? I'm like that fellow. When I drink water, Fitzgerald said, I drink water. When I drink whiskey, I drink whiskey." My wife laughed. The blind man brought his hand up under his beard. He lifted his beard slowly and let it drop.

I did the drinks, three big glasses of Scotch with a splash of water in each. Then we made ourselves comfortable and talked about Robert's travels. First the long flight from the West Coast to Connecticut, we covered that. Then from Connecticut up here by train. We had another drink concerning that leg of the trip.

I remembered having read somewhere that the blind didn't smoke because, as speculation had it, they couldn't see the smoke they exhaled. I thought I knew that much and that much only about blind people. But this blind man smoked his cigarette down to the nubbin and then lit another one. This blind man filled his ashtray and my wife emptied it.

When we sat down at the table for dinner, we had another drink. My wife heaped Robert's plate with cube steak, scalloped potatoes, green beans.

I buttered him up two slices of bread. I said, "Here's bread and butter for you." I swallowed some of my drink. "Now let us pray," I said, and the blind man lowered his head. My wife looked at me, her mouth agape. "Pray the phone won't ring and the food doesn't get cold," I said.

We dug in. We ate everything there was to eat on the table. We ate like there was no tomorrow. We didn't talk. We ate. We scarfed. We grazed that table. We were into serious eating. The blind man had right away located his foods, he knew just where everything was on his plate. I watched with admiration as he used his knife and fork on the meat. He'd cut two pieces of meat, fork the meat into his mouth, and then go all out for the scalloped potatoes, the beans next, and then he'd tear off a hunk of buttered bread and eat that. He'd follow this up with a big drink of milk. It didn't seem to bother him to use his fingers once in a while, either.

We finished everything, including half a strawberry pie. For a few moments, we sat as if stunned. Sweat beaded on our faces. Finally, we got up from the table and left the dirty plates. We didn't look back. We took ourselves into the living room and sank into our places again. Robert and my wife sat on the sofa. I took the big chair. We had us two or three more drinks while they talked about the major things that had come to pass for them in the past ten years. For the most part, I just listened. Now and then I joined in. I didn't want him to think I'd left the room, and I didn't want her to think I was feeling left out. They talked of things that had happened to them—to them—these past ten years. I waited in vain to hear my name on my wife's sweet lips: "And then my dear husband came into my life"—something like that. But I heard nothing of the sort. More talk of Robert. Robert had done a little of everything, it seemed, a regular blind jack-of-all-trades. But most recently he and his wife had had an Amway distributorship, from which, I gathered, they'd earned their living, such as it was. The blind man was also a ham radio operator. He talked in his loud voice about conversations he'd had with fellow operators in Guam, in the Philippines, in Alaska, and even in Tahiti. He said he'd have a lot of friends there if he ever wanted to go visit those places. From time to time, he'd turn his blind face toward me, put his hand under his beard, ask me something. How long had I been in my present position? (Three years.) Did I like my work? (I didn't.) Was I going to stay with it? (What were the options?) Finally, when I thought he was beginning to run down, I got up and turned on the TV.

My wife looked at me with irritation. She was heading toward a boil. Then she looked at the blind man and said, "Robert, do you have a TV?"

The blind man said, "My dear, I have two TVs. I have a color set and a black-and-white thing, an old relic. It's funny, but if I turn the TV on, and I'm always turning it on, I turn on the color set. It's funny, don't you think?"

I didn't know what to say to that. I had absolutely nothing to say to that. No opinion. So I watched the news program and tried to listen to what the announcer was saying.

"This is a color TV," the blind man said. "Don't ask me how, but I can tell."

"We traded up a while ago," I said.

The blind man had another taste of his drink. He lifted his beard, sniffed it, and let it fall. He leaned forward on the sofa. He positioned his ashtray on the coffee table, then put the lighter to his cigarette. He leaned back on the sofa and crossed his legs at the ankles.

My wife covered her mouth, and then she yawned. She stretched. She said, "I think I'll go upstairs and put on my robe. I think I'll change into something else. Robert, you make yourself comfortable," she said.

"I'm comfortable," the blind man said.

"I want you to feel comfortable in this house," she said.

"I am comfortable," the blind man said.

After she'd left the room, he and I listened to the weather report and then to the sports roundup. By that time, she'd been gone so long I didn't know if she was going to come back. I thought she might have gone to bed. I wished she'd come back downstairs. I didn't want to be left alone with a blind man. I asked him if he wanted another drink, and he said sure. Then I asked if he wanted to smoke some dope with me. I said I'd just rolled a number. I hadn't, but I planned to do so in about two shakes.

"I'll try some with you," he said.

"Damn right," I said. "That's the stuff."

I got our drinks and sat down on the sofa with him. Then I rolled us two fat numbers. I lit one and passed it. I brought it to his fingers. He took it and inhaled.

"Hold it as long as you can," I said. I could tell he didn't know the first thing.

My wife came back downstairs wearing her pink robe and her pink slippers.

"What do I smell?" she said.

"We thought we'd have us some cannabis," I said.

My wife gave me a savage look. Then she looked at the blind man and said, "Robert, I didn't know you smoked."

He said, "I do now, my dear. There's a first time for everything. But I don't feel anything yet."

"This stuff is pretty mellow," I said. "This stuff is mild. It's dope you can reason with," I said. "It doesn't mess you up."

"Not much it doesn't, bub," he said, and laughed.

My wife sat on the sofa between the blind man and me. I passed her the number. She took it and toked and then passed it back to me. "Which way is this going?" she said. Then she said, "I shouldn't be smoking this. I can hardly keep my eyes open as it is. That dinner did me in. I shouldn't have eaten so much."

"It was the strawberry pie," the blind man said. "That's what did it," he said, and he laughed his big laugh. Then he shook his head.

"There's more strawberry pie," I said.

"Do you want some more, Robert?" my wife said.

"Maybe in a little while," he said.

We gave our attention to the TV. My wife yawned again. She said, "Your bed is made up when you feel like going to bed, Robert. I know you must have had a long day. When you're ready to go to bed, say so." She pulled his arm. "Robert?"

He came to and said, "I've had a real nice time. This beats tapes, doesn't it?"

I said, "Coming at you," and I put the number between his fingers. He inhaled, held the smoke, and then let it go. It was like he'd been doing it since he was nine years old.

"Thanks, bub," he said. "But I think this is all for me. I think I'm beginning to feel it," he said. He held the burning roach out for my wife.

"Same here," she said. "Ditto. Me, too." She took the roach and passed it to me. "I may just sit for a while between you two guys with my eyes closed. But don't let me bother you, okay? Either one of you. If it bothers you, say so. Otherwise, I may just sit here with my eyes closed until you're ready to go to bed," she said. "Your bed's made up, Robert, when you're ready. It's right next to our room at the top of the stairs. We'll show you up when you're ready. You wake me up now, you guys, if I fall asleep." She said that and then she closed her eyes and went to sleep.

The news program ended. I got up and changed the channel. I sat back down on the sofa. I wished my wife hadn't pooped out. Her head lay across the back of the sofa, her mouth open. She'd turned so that her robe had slipped away from her legs, exposing a juicy thigh. I reached to draw her robe back over her, and it was then that I glanced at the blind man. What the hell! I flipped the robe open again.

"You say when you want some strawberry pie," I said.

"I will," he said.

I said, "Are you tired? Do you want me to take you up to your bed? Are you ready to hit the hay?"

"Not yet," he said. "No, I'll stay up with you, bub. If that's all right. I'll stay up until you're ready to turn in. We haven't had a chance to talk. Know what I mean? I feel like me and her monopolized the evening." He lifted his beard and he let it fall. He picked up his cigarettes and his lighter.

"That's all right," I said. Then I said, "I'm glad for the company."

And I guess I was. Every night I smoked dope and stayed up as long as I could before I fell asleep. My wife and I hardly ever went to bed at the same time. When I did go to sleep, I had these dreams. Sometimes I'd wake up from one of them, my heart going crazy.

Something about the church and the Middle Ages was on the TV. Not your run-of-the-mill TV fare. I wanted to watch something else. I turned to the other channels. But there was nothing on them, either. So I turned back to the first channel and apologized.

"Bub, it's all right," the blind man said. "It's fine with me. Whatever you want to watch is okay. I'm always learning something. Learning never ends. It won't hurt me to learn something tonight. I got ears," he said.

We didn't say anything for a time. He was leaning forward with his head turned at me, his right ear aimed in the direction of the set. Very disconcerting. Now and then his eyelids drooped and then they snapped open again. Now and then he put his fingers into his beard and tugged, like he was thinking about something he was hearing on the television.

On the screen, a group of men wearing cowls was being set upon and tormented by men dressed in skeleton costumes and men dressed as devils.

The men dressed as devils wore devil masks, horns, and long tails. This pageant was part of a procession. The Englishman who was narrating the thing said it took place in Spain once a year. I tried to explain to the blind man what was happening.

"Skeletons," he said. "I know about skeletons," he said, and he nodded.

The TV showed this one cathedral. Then there was a long, slow look at another one. Finally, the picture switched to the famous one in Paris, with its flying buttresses and its spires reaching up to the clouds. The camera pulled away to show the whole of the cathedral rising above the skyline.

There were times when the Englishman who was telling the thing would shut up, would simply let the camera move around over the cathedrals. Or else the camera would tour the countryside, men in fields walking behind oxen. I waited as long as I could. Then I felt I had to say something. I said, "They're showing the outside of this cathedral now. Gargoyles. Little statues carved to look like monsters. Now I guess they're in Italy. There's paintings on the walls of this one church."

"Are those fresco paintings, bub?" he asked, and he sipped from his drink.

I reached for my glass. But it was empty. I tried to remember what I could remember. "You're asking me are those frescoes?" I said. "That's a good question. I don't know."

The camera moved to a cathedral outside Lisbon. The differences in the Portuguese cathedral compared with the French and Italian were not that great. But they were there. Mostly the interior stuff. Then something occurred to me, and I said, "Something has occurred to me. Do you have any idea what a cathedral is? What they look like, that is? Do you follow me? If somebody says cathedral to you, do you have any notion what they're talking about? Do you know the difference between that and a Baptist church, say?"

He let the smoke dribble from his mouth. "I know they took hundreds of workers fifty or a hundred years to build," he said. "I just heard the man say that, of course. I know generations of the same families worked on a cathedral. I heard him say that, too. The men who began their life's work on them, they never lived to see the completion of their work. In that wise, bub, they're no different from the rest of us, right?" He laughed. Then his eyelids drooped again. His head nodded. He seemed to be snoozing. Maybe he was imagining himself in Portugal. The TV was showing another cathedral now.

This one was in Germany. The Englishman's voice droned on. "Cathedrals," the blind man said. He sat up and rolled his head back and forth. "If you want the truth, bub, that's about all I know. What I just said. What I heard him say. But maybe you could describe one to me? I wish you'd do it. I'd like that. If you want to know, I really don't have a good idea."

I stared hard at the shot of the cathedral on the TV. How could I even begin to describe it? But say my life depended on it. Say my life was being threatened by an insane guy who said I had to do it or else.

I stared some more at the cathedral before the picture flipped off into the countryside. There was no use. I turned to the blind man and said, "To begin with, they're very tall." I was looking around the room for clues. "They reach way up. Up and up. Toward the sky. They're so big, some of them, they have to have these supports. To help hold them up, so to speak. These supports are called buttresses. They remind me of viaducts, for some reason. But maybe you don't know viaducts, either? Sometimes the cathedrals have devils and such carved into the front. Sometimes lords and ladies. Don't ask me why this is," I said.

He was nodding. The whole upper part of his body seemed to be moving back and forth.

"I'm not doing so good, am I?" I said.

He stopped nodding and leaned forward on the edge of the sofa. As he listened to me, he was running his fingers through his beard. I wasn't getting through to him, I could see that. But he waited for me to go on just the same. He nodded, like he was trying to encourage me. I tried to think what else to say. "They're really big," I said. "They're massive. They're built of stone. Marble, too, sometimes. In those olden days, when they built cathedrals, men wanted to be close to God. In those olden days, God was an important part of everyone's life. You could tell this from their cathedral-building. I'm sorry," I said, "but it looks like that's the best I can do for you. I'm just no good at it."

"That's all right, bub," the blind man said. "Hey, listen. I hope you don't mind my asking you. Can I ask you something? Let me ask you a simple question, yes or no. I'm just curious and there's no offense. You're my host. But let me ask if you are in any way religious? You don't mind my asking?"

I shook my head. He couldn't see that, though. A wink is the same as a nod to a blind man. "I guess I don't believe in it. In anything. Sometimes it's hard. You know what I'm saying?"

"Sure, I do," he said.

"Right," I said.

The Englishman was still holding forth. My wife sighed in her sleep. She drew a long breath and went on with her sleeping.

"You'll have to forgive me," I said. "But I can't tell you what a cathedral looks like. It just isn't in me to do it. I can't do any more than I've done."

The blind man sat very still, his head down, as he listened to me.

I said, "The truth is, cathedrals don't mean anything special to me. Nothing. Cathedrals. They're something to look at on late-night TV. That's all they are."

It was then that the blind man cleared his throat. He brought something up. He took a handkerchief from his back pocket. Then he said, "I get it, bub. It's okay. It happens. Don't worry about it," he said. "Hey, listen to me. Will you do me a favor? I got an idea. Why don't you find us some heavy paper? And a pen. We'll do something. We'll draw one together. Get us a pen and some heavy paper. Go on, bub, get the stuff," he said.

So I went upstairs. My legs felt like they didn't have any strength in them. They felt like they did after I'd done some running. In my wife's room, I looked around. I found some ballpoints in a little basket on her table. And then I tried to think where to look for the kind of paper he was talking about.

Downstairs, in the kitchen, I found a shopping bag with onion skins in the bottom of the bag. I emptied the bag and shook it. I brought it into the living room and sat down with it near his legs. I moved some things, smoothed the wrinkles from the bag, spread it out on the coffee table.

The blind man got down from the sofa and sat next to me on the carpet.

He ran his fingers over the paper. He went up and down the sides of the paper. The edges, even the edges. He fingered the corners.

"All right," he said. "All right, let's do her."

He found my hand, the hand with the pen. He closed his hand over my hand. "Go ahead, bub, draw," he said. "Draw. You'll see. I'll follow along with you. It'll be okay. Just begin now like I'm telling you. You'll see. Draw," the blind man said.

So I began. First I drew a box that looked like a house. It could have been the house I lived in. Then I put a roof on it. At either end of the roof, I drew spires. Crazy.

"Swell," he said. "Terrific. You're doing fine," he said. "Never thought anything like this could happen in your lifetime, did you, bub? Well, it's a strange life, we all know that. Go on now. Keep it up."

I put in windows with arches. I drew flying buttresses. I hung great doors. I couldn't stop. The TV station went off the air. I put down the pen and closed and opened my fingers. The blind man felt around over the paper. He moved the tips of his fingers over the paper, all over what I had drawn, and he nodded.

"Doing fine," the blind man said.

I took up the pen again, and he found my hand. I kept at it. I'm no artist. But I kept drawing just the same.

My wife opened up her eyes and gazed at us. She sat up on the sofa, her robe hanging open. She said, "What are you doing? Tell me, I want to know."

I didn't answer her.

The blind man said, "We're drawing a cathedral. Me and him are working on it. Press hard," he said to me. "That's right. That's good," he said. "Sure. You got it, bub. I can tell. You didn't think you could. But you can, can't you? You're cooking with gas now. You know what I'm saying? We're going to really have us something here in a minute. How's the old arm?" he said. "Put some people in there now. What's a cathedral without people?"

My wife said, "What's going on? Robert, what are you doing? What's going on?"

"It's all right," he said to her. "Close your eyes now," the blind man said to me.

I did it. I closed them just like he said.

"Are they closed?" he said. "Don't fudge."

"They're closed," I said.

"Keep them that way," he said. He said, "Don't stop now. Draw."

So we kept on with it. His fingers rode my fingers as my hand went over the paper. It was like nothing else in my life up to now.

Then he said, "I think that's it. I think you got it," he said. "Take a look. What do you think?"

But I had my eyes closed. I thought I'd keep them that way for a little longer. I thought it was something I ought to do.

"Well?" he said. "Are you looking?"

My eyes were still closed. I was in my house. I knew that. But I didn't feel like I was inside anything.

"It's really something," I said.

ACKNOWLEDGMENTS

Writing Fiction emerged from the experience and insight of ten Gotham Writers' Workshop teachers and our dean of faculty, Alexander Steele, who edited and oversaw this project with his customary keen eye and grace under pressure.

This book also represents the concerted efforts of Andre Becker, president of Gotham Writers' Workshop, Faith Hamlin of Sanford Greenburger Associates, Colin Dickerman at Bloomsbury USA, and Nikki Moustaki, for her efforts in the initial stages of this project and for lending us her publishing and editorial expertise.

Moreover, we recognize and gratefully thank the dedicated Gotham staff: Joel Mellin, Dana Miller, Linda Novak, Betsey Odell, Stacey Panousopoulos, and Charlie Shehadi.

Writing Fiction is also indebted to the talented Gotham teachers who, over the years, have helped to distill and define the craft of fiction writing into a form that is easily understood. Finally, this book is dedicated to our students, who continually challenge and inspire us all.

CONTRIBUTORS

Allison Amend has published short fiction in *Other Voices, StoryQuarterly, One Story, Arts and Letters,* and *Atlantic Unbound,* and serves as fiction editor at *StoryQuarterly* magazine. She lives in New York City.

Terry Bain has published short fiction in *Book Magazine, Prize Stories 1994: The O. Henry Awards,* and *The Gettysburg Review,* among others, and he writes humor pieces for *Sweet Fancy Moses.* He lives in Spokane, Washington.

David Harris Ebenbach has published short fiction in such magazines as *Denver Quarterly,* the *Beloit Fiction Journal,* and the *Crescent Review,* and his poetry has appeared in *La Petite Zine* and the *Red River Review.* He lives in New York City.

Hardy Griffin has published short fiction in *The Hangman's Lime* and *Ox,* and his nonfiction has appeared in *The Washington Post, American Letters & Commentary,* and *Fodors.com.* He lives in Istanbul, Turkey.

Caren Gussoff is the author of the novel *Homecoming* (Serpent's Tail) and the short-story collection *The Wave and Other Stories* (Serpent's Tail). She lives in Seattle, Washington.

Corene Lemaitre is the author of the novel *April Rising* (HarperCollins UK and Carroll & Graf US) and was awarded first prize in the World Wide Writers international short fiction competition. She lives in Wayne, Pennsylvania.

Chris Lombardi has published short fiction in *minnesota review, Anything That Moves, living room,* and assorted anthologies, including *HEY PAESAN! Lesbians and Gays of Italian Descent.* Her nonfiction has appeared in *The Nation, Ms, Poets & Writers,* and *Inside MS,* among others. She lives in New York City.

Brandi Reissenweber has published short fiction in such magazines as *Rattapallax* and *Aspects,* serves as an editorial assistant at *Zoetrope: All-Story,* and founded a therapeutic writing workshop at Safespace, a center for homeless teens. She lives in Chicago, Illinois.

Peter Selgin has published short fiction in *Glimmer Train* and *Salon,* among others. His artwork has appeared in such publications as *The New Yorker* and *The Wall Street Journal,* and he is the author/illustrator of the children's book *S.S. Gigantic Across the Atlantic* (Simon & Schuster). He lives in New York City.

Alexander Steele serves as dean of faculty of Gotham Writers' Workshop. He has written numerous plays, screenplays, and nonfiction pieces, and has published seventeen books for children. He lives in New York City.

Valerie Vogrin is the author of the novel *Shebang* (University of Mississippi Press), has published short fiction in such magazines as *New Orleans Review* and *Black Warrior Review,* and cofounded Smallmouth Press. She lives in St. Louis, Missouri.

INDEX

Looking for exceptional stories to read or study?
Fiction Gallery is the perfect companion to *Writing Fiction*

Gotham Writers' Workshop is pleased to introduce *Fiction Gallery*, an anthology of excellent and accessible short stories. Every story will hold the reader spellbound from first to last page, while also exemplifying the very best in literary fiction.

The twenty-five authors include such acknowledged masters of short fiction as Anton Chekhov, Dorothy Parker, John Cheever, and Raymond Carver, and such acclaimed contemporary writers as Edwidge Danticat, Pam Houston, Ethan Canin, T. C. Boyle, Jhumpa Lahiri, and ZZ Packer.

Aspiring writers will find this anthology an invaluable source of inspiration and instruction. This gallery of stories presents diverse examples of all the elements of fiction craft and demonstrates how writers seamlessly sew these elements into unforgettable tales.

As a bonus, the anthology includes original interviews with T. C. Boyle, Jhumpa Lahiri, and Hannah Tinti, in which they illuminate the process of creating a short story.

For writers and readers alike, *Fiction Gallery* is a book to be treasured.

ISBN: 1-58234-462-0

Preview stories and learn more at www.FictionGallery.com